GOOD MORNING, DESTROYER OF MEN'S SOULS

"Ferocious . . . Aron's hatchet is the sharp prose she uses to slash through broken promises and empty apologies. Whether she's describing her mental state ("Depression made a nest of my mind") or the landscape of addiction ("A bus depot at night is always a site of small horrors"), each page of Aron's memoir glints with hard-won truths. . . . Aron lights a path through the darkness of her past toward a better future."
— *Los Angeles Times*

"Stunning . . . Reading it was like a first sip of water after a 20-mile run in the heat. . . . If you've been an addict or loved an addict, *Good Morning, Destroyer of Men's Souls* will enter your bloodstream and overtake your mind in the most serious way. But even if you have no experience with addiction or codependency, this book is an essential read. It shows us that addicts are more than statistics, their codependents more than 'sniveling, whimpering, and brokenhearted.' These are real people, rendered by Aron with eye-opening complexity and dynamism. In this book, the underrepresented and overlooked world of the codependent emerges from the bargain basement of self-help and shopworn homilies into the realm of love and loathing, birth and death, blood and urine. Into the realm, in other words, of the literary."
—*The Washington Post*

"Unflinching . . . Aron writes in gripping prose about the thrills and dangers of her own substance use and relationship with K—their weak-kneed passion and wolfish needs, as well as her guilt-ridden enabling and savior-complex optimism."
—*San Francisco Chronicle*

"In Nina Renata Aron's scorching, unvarnished memoir, an addiction story gets spun from the perspective of the helpless partner, the lover too stuck in a dangerous dynamic to find her way out."
—*Entertainment Weekly*, Best Books of April

"In Aron's candid and heart-wrenching memoir, the gnarled knots of love and addiction are untied and tangled and tied again. . . . Her compassion for victims of addiction never wavers, and her presentation of the addicted people in her life is dynamic and fair. A beautiful, nuanced portrait of living alongside addiction."
—*Booklist* (starred review)

GOOD MORNING, DESTROYER OF MEN'S SOULS

GOOD MORNING, DESTROYER OF MEN'S SOULS

a memoir of women, addiction, and love

NINA RENATA ARON

CROWN
NEW YORK

2021 Crown Trade Paperback Edition

Copyright © 2020 by Nina Renata Aron
Book club guide copyright © 2021 by Penguin Random House LLC

Published in the United States by Crown, an imprint of Random House, a division of Penguin Random House LLC, New York.

CROWN and the Crown colophon are registered trademarks of Penguin Random House LLC. RANDOM HOUSE BOOK CLUB and colophon are trademarks of Penguin Random House LLC.

Originally published in hardcover in the United States by Crown, an imprint of Random House, a division of Penguin Random House LLC, New York, in 2020.

Grateful acknowledgment is made to Milkweed Editions for permission to reprint an excerpt of "Wife" from *The Carrying* by Ada Limón, published by Milkweed Editions, Minneapolis, in 2018. Copyright © 2018 by Ada Limón. Reprinted with permission from Milkweed Editions (milkweed.org).

Library of Congress Cataloging-in-Publication Data
Names: Aron, Nina Renata, author.
Title: Good morning, destroyer of men's souls / Nina Renata Aron.
Description: First edition. | New York: Crown, [2020]
Identifiers: LCCN 2020003061 (print) | LCCN 2020003062 (ebook) |
ISBN 9780525576686 (trade paperback) | ISBN 9780525576693 (ebook)
Subjects: LCSH: Aron, Nina Renata. | Drug addicts—United States—Biography. | Drug addicts—Family relationships—United States. | Man-woman relationships. | Codependency.
Classification: LCC HV5805.A76 A3 2020 (print) | LCC HV5805.A76 (ebook) |
DDC 362.29/13092 [B]—dc23
LC record available at https://lccn.loc.gov/2020003061
LC ebook record available at https://lccn.loc.gov/2020003062

Printed in the United States of America on acid-free paper

crownpublishing.com
randomhousebookclub.com

9 8 7 6 5 4 3 2 1

First Edition

Book design by Jo Anne Metsch

For my mother and father

part 1

On a Hunter's Moon, I burned his name. The drummer in my band told me to do it. We were sitting at the bar drinking well whiskeys and cans of beer. *A Hunter's Moon is powerful for intention setting,* she said, winding her long, chemically straightened hair into an apple fritter–sized bun atop her head. She secured it not with an elastic but with a wrist flick and a twist of another piece of her hair, some sleight of hand I'd always envied in the girls who could do it. It stayed in place perfectly. She pulled a few baby hairs out to fall in front of her ears, and they made small, wispy parentheses around her face. Fleetwood Mac was playing.

Write down what you want and burn it, she said, knocking back the last of her drink.

Women suggest these types of things to one another.

A Hunter's Moon is powerful for intention setting. This was the kind of oblique advice I was getting a lot. I didn't know where to hook into it, how to listen better to make it feel real, like something I could act on. Still, I let it wash over me, this language I was trying to learn. My earnest, beautiful, California girlfriends, knowing I needed them, were doing their very best, circling with candles and crystals. I welcomed their warmth the way I imagined I was supposed to, with an open, wistful gaze, and slow, New Age nodding.

Just that week, one had shown up with a bottle of rosé and made the measured, straight-faced suggestion that I "sage" him from the premises. *This will cleanse your space of him,* she said, proffering a bound, faded bundle of expired flora and a lighter.

I was constantly cleansing him from my space. Every few days, for example, I'd clean our bathroom, wiping with Lysol-drenched paper towels the delicate spray of dried blood that lay over most surfaces and reminded me of the splatter of colored dye on the outside of a jawbreaker, the first layer that makes a white paste in your mouth as you suck it away. Living with a junkie involves a lot of effluvia. Everywhere, there are oozes that must be wiped away. It seems there's simply more of it all: The sweat that goes immediately cold on the disregulated slab of his body. Piss that didn't make it into the toilet bowl. There's blood and vomit—vomit every day—and the rotten, volcanic secretions of abscesses. And when I come home from work and he lunges for me, kisses me, all *babybaby* and half on the nod, and we fuck dreamily, devotedly on the couch, there's spit, and there's come.

Sometimes in the trash can I find wadded-up paper towels or bits of toilet paper he's used to wipe the blood away himself, and sometimes blood-stained T-shirts or socks or floral dish towels, which stiffen as they dry as though rigor mortis has set in.

I didn't know how to tell my friends, those well-meaning rays of blond hope, that intention setting was already my life. Intention setting was the blistering fever that came over me when I couldn't reach him and I had to type *fuck you fuck you fuck you fuck you fuck you fuck you fuck you* over four inches of an email box—my version of a breathing exercise—until I could calm down and go back to my work. My drafts folder was full of these ten-point *fuck you* blocks, and hundreds of other half-written love letters and hate letters I'd nearly lobbed his way, all intentions to reform or renounce him. Intention setting was what I was doing all those mornings I pulled the car over to cry with my head on the steering wheel, it was the cement resolve I felt harden in my gut when I saw how much money was missing from my bank account. It was the ominous thump of my own helplessness, the rhythm of my days and nights. What I needed was something for intention *keeping. Do they make a tinc-ture for that,* I wanted to ask, *some rose-petal elixir to heal me?*

Later that night, I did as my drummer friend said. I stood above my kitchen sink—swaying slightly, rocking the bourbon baby of my body—and burned a small strip of printer paper on which I'd writ-ten K—M—S—I AM LETTING GO OF YOU in junk-drawer ball-point pen. I'd considered I WANT TO LET GO OF YOU—*Write down what you want,* she'd said—but that seemed too aspirational, not present tense enough. No, I don't *want* to, I *am.*

The paper curled hot orange and tears welled in my eyes as the flame climbed slowly closer to my hand. I wanted it to be Satanic, the dark, measured wildness of casting a spell, untying and setting loose some force in the universe. It felt more like something out of a Taylor Swift video. A pathetic, overearnest micro-victory against obsessive love while my eyeliner ran. The tiny blaze appeared per-fectly controlled. I let the ashes fall into the dirty cereal bowls, nar-rowing my eyes to summon the sense that this time would be consequential. *I really mean it this time:* the refrain of sick people the world over. The thing is, you do mean it each time. That night I certainly did. I swallowed the lump in my throat and thought, *I am letting go, motherfucker. Starting right now.*

. . .

The disease he has is addiction. It's in the headlines every day, kill-ing more people than ever before, taking over the country. I look at graphs in the newspapers showing steep, almost vertical upticks in overdoses and deaths. I read all the stories—about the cheap, pure Mexican heroin flooding the market, about school-age kids left to fend for themselves as their parents descend, then disappear, about small-town librarians carrying NARCAN to reverse the overdoses happening in their bathrooms, about the cops in a futile, all-out war to stem the tides of supply and skyrocketing demand. At work, I surreptitiously watch *Vice* videos about Canadian teenagers pan-handling so they can snort crushed-up Smurf-blue Fentanyl, chas-ing ever-shorter highs. They amble around hot parking lots, sending text messages in search of ten more minutes of oblivion, more pills they can crush into the powder they snort off the backs of public toilets. You can see any prospect of future joy receding as their faces slacken and their lids grow heavy.

But even the constant reporting on the recent surge in drug horrors—seen as more horrifying now that the people affected are increasingly whiter and younger—cannot adequately document its monstrousness. Each time I read one of these stories, watch a film, or look at a graph, I think about all that lies outside the frame, the heartaches those headlines don't show, the creeping messes they won't account for and couldn't possibly contain. They say addiction is a "family disease," and I ponder this a lot, the astonishing rippling outward of bad decisions and risky behaviors—the impound lots, eviction notices, and pawned heirlooms, lives caught up, just as mine is, in managing everyday grief, accommodating each day a little bit more, more than you ever thought you could handle.

.   .   .

A cool morning in early autumn, Oakland, California. K is poised to get out of the car and onto the BART train to head to a job I'm not certain he actually has anymore. He presses play on the music on his phone and pulls the hood of his black sweatshirt—the addict's veil—gruffly up over his headphones. In the way a different person (me) might straighten her skirt or reach for her purse, K readies himself for public view with a series of small, personal movements. They are designed to hide as much of himself as possible. In more desperate times, he has ridden the train looking for people to rob, seizing upon couples he could intimidate by threatening to hit the woman. He wouldn't hit a woman, he said when he first revealed this to me, but the tactic always worked. *And the guy gets a moment to shine,* he added. *All he has to do is fork over the cash and he looks like a hero.* But K's habit is not that out of control at the moment, and besides, he has me.

His waking hours are a careful calculus. To get from sunrise to sundown, he needs forty dollars—thirty for heroin and ten for crack. Maybe a couple bucks more from the change jar for one of those plastic containers of lemon or lime juice that junkies use to break down crack. Bodegas in bad neighborhoods sell them on the counter. I used to wonder what they were for. He doesn't actually shoot drugs in front of me; the actual moments when he's getting high are more like an open secret between us. He usually goes to the bathroom to do it, and I can often hear him humming innocuously from behind the door, sometimes whistling, sounding carefree and maybe a little excited, like he's Mr. Rogers buttoning his cardigan and donning his loafers, readying himself for a wholesome adventure.

He'll do the first shot, a combination of the two, to get the first high of the day, the only true high. After so many years of shooting dope, speedballs are the quickest way to feel something. He'll do a second shot of the heroin he's saved later, to come down a bit from that bell-ringing height. And he'll need another one at night, but will rarely have enough left. His evening shot will just be a rinse—the weak residue of heroin left over in the cotton. It would be best if he could save himself a wakeup shot for the following morning, but he never finds a way to. (Does anyone? The wakeup shot might be a junkie myth.) At night, he might have a drink or take some pills or smoke some weed, but none will quell the mushrooming dopesickness—or the fear of dopesickness, which he tells me is just as strong as the sickness itself—that will peel him out of sleep around 4:00 A.M. and linger, a light panic, throughout the morning.

Dirty as it sounds, there's something neat and straightforward about his routine. It depends upon other humans—through cooperation, manipulation, coercion, force—yet it also remains pristinely single-minded, self-directed, and selfish.

So many of our habits come to feel like rituals, but if you think about it, few are truly nonnegotiable. I like to have a cup of coffee with a splash of milk every morning, but if there isn't coffee or milk at home, I simply wait. The day might take on a different shape, a detour to stop at a café or a trip to the market. Maybe I'll go without coffee until later in the afternoon. This isn't like that. The necessity of getting drugs and the wolfish entitlement to be high arrive anew each morning with the rosy light of daybreak, and he sets about, diversionless, feeding that urge.

Addiction is biological, of course, but that isn't all. It's emotional and psychological. Often, the addict retrofits an entire philosophy of life in order to justify his behavior. For example, K might say he's always been a nihilist, but I think that was just a way to account for his penchant for drugs. There's also something almost religious in the devotion this type of addiction, this practice, requires. The focus of the addict is chilling in its intensity. It's not like my morning coffee. It's more like the monk at the sound of the meditation gong. A zombie at the whiff of blood. A pattern that won't be interrupted, challenged, or moved. Its lack of variation feels like the purest dedication, though it also appears almost robotic. It is not enviable, but it *is* stunning—awe-inspiring—in its way.

I gotta get to work, he says as we sit parked in front of the train station. Outside the window, commuters stream by with briefcases, students with earbuds and backpacks. All have a bounciness that seems foreign to the moment, to the air inside the car, to the culture of our relationship. I watch them pass with longing and judgment.

I know he's going to ask me for money, and that he'll save it until the end so that the shame of the question might be lost among the last of his shufflings. His eyes dart around the car's interior and then eventually up to my eyes, where they pause flatly. He rolls the window down just a couple of inches, then rolls it back up. Nervous energy. He so often appears poised to bolt. *Can I borrow forty bucks,* he says, with no question mark. My pulse picks up at the sound of that word, "borrow." Just the sound of it, the nerve of it, rankles me. (Pro tip: a drug addict is never, ever borrowing money.) My eyes close for a long moment and then open again, and the daylight pours back in.

My calculations are ceaseless, too. My bank account has $211 in it. Our phone bill is overdue, and I need to buy groceries on my lunch break. But I get paid tomorrow, and it isn't the paycheck that goes entirely to rent, it's the fifteenth's paycheck, the one for bills.

I'm owed a few hundred dollars for a copyediting job. And there's child support coming. But forty dollars a day is two hundred and eighty dollars a week. Eleven hundred and twenty dollars a month. Enough to open a savings account, rent a room, take a trip, run away. An extra grand a month would be a life-changing sum. Or maybe I just crave a literal life change. That's the itch coursing angrily through my blood, a fix I don't know how to get. The money he needs we don't technically have, or we have it but we shouldn't spend it, we can't go on spending it like this. I can't make it fast enough, and if he's making any, it isn't making its way home. Not a dollar, not ever. On a different morning, I might ask if he is really going to work. With exhaustion and exasperation in my voice, I'd say, *You can just tell me if you don't have that job anymore.* I might even get angry, berate him for a few parting minutes for being aloof or opaque or conniving or a liar. Sitting in the car at the BART station seems to call forth the worst of my rage—why are these transitional spaces, these thresholds, the moments before separation, so ideal for quick, machine-gun bursts of fighting?

But not this morning. To comment is to risk lighting up the entire, intricate network of resentments that lay like a power grid beneath our relationship. Today the surface is fragile enough. I can tell he doesn't feel well.

Honesty is supposed to be the hallmark of a loving relationship, but I'm expert at swallowing my next thought just as it's about to make its way out of my mouth. I say nothing. I don't know if I even think anything. I open my black leather envelope wallet, a grown woman's wallet, the one my mother bought me for my birthday, saying, I'm *a professional who needs a few nice things,* and I pull out two twenties. I hold the money in my hand and look at K for a long minute, talking with my eyes, feeling the perverse power I hold as the gatekeeper, breadwinner, granter of wishes. I can make dope-sickness disappear. It's money I withdrew from the ATM on San Pablo on the way home from work the night before, anticipating this very interaction, knowing my role. That I will give it to him is a foregone conclusion. I don't know why. I only know that every day I think I'll do something different and then I don't. I set out to do the opposite of this—to make my life the opposite of this—and then discover that *this* is a decision I seem to have already made.

. . .

The disease I have is loving him. They don't write articles about it or send camera crews to follow us. The disease I have is called co-dependency, or sometimes enabling, and it isn't really a disease, though it can feel like one. It's more like an ill-defined set of tendencies and behaviors, and depending on how badly it's flaring, it can manifest as a lot of different things—a disorder, a nuisance, an encumbrance, a curse, or sometimes merely a sensibility, a preference, a cast of mind. It can manifest as the gentle tinkling piano notes before Patsy Cline sings that first long, plaintive "craaaaazy." *Crazy for thinking that my love could hold you.* One of a hundred anthems that have come to sound vaguely psychotic as I've applied them to my own circumstances. So many songs are about men wriggling away from love. This one in particular would make a good codependent cross-stitch: *Crazy for trying, and crazy for crying, and crazy for loving you.* That would look nice above the mantel. Incidentally, the song "Crazy" was originally written by Willie Nelson for country singer Billy Walker, but Walker turned it down, reportedly calling it a "girl's song." According to Nelson's biographer, Cline "didn't much cotton to songs that made her sound so wounded." But the song broke into the Top Ten on the pop charts and became her signature.

Codependency is a girl's song. The sounds of the busying and tidying of the quietly controlling. The sniveling and whimpering of the long overlooked, the caterwaul of the brokenhearted. The word has a long and complex history, but it has never been taken particularly seriously. To the extent that it is understood at all, codependency is thought to be the province of crazy girlfriends, overbearing mothers, and pathetic wives. In popular culture, women's obsessive, controlling, or enabling behaviors are represented as assorted forms of weakness or madness. Sometimes pitiable, sometimes just sad.

We codependents used to be called "co-alcoholics," which is

kind of funny. It gets at just how much of an accomplice you are: for them to drink like that takes someone like you to make it possible, some gullible idiot idling in the getaway car. Some people think this condition is the same as relationship addiction or love addiction, a debilitating focus on an external source of validation. Some believe that the constellation of behaviors referred to as codependent are maladaptive responses to childhood trauma that may be unrelated to substance abuse. Still others think the very idea of codependency is nonsense and that the kinds of relationships that come to be defined this way needn't be pathologized, that they're not that much more messed up than any other relationship. In recent years, attachment theory has come to dominate some corners of the mental health establishment, and an insecure or anxious attachment has become a more popular way to denote these dysfunctional bonds. If the style of attachment you learned in infancy and childhood is insecure, you may forever seek relationships that are laced with fear or shaded by rejection.

The definitions are varied and sometimes weak, the diagnostic tools shoddy, and the treatments wide-ranging, but this way of being is real. In the 2003 book *Love Is a Choice: The Definitive Book on Letting Go of Unhealthy Relationships,* Robert Hemfelt, Frank Minirth, and Paul Meier write that codependency affects roughly four people for every one alcoholic. And current estimates of the number of alcoholics in the United States are shockingly high. A 2017 paper published in *JAMA Psychiatry* found that one in eight American adults suffer from alcoholism. Considering challenges in accurate reporting and the sharply rising number of drug addicts in this country, that number of sufferers from addiction in general is conservative. Hemfelt, Minirth, and Meier —all doctors who treat codependency—are not alone in arguing that "we are embattled by an epidemic of staggering degree. The unhappiness, despair, and wasted life lie beyond comprehension."

But if codependency is a condition that produces widespread despair, if it's responsible for an "epidemic of . . . wasted life," why don't we know more about it? Alcoholism and its treatment entered popular consciousness long ago, and though arguably still stigmatized and misunderstood, the disease has become ever-more medicalized and normalized in our culture. Co-alcoholism, or co-dependency, was defined alongside alcoholism, but continues to be seen as a set of desperate behaviors practiced by sad women. The term enjoyed a moment of widespread exposure in the late 1980s and early '90s, as the Twelve Step recovery movement ballooned, but it has since been largely sidelined and sometimes ridiculed. Even as alcoholism treatment emphasizes that addiction is a "family disease," the codependent struggle—so often a woman's struggle—is marginalized.

In movies, TV shows, and magazine articles about addiction, the family is usually present, but on the sidelines or in the shadows, their anguish an unfortunate effect of the disease, not a contributing factor, a puzzle to be worked on, or a condition unto itself. We are inclined to think that family members are not, after all, the principal characters in the drama, just its supporting cast. But living alongside addiction is a distinctly bewildering experience. It is grueling, depressing, infuriating, and often terrifying. Perversely, it is not without its perks—for many, there is some kind of emotional payoff involved. Living in proximity to addiction enables codependents to feel righteous and smug, or victimized and manipulated. This illness gives our lives their texture, in some cases their purpose.

I've come to see that the tale of the lonely alcoholic, the lonely junkie—peddled largely in the literary accounts of male addicts, from Thomas De Quincey to Alexander Trocchi to John Cheever, and cemented in film representations of tortured, scruffy souls—entails an act of obfuscation. Of course, we know that a profound solitude attends the machinations of the addict. Being in the throes of the disease entails a miserable, yawning existential aloneness, a confrontation with one's weakness and powerlessness that has proven rich fodder for artistic expression. But addiction is also necessarily a relational condition. In all but the most abject circumstances, someone, somewhere, is making the money, covering for the addict, cleaning up the mess. Someone is sitting by the window, waiting. Someone is believing, hoping that today might be different.

The mythic male genius artist was long thought to be divinely inspired to create masterpieces in isolation. Except that was never the complete picture. We have by now come to understand the ways that story conveniently conceals the labor of wives, apprentices, and assistants, as well as all of the structural forces and institutional particularities that elevate certain work and idolize certain individuals. Often, at the center of addiction narratives, we find a sole individual: the addict, on a lonely hero's journey toward salvation or else free-falling toward death. But why should he be seen in isolation? Why do we not as a matter of course acknowledge that behind every junkie is a veritable symphony of hidden energies? And why shouldn't we care about those?

This book arose from a desire to interrogate the ideas that underpin codependency and reinvigorate a conversation around what it means to love those who are dependent on substances. I wanted to write about the ways that living around addiction habituates us to chaos and fear, invites us to dwell in perpetual victimhood, and drives our decision-making in self-destructive directions. I wanted to better understand how this problem was articulated in the first place, by whom and for whom. In the days before they could own property, hold paying jobs, or vote, women were arguably the people most severely impacted by alcoholism. Was codependency a schematic they designed themselves in order to describe their own reality? Or, as with so many conditions specific to women, was it identified and elaborated by a mostly male psychological establishment? Does it really exist? Can it really be treated? Ameliorated? Cured? Should it? Is there something liberating about choosing to apply this lens to our lives, or are we simply reproducing tired ideas about gender, family, relatedness, and love, not to mention addiction?

This book is not just about my life. It's also the story of nineteenth-century American women who for so long felt helpless watching men in their lives succumb to alcoholism, and who eventually fought to ban alcohol entirely. It's about the women who, after their husbands found their way to Alcoholics Anonymous (AA) in the early twentieth century, discovered they had a great deal in common and formed the coffee klatch that became Al-Anon. It's about the men and women who ushered in a boom in self-help literature in the 1980s and '90s and the ways they broadened existing notions of codependency beyond alcoholism.

Our views of love and dependency are complex, informed by our family stories and personal experiences, and shaped by the culture we live in. Codependency as it expresses itself in romantic relationships looks a lot like the representations of "true love" we see in literature and film (and that many women like me grow up gorging themselves on). The work of separating the threads of our love relationships, exploring what makes them tick and what makes them toxic, is daunting and also exciting. I wonder what it would look like for us to bear witness differently to the exquisite pain addiction causes in people's lives and the ways we try to square that pain with love.

chapter two

"This is the love our grandparents had," I once said to K, and it became something like a tagline for our love, a line he repeated to me many times when he admired me in a new dress or sought to soothe me after an argument. I think he repeated it also to remind me not to expect too much from him—ours was not a therapized love, after all, not a gender-neutral love, a love between evolved equals. It was an old-world romance, loud and lively—roaring with violent uncertainty—into which some tears and some lies were bound to fall. Some objects were bound to be hurled across the room. That seemed the price for such gargantuan affection, for the love notes stashed in the books I was reading, the pleasure he took in bringing me flowers and buying me records, in scaring me half to death and ravenously kissing my neck while I stood soaping the dishes. Date nape, we called it.

"Young girls, they do get weary, wearing that same old shaggy dress," sang Otis Redding in "Try a Little Tenderness." "Looo-ooo-ooove is their only happiness."

Before K, I'd grown weary in record time, in a marriage that should have, maybe could have, nourished me. My husband and I were wed just a few years earlier under a weak North Bay sun, in a little backyard ceremony at his sister's house, where the guests had applied fake heart-and-banner tattoos of our names to their biceps and forearms. Our mothers, smiling proudly, posed for a photo together, arm-to-arm, showing off their matching tattoos. *I can't believe I get to marry you,* I'd said during my vows, looking up into his big, aqua eyes, gulping forcefully to stop myself from more crying. I was prone not to demure tearfulness but to real sobbing in these moments, the slightly fearful sense of being positively overcome. That evening, a cool breeze blew in. My husband and I fed each other bites of a layered white sheet cake bedecked with fresh flowers and fresh strawberries and cream in the middle. Our son was the size of a strawberry, too, growing there behind my dress and a tacky lace BRIDE thong, my something blue.

It felt like a beginning as auspicious as any other, but it wasn't long before I felt emotionally alone, before I was pining for a more desperate variant of love, something a little wilder to make me feel more alive. Not long after K walked back into my life, I detonated my young marriage for a chance to step fully and honestly into a life with him. I had a two-year-old and a two-month-old. I was insane, in other words.

K was sober at the time, but it didn't last. He overdosed and died the day we moved in together, into a tiny sublet I'd found, secured, and paid for. He was shooting speedballs with his friend Will, an unrepentant junkie I would come to know well, who had the presence of mind to call 911 (no small or un-risky thing for someone whose whole life is illegal). The EMTs arrived, defibrillated the flatlined K back into being, and delivered him to me, the button electrodes still stuck to his chest with tacky adhesive. The apartment was full of unpacked boxes. That night, we lay in silence in bed. He smoothed the baby's colorless sprouts of hair as I nursed her.

Sobriety, it turned out, was not a thing I could expect from him. The things I *could* expect, however, seemed to be the important things, to me, perhaps sadly, the only things—protection, fun, laughter, extraordinary sex. Drinking Slurpees together in my car on a street corner was pure joy. The once soul-deadening errands that defined my days—food shopping, dry cleaning—were, with him, extravagantly entertaining.

As if to resist the always-imminent threat of his death, we made a romance from a distant era. He was handsome and I was pretty. I learned his mother's recipes. We decorated the Christmas tree and changed diapers and threw dinner parties and had date nights and wheeled the trash cans out to the curb on Wednesday nights. We took comfort in the traditions we built or sustained as a bulwark against the chaos we lived with. And for long stretches, we made do—on no money, no sleep, no one's approval, just love. It existed only for us, this clunky, blind, and stupid love, it was a solar system that held our two planets alone, and gave our lives myth and meaning.

"I love you as certain dark things are to be loved, in secret," wrote Neruda.

Anytime we could, we fucked all day, every conceivable permutation of fucking, and then one sweet missionary one, his body covering me completely as though we were brothers in arms and might be lying next to a grenade. In the beginning it was summer, and sex with him was summer sex, powered by the sun, grimy and gruff. We smelled of bicycle chains, something industrial, metallic, and sweet that passed between us as we bit at each other's lips. Pineapple juice and heroin. I liked it best when he was rough, the look on his face when I was Bambi-eyed and frozen in fear. Be a dear. Be a little deer. Afterward, I slept beneath his muscled arm as though tied down by heavy rope.

Weeknights I was weak-kneed, tiptoeing over and over again to the freezer in an apricot vintage slip, refreshing the ice in our drinks, pouring just a couple fingers more. We slow-danced in the dark, with the kids sweetly snoring in their beds and the dishwasher sloshing and whirring. The day's drudgery lightened by lust. Is this not every young mother's dream?

Sometimes we got stoned and watched reruns of *Chopped,* and he made me laugh so hard I peed. It was like getting away with something, laughing like that every day.

. . .

Fifteen years before his blood was splattered on our bathroom walls, we met on Thanksgiving Day, 1997, at the Tower Records on the corner of Market and Castro Streets in San Francisco, where I was a clerk working the 4:00 P.M. to 1:00 A.M. closing shift with a motley crew of disaffected minimum-wage earners. We passed the time pranking one another or using the label maker or bits of foam core from the art department to make funny signs and little art projects. From the masthead of one of the porn magazines we sold in the store, I'd clipped the words *Barely Legal* and taped them to the yellow plastic name tag I wore around my neck, where my name was supposed to go—a small act of guerrilla crafting that says virtually everything about me as a teenager. I lusted after boys, but more than that I lusted after being lusted after. I applied creamy lipsticks in mauves and wines and brilliant reds, pulled my black hair into a high ponytail, and daily practiced my gait, the sly, steady pendulum of my hips and my heart-shaped ass as I walked upstairs to the count-out room. The name tag was an act of interpolation, a way of insisting I'd be viewed in a particular way by every stranger who walked in. *Welcome, I'm fuckable!* But it wasn't all advertisement. "Barely Legal" was also literally true: by Thanksgiving that year, I'd been eighteen for exactly two weeks.

The days at Tower were punctuated by smoke breaks, when I leaned against the red banister outside the store, sucking down Marlboro Mediums and ashing into a large potted plant. Sometimes I would pad down Market to the bookstore to make eyes at the clerk or to Sweet Nothings for a coffee and a slice of apple cake to be picked apart throughout the remainder of my shift. At work I was gregarious, but once thrust outside alone, I felt shy, uncomfortable, and exposed. I felt young. It was cold. In California, I was always freezing. I wore tights and boots and pulled my sweater sleeves down over my hands, tapping at the cash register keys with the exposed tips of my frigid fingers, rocking onto the balls of my feet for the chill and my anxiety. This is how he found me.

K, with his thick, black, Italian hair slicked into a throwback pompadour with Tres Flores brilliantine, greasy as Vaseline, its cloying petroleum-geranium fragrance trailing him. He came into the store—tall and lean and clean and beautiful, tattooed everywhere with sacred hearts and the lyrics of Smiths songs—and bought an Alice in Chains CD called *Dirt*. My eyes burned at the sight of him.

He knew instinctively, by my clothes or my attitude, the special sneer of the record-store employee, that I would disapprove of his selection—I'd made a point of looking like someone who was clearly into deeper cuts. He walked to the register with a defense already prepared. *I drove all the way across town so that no one would recognize me buying this,* he said, smiling as I rang him up. I smiled, too, and looked at him skeptically.

I'm on my way out to my mom's, he continued, *and just needed something to listen to on the drive, but now I feel suddenly ashamed.*

You should, I said. *That record is terrible.* We laughed and I shrugged as if to say I don't make the rules.

K pulled his wallet from his pocket and I completed the transaction nervously, under the hot spotlight of fresh desire. I knew for certain he could see me squirm. The CD and receipt I put inside the little yellow plastic bag and thrust it out to him, my eyebrows raised in anticipated parting.

Working on Thanksgiving? he said, as he opened his pea coat to drop the CD into the large inside pocket. *That's too bad.*

Outside, the greyness hovered. Cars sped down Market. The door jangled as another customer entered the store. I wanted to curl up in that warm coat pocket and be moved by the weight of him, all over this city I didn't yet know.

It's okay, I replied. *I have nowhere else to be.*

For the rest of the day I turned the exchange over and over in my mind, burnishing it like found treasure, willing it to mean more than it did. I smoked a clove cigarette with Winter, a goth girl I worked with who smelled strongly of vanilla oil and wore her fire-red dreadlocks in high pigtails, and told her about the cute boy I'd rung up. *Oh really,* she said, unfazed. A cute boy coming into the record store was a thing that sometimes happened.

That I had nowhere to be was not at all true. The following day, a shared day off, I would over-butter the Stove Top stuffing and the green beans, and share them, along with a teriyaki tofu stir-fry and a six-pack, with Rachel and Kat, my best friends. We would lounge, overfull, on the fuchsia carpet of our Fourteenth Street apartment, stoned and giggling under the twinkle of pink Christmas lights, 2,900 miles from home—plum across the world, it felt like—and elated. We'd driven to San Francisco from New Jersey three months earlier, after high school finally, blessedly came to an end. Straight across I-80 in a dying Honda hatchback, with a few zigzagging detours, to begin a self-imposed exile from the suburbs. We mapped our route in a lap-sized atlas: New Jersey to Michigan to Illinois to Colorado to Utah to Nevada to California, playing the same shoebox of mixtapes over and over. Aged seventeen, hair whipping in the highway wind, I only wanted to feel the freedom of the passenger seat, to look at myself in the side-view mirror, see myself being seen. Is all youth the same? That bottom quadrant of my face, an object in the mirror, closer than it appeared, all plump skin, lip gloss, and soda straws. The stick of a lollipop—*Lo. Lee. Ta.*—jutting out from between my teeth. We wrote postcards home in all-night diners and broke down outside Chicago, coasting down an exit ramp into a service station where Rachel flirted with the mechanic. He took her on a motorcycle ride while the other guys worked on the car and I felt some raw, foreign combination of after-dark panic and jealousy. Around every corner, it seemed, there were men willing to extend to us various courtesies, to give us things for free, to let us in underage, batting away our youth as though it was a nuisance, a gnat, nothing. New worlds were becoming visible, new constellations beginning to hotly twinkle in the night skies of our minds.

When K and I next ran into each other four months later, I was at my other job, at a Mission gift shop. *Tower Records girl,* he blurted out when he saw me. He was with two friends, similarly dressed and tattooed boys who were cute enough but looked rougher. They didn't radiate the way K did. He appeared luminous to me. The three of them scuffled around the shop cracking jokes, trying to be inconspicuously conspicuous, flirting without even looking at me. "Sitting On the Dock of the Bay" was playing, and just at the part where Otis begins to whistle, K raised a finger in warning, looked around the store, and said out loud, *Nobody better do the corny whistling part,* which made me laugh. A few minutes later they left, but a few minutes after that, he came back, and walked up to the counter where I stood.

So, he began.

Yes? I smiled.

Do you have a strict policy against going out with people who've purchased that Alice in Chains record? he asked.

It was fairly strict, I was sorry to say, but I would make an exception in this case. *Just this once,* I said, writing my phone number down on the back of one of the store's gold business cards.

He began calling me after he got off work in the middle of the night. I was wide awake at the blond wood kitchen table, waiting for the sharp rolling *brrrring!* of the wall phone. I rolled the ash of my cigarette along the perimeter of a novelty Las Vegas ashtray, working its lit end into a grey and glowing cone. After smoking a few, I lay by the heater in our hallway, which required stretching the telephone cord as far as it would go, and we talked for two, three, four hours. Our kittens walked up and down my back as I did my best to charm him.

Our relationship was brief and intense. K was gorgeous and inscrutable and funny, unfairly funny, and a little bit mean. His hair looked like something from the fifties, or the forties? Sometimes the twenties, when it hadn't yet been pomaded for the day and made a shiny dark mop messily befitting a rakish Left Bank poet. Can you fall for a hairline? Some are unflattering or uneven, but his stretched perfectly, ever so slightly bowed across his forehead, so precise as to look like a wire penning in his voluminous straight greasy hair. I wanted his love desperately and I knew I couldn't be the only one. Some people have that kind of magnetism. I could sense a certain current directed toward him, could almost feel writhing within the city the bodies, the energy of many more girls in many other apartments, hoping he would call. I pictured them and broke out in a fever of jaw-clenching jealousy, even though I knew he liked me. He was hard to pin down, but when I got myself in front of him, he looked at me like I was an ice cream sundae.

K would disappear for a few days and then call, all breezy confidence and purpose.

What are you doing right now? he asked.

What to say, baking a cake? Writing a song? Getting ready to go out? Anything but "nothing."

Nothing, I said. *What are you doing?* I could never think of anything cool.

Hanging out with you, he said. *I'll pick you up in twenty minutes.*

His was the kind of attention I felt I just had to take as it came—because I was too young and too shy or because he was intimidating, older, and clearly more experienced. Or was he? I never worked up the courage to ask him where he'd been, why I hadn't heard from him, what exactly he wanted from me, how many others like me there were. That day, I waited for him outside my apartment in a burgundy skirt. I wore my faded black sweatshirt, the one that said JENN in white felt lettering on the breast, underneath Rachel's jean jacket, which had clusters of black bobby pins in the pockets and smelled of our smoky apartment. On the pavement in front of our door were smashed avocados that had fallen from a tree. The fruit made matte smudges of lime green and yellow on the ground. The sun was shining and birds were singing like symbols of happiness and naïveté in a cartoon. I rode up Potrero on the back of his motorcycle, the city blurring by me, and when we stopped at a stop sign at the top of the hill, I pictured us from above, a bird's-eye view of us from a telephone pole. We were a movie poster unrolled against the sky.

K was a smooth operator. On the floor of his Oak Street bedroom, we made out by the light of VHS tapes: ultraviolent Japanese slasher movies, Morrissey music videos, *The Godfather*. On my walk downhill from Tower after work, I stopped to flirt with him at the bar where he worked the door, and once watched him settle an altercation by strong-arming a drunk and belligerent frat boy into the back of a cab. *All right, Joe College, take it easy,* he said as he fluidly twisted the guy's forearm behind his back, hailing a taxi at the same time. *Fuck you!* the guy was shouting through the window, and K just smiled, cool as a speakeasy gangster, and said, *You're gonna be okay, pal,* rapping his knuckle on the top of the car as it drove away.

Everyone in his orbit had a nickname. Mine was Pimentoloaf— I have absolutely no memory of its genesis, I only know that it soon became the only thing he called me and despite being an ugly word for a disgusting luncheon meat, somehow it didn't even sound odd. We went out for coffee in North Beach and sushi in the Sunset and he made me laugh loudly, a bright, squeaky, sunny sound I barely recognized. He said he thought he should move back to New York with me when I started college in the fall, and we spun a story about what our life could be like there. Plants on the sill of an East Village apartment. A little dog.

While sitting at the laundromat watching the dryers spin my clothes, he told me he'd had cancer, and I drove him to St. Mary's one day and waited as they scanned him to see if it had come back. Fingering the pages of a paperback as I sat nervously in the plastic waiting-room chair, I felt the familiar charge of responsibility. It had a narcotic effect on me, this sense of mild suffering, the feeling of being needed, of being poised to *go through* something. If he was sick, I would nurse him back to health. I relished the idea. As it turned out, the cancer wasn't back that time, but it soon would be, and K would experience his first taste of opiate painkillers, which would alter the course of his life.

.   .   .

I was particularly keen to leave home for California. My parents were in the middle of a divorce and had both taken up with new partners. For my father, who was living in a small, yellowed apartment with a mattress on the floor and one fork, it was a revolving cast of local moms. For my mother, it was Jim, a much younger man she met through work and with whom she seemed suddenly, shockingly in love. My younger sister, Anya, frequently enveloped by pot smoke in her bedroom, still pulled straight As. She came and went from friends' houses and field hockey practices with her thick athletic braid reaching almost to her waist, seeming, with her long legs and unsettling type-A aptitude for everything, somehow both apart from and already above any family drama. My older sister, Lucia, had graduated from drug-fueled weekend raves to cocaine to full-blown heroin addiction, and I carried her secrets around like a backpack full of body parts, guilty, angry, and exhausted. At home as a young teenager, I learned the detective work of codependency, nurturing along with my fear-crazed parents the delusion that if we could just put our hands on the evidence, we could somehow stop my sister, save her, find out the truth. It had been this way for a few years. *Go in there and see if you find anything,* my mother whispered conspiratorially whenever Lucia was out or distracted, and I'd slip into my sister's bedroom, sweaty and stealthy as special forces, to root around in her belongings and retrieve some proof that things were how we thought they were, that we were not insane. No, we were *right.* I'd return minutes later with her needle exchange ID card, bottles of pills, bits of folded up aluminum foil from the bottom of her purse, tiny plastic bags imprinted with skulls, bearing the ghostly residue of white powder. I dropped these like a loyal dog and was awarded the treat of my mother's love. Much as I came to resent it, I felt most alive and most treasured when I was called upon to do this important work, to be my mother's partner in crime-solving. I always rose to meet the challenge of trying to figure out and control my sister's life, of invading her privacy. It felt like a righteous pursuit, a battle of light over darkness, good against evil. Backed into a corner by heroin, we felt we had no choice. Tracking my sister's movements was what we must do or else we would lose her. Her survival became a kind of crooked victory we audaciously believed we'd engineered.

Lucia had always seemed too big for our town. She had a certain star quality, even as a child. She loved performing and the excitement of all its preceding necessities: rehearsing, yes—that she did with Fosse-like focus—but also corralling and orchestrating others' energies, gathering an audience, dimming the lights, and pulling back a bedsheet curtain. A born ringleader, she made programs for our living-room plays, menus for our kitchen-table café, and once the show began, she never broke character. *Can I get you anything else or are you ready for the bill?* she'd asked our parents earnestly as she cleared plates from our pretend restaurant while Anya and I stood tittering in the wings. *Perhaps you'd like to meet the chefs? They're sisters, you know.*

While our grandmother napped one day, Lucia convinced us to put on her clothes and perform a bizarre funerary-style ritual at her bedside, walking in one by one to lay jewelry and other household offerings on her sleeping body. She directed Anya and me in silence, waving us toward the bed and nodding as we placed a comb and a bracelet on Nanny's gently rising and falling bosom. Lucia took pride in forcing solemnity over a room, holding us as if under a spell. In the backyard, atop the picnic table, wearing jelly bracelets up to the elbow and one lace glove, she commandeered an army of cousins and neighbors, directing lip sync performances of Madonna and Debbie Gibson. Once, she pretended she was a scientist and locked Anya in our dog's crate to study her. When Anya complained of hunger, Lucia slipped bites of a bagel through the bars. *Let her out!* I protested. *But I like it,* said Anya from inside the cage.

In a way, Anya was better matched to Lucia's intensity than I was. A string bean with a wild, tangled mane of mysteriously blond hair, she had seemed to be in possession of an excess of ardor from the very beginning of life. It emerged as a tantrum or through her drillbit kisses, moments when she glommed on to me and wouldn't let go, or in the form of frantic dancing. For a time, around five or six years old, she carried a cassette player around the house. After a sleepover once, she barged in and woke up my friend and me with a 6:00 A.M. rendition of Ella Fitzgerald's "A Tisket, A Tasket."

My sisters liked a spectacle, and it could be thrilling to be their assistant, apprentice, understudy. Lucia especially made you want to go along with her. I wasn't shy, exactly, but I drew no power from being the center of attention. I retreated with a book when their games grew most elaborate. When my sisters belted out show tunes, harmonizing perfectly at ages seven and twelve, I didn't know where my weaker voice fit. It often got lost in the middle. *You be the boy,* Lucia would say, *you can't be Cosette, you're Jean Valjean.*

Naturally, the older we got, the more dangerous the spectacle. We started going to punk rock shows at City Gardens in Trenton, and I watched her abandon herself to the sweaty throng, get tossed around by the undulations of the crowd or whipped about by a mosh pit. It was the same fearlessness and surrender as when she swam in the ocean. She once laughed while confiding in me that she'd been tripping on acid in math class that day, and the carefree sound of the laughter terrified me: Was it a confession or a provocation? Didn't she know it would frighten me? I realized that she was often stoned while driving us to and from school in our mom's old silver Saab, but I didn't want to get her in trouble, so I asked if she would teach me to drive. It was only a couple miles anyway, and I was almost fifteen.

Lucia was glamorous. She became best friends with an equally glamorous British girl whose parent was a visiting professor at Princeton, and the pair seemed to have more fun than anyone else in school. They watched episodes of *Absolutely Fabulous* and dyed their hair the same colors as Patsy and Edina. They bought cigarettes from a hesher at school who carried a guitar case filled with cartons of them, and smoked where the cool kids did, in the area we called Varsity Smoking. One spring, Lucia contracted mono and stayed home for a month, tanning on the roof and listening to Saint Etienne on a boom box.

The only time our parents ever left us alone overnight, Lucia threw a party in the backyard. It was summer, and they'd driven upstate to collect Anya from her first sleepaway camp. At the impromptu party, where guests multiplied like swarming insects—so many people I'd never seen before, where had they come from?—my boyfriend and I walked through the smoky mob, then retreated upstairs to observe the debauchery from a bedroom window.

You'll take care of the house and be responsible, right, my darlings? my mother had said that morning. How convincingly Lucia had nodded, tilting her head to question the question itself. *Why yes, of course, Mother,* she'd said, in a posh English accent. Now I could see her in a lawn chair below, holding court from her perch on a skater's lap.

You're Lucia's sister? a boy asked me as I stood by my locker not long after that party, his face full of all that that meant to him. What did it mean—that I was cool? Easy? That now we had a party house?

Yeah, I answered.

He just raised his eyebrows and smiled.

For all the uncertainty, the fear, that Lucia introduced, she was also brilliant, glittering with an enviable knowingness, and when it came to getting something done or getting the grade, she always pulled it off at the last minute. She made things look easy. Often at night, with the whole household winding down, she was just sitting down at the dining room table to plow through the day's homework, which she was smart enough to do in fifteen minutes. Once, we awoke in the morning to find that she'd baked two large trays of perfect madeleines in the night. *What is this?* I asked. *For French class,* she answered nonchalantly. *I have to make some presentation.* For college, she had her heart set on going to Tisch, the competitive drama school at NYU. Before her audition, she stayed up all night learning Ophelia's monologue from *Hamlet*—*O my Lord, my Lord, I have been so affrighted!* she exclaimed in the kitchen as I packed my lunch—and was, of course, accepted. The deeper into addiction she got, the less common these moments were, but Lucia never completely lost this magic. It's part of what kept hope alive in our family.

chapter three

When I was five or six, I asked my mother about religion. I had become curious about the churches in our town, around which on the weekends clustered well-heeled, sandy-haired congregants clad in taupes and ecrus. *What is church?* I asked, and she answered that it was a place where people went to practice their religion. *What is religion?* I pressed. That drew a pause.

A lot of beautiful pictures and stories, she eventually said. *Some of them are very scary. People have been looking at them for a long, long time—they use them to make sense of the world.*

Are the pictures and stories real? I asked.

No, she said flatly, not missing a beat.

A few years later, my mother shed her skin, leaving domesticity behind to go back to school and earn a graduate degree in art history. Something was stirring in her. Months earlier, she'd torn an image of a David Hockney swimming pool—monochromatic blue, more cornflower than aqua—from an art magazine and stuck it with a magnet to the fridge beneath some words she'd cut from an advertisement in the newspaper: "Other worlds do exist."

While she read or checked out books, my sisters and I played hushed games of hide-and-seek among the Rutgers library carrels and went on group excursions to the hallway water fountain, dragging our Velcro sneakers along the carpet to make static electricity to administer little shocks. Mommy shot us a serious look if we were getting too noisy, and we fell in line, shushing one another. Sometimes at night after dinner, we were enlisted to quiz her for exams from a giant stack of index cards on which she'd written the names of painters on one side and paintings on the other, in her pretty, efficient, semi-script handwriting. In my memory, the stack of index cards was as high as my knees, but it couldn't have actually been that tall. Some of the images in her textbooks were the same ones I knew she'd been talking about when we'd discussed religion. All those beautiful pictures and stories: angels and fire and breasts.

My mother wrote her thesis about representations of women during Westward Expansion, and for half a year there were books scattered around the house or stacked on the dining room table depicting these embattled souls. Women's struggles and women's dreams were a theme in our home. There were three of us girls— ducklings toddling in a row—and our mother and her index cards, and we all wanted so much. In her master's thesis, plucked from a box during one of her post-divorce moves, my mother sought to grant interiority and depth to women who'd been painted out of their complexity, their humanity. The hardy pioneer family was the primary "civilizing" agent at the center of the violent, racist doctrine of Manifest Destiny, but the women at the helm of these families were rendered (by men) without agency. Many were small and peripheral—specks of femininity—representing something without actually *being* anything. The frontier painters drew on Christian iconography, and my mother catalogued the female figures they painted as "frontier Madonnas," "happy nesters," and "captives." Then she used the accounts in pioneer women's diaries to demonstrate how rich and how difficult their experiences actually were. To their blurred faces and windswept skirts, she added the details of their exhaustion, determination, fear, and hope. She asserted that they had as much expertise as their intrepid hunter-husbands who, along with their horses, were always depicted in action—upright, dynamic, and strong. It was an admirable act of recuperation.

I grew up believing there is always more to the story. I was primed to be interested in women's history and particularly in the spaces where it seemed there *ought* to be a women's history, yet there was nothing. I suppose I was trained by my mother to remember that other worlds exist, to always look at the woman frozen in the window and wonder what her life was like. I grew up in love with women's stories, with the ways their labor made itself visible everywhere, even when men would prefer to pretend that it wasn't the scaffolding of their very existence. I was especially taken with their anger.

At thirteen, my friends and I became riot grrrls. We were hormonal, stewing in new bodily shames, processing the experiences of sexual assault we'd already had by the handful. We embarked on an ambitious regimen of at-home piercing, bleaching, head-shaving. I was reading nightly from a hardbound, secondhand copy of *Sisterhood Is Powerful* and having my mind blown. And then I ordered the first Bikini Kill LP from Kill Rock Stars and we listened to it on my parent's record player, draped on the den futon, and our lives changed forever.

Radicalized by mail order, our baby claws came out. We made zines and traded them with other girls around the country who became our pen pals and our friends. In sparkly homemade envelopes, we sent one another candy and toys and stickers and long letters, sharing our secrets, trying to build a movement. We wheat-pasted flyers around town with messages that made our fathers raise their eyebrows. ("Hi, I just wanted to let you know that I am not going to smile, act dumb, hide my body, pretend, lie, or act silent for you," read one flyer made by Omaha riot grrrl Ann Carroll that we plastered everywhere. "I'm not going to let you laugh at me, harass me, abuse me, or rape me anymore. Because I am a girl and me and my girlfriends are not afraid of you!") We went to punk rock shows and eventually started our own pissed-off, three-piece band. We got other bands to play shows at the local arts council or the basement of the Unitarian church. When the first of us got a license, we drove to New York and Philadelphia to go to house shows and vegetarian Chinese restaurants, to run around. We let our leg hair grow. It was before we knew sugar was toxic, before anyone thought to eschew gluten. Junk food was a rebellion. *Riot don't diet,* I scrawled in lavender paint marker on the locker-room mirror. We slept over at the houses where parents were the most permissive, and sat talking and listening to music, gorging ourselves on candy and soda and chips, grouping jelly beans by color, making straws out of Twizzlers to drink our Dr Pepper through. In the darkness of 2:00 or 3:00 A.M., we snuck out and walked around town, stealing a taste of freedom, listening for boys on skateboards, watching the streetlights cast our shadows and taking ourselves in, our forms suddenly tall and forbidding, with power in numbers. A proper girl gang.

We became foot soldiers of a feminism that, like my mother's, began with an impulse to wedge women's reality, specifically women's pain, back into the stories we tell about the world. Riot grrrl was very white and very suburban—it was rightly criticized for becoming an echo chamber for girls like us—but I cherished the scene for giving me a new language and a purpose. Riot grrrl continued the work of Second Wave consciousness-raising by foregrounding the first-person narrative, which we believed had radical potential, and by recasting human history as riven by incest, rape, and other abuses of power. The movement also continually acknowledged its own messiness and the mess that was womanhood—particularly sexuality—and validated our growing sense that patriarchy was not only a thing that was being enacted upon us but a throbbing, oozing, living system in which we were complexly complicit.

But as I was embracing radical feminism, my relationships with my family, friends, and boys were growing evermore enmeshed. Friendships and crushes were consuming and obsessive. I felt targeted and trapped by the intensity of boys' feelings for me. And though I was learning about political experiments in collectivity, I knew that the more primary feminist project lay in cultivating autonomy, and that seemed impossible to imagine. My responsibility to my family alone precluded any possibility of real independence. Between my budding feminism and the demands of my relationships, there was a disconnect. I found myself utterly unable to put my new principles into practice in my personal life.

As a teenager, I spent hours enveloped by the tall, overfull pine bookshelves at the used bookstore in our town, looking for a book about someone like me. Someone who searched for drugs in her sister's shoulder bag, in the aperture of her sister's pupils. Someone whose parents had gone limp and ragged with worry. Women had lived for centuries as we were, beside the beast of addiction, tormented both by its predictable heartbreaks and by the specter of death, its menacing, unpredictable end. I thought there must be something soulful, something wise written by a grown woman, someone who had felt this way before, who would know how to handle it. I found a couple crappy self-help books and page-a-day compendia of hackneyed "wisdom." The well-thumbed books that mentioned codependency seemed so pandering, so simple. They were collections of complaints with chapter titles like "Cindy" and "Jessica." Was this therapy-speak the reason my father had been so dismissive of Al-Anon meetings? Maybe I was no better than he was.

What I mostly found was the *I, I, I* of the addict, shelf upon shelf of their lush, gorgeous, narcissistic tomes. The canon of personal and cultural reflection on the disease produced by alcoholics and addicts is enormous, varied, and often brilliant. I became an addiction literature junkie. I read *Junky; The Basketball Diaries; Jesus' Son; Bright Lights, Big City; Confessions of an English Opium-Eater; Drinking: A Love Story; Postcards from the Edge; Trainspotting.* I've since read *Lit, Tweak, Cherry, Blackout, Permanent Midnight, The Night of the Gun, Running with Scissors, A Million Little Pieces, How to Murder Your Life, Portrait of an Addict as a Young Man, Drunk Mom,* and on and on. I came to resent that there were so many books and films for "them" (addicts) and none for "us" (codependents).

But back then, I never found what I was looking for. There were women alcoholics, but what about the women who lived *with* alcoholics? Who cooked and cleaned for alcoholics, raised their children? What about the mothers who watched their babies grow possessed by drugs, as mine had? Were they too tired to write anything down? Too busy making their own mistakes?

The particular emotional storms that attend this experience were collected and named codependency, but those who had named it hadn't adequately answered the only questions I seemed to care about: Why did taking care of other people feel so good and hurt so much? Why was I able to build an ironclad feminist politics but not able to live according to its most elemental message: that I was a person equal to any other?

. . .

My parents reluctantly dipped a toe into the Al-Anon pond in the late 1990s as my sister's addiction crescendoed. The suggestion they received in the rooms was to "detach with love," show my sister some "tough love," and refuse to shield her from the consequences of her drug use. Protecting her from having to pay the price for her own actions was a form of enabling, after all.

They couldn't embrace this thinking one bit. My father seemed uninterested even in the meetings themselves. He didn't want to have to sit through the sharing of all of these different types of people with their different ways of relating to their common problem. He wanted something he knew would work for him. *I wish there was a meeting for college-educated fathers of heroin-addicted daughters,* he said when I asked what he thought of Al-Anon.

Maybe you should start one, I said curtly. But that wasn't likely. That's not how Twelve Step recovery works, for one thing. It is precisely based on the idea of transcending differences, listening to the experiences of others, and believing that, as in a church, support and salvation come to everyone, regardless of their background or the specificities of their situation. Moreover, my parents were ashamed. If the perfect support group had come to them, knocked on their door, and perhaps promised not to alert their broader community to my sister's heroin addiction, they might have taken more of an interest. But they weren't entirely ready to announce themselves as the parents of a drug addict to a roomful of strangers, especially when one of the strangers might turn out to be someone they knew. We lived in the suburbs, my parents were well respected and normal, and they had raised us well. By that logic—the logic that has kept addiction stigmatized for so long—Lucia's problem wasn't supposed to happen. The revelation would have been an indictment of my mother in particular, or at least it was likely to feel that way, since discord in the home traditionally reflects the inadequacy of the wife/mother. They were not inclined to talk about it outside of our family, which made telling my friends or even the guidance counselor at school feel suspect, a mini-betrayal that, even if it would never make its way back to them, still counted as a mark against our clan.

Another reason Al-Anon didn't take was because its message, particularly then, was that family members of alcoholics and addicts must focus on themselves and stop letting the ups and downs of addiction rule their lives. They must stop trying to manage someone else's decisions and disease and stop buffering against the repercussions of another's actions. But there was simply no way my mother could ever be convinced to change our locks, stop giving my sister help, support, money, or time. Sometimes, when I was frustrated by how consumed she was, I wished she would just banish Lucia. For once, just tell her that we'd had enough. Sometimes the impulse was well-meaning: I thought for a time, naïvely, that maybe a stint in jail or being homeless would jolt her into recognizing the severity of the problem and convince her to get and stay clean. Other times it was powered by resentment: maybe if she got kicked out, I could get some attention from my parents. Either way, my mother disagreed.

In her 2005 book, *The Too-Good Wife: Alcohol, Codependency, and the Politics of Nurturance in Postwar Japan,* anthropologist Amy Borovoy, who studied Japanese women's codependency support groups, writes that "tough love" held little sway in that context. "US substance abuse discourse relies heavily on the American language of rights and autonomy," writes Borovoy. "Yet Japanese discourses of family and motherhood do not emphasize the independence of the child from the parents; neither do they grant the parents rights by which they may separate themselves off from the needs of the child." The women Borovoy observed and interviewed had an understanding of motherhood as completely central to their identities, and their understanding of the mothers' role was incompatible with the individualism at the center of Al-Anon. In the context of "American ideologies that fetishize individual rights," Borovoy writes, ". . . there is little language for conceptualizing the necessary compromises in self-determination that sociality entails." Relationships that jeopardize or compromise individual rights or autonomy are "classified as abusive or exploitive." Only "self-loathing, uncontrollable compulsion, or a troubled family background" could explain why an individual would enter into such relations. My mother, a Jewish American woman who'd spent most of her life on the East Coast of the United States, had a great deal in common with these Japanese moms. She practiced the art of motherhood in a way that celebrated our profound dependencies. The idea that she should reclaim her individual rights by relinquishing responsibility for her child's illness was repellent to her, and one reason why she never stayed long in the rooms of Al-Anon.

.   .   .

Eventually, I tried Al-Anon, too. I was sixteen. A day after my math teacher returned a quiz with only one correct answer and the words "Wake up!" written in red ballpoint cursive at the top, a note from the guidance counselor appeared on my locker. It wasn't an invitation to see her, but an appointment already scheduled. I just had to show up. I had seen the school nurse, who kept a dish of tiny plastic babies in her office that she used to warn teenage girls against abortion. But the guidance counselor seemed normal enough, and when prompted I described for her "the scene at home." My parents were splitting up, my sister was a heroin addict, and I was in the middle. I had been called upon to listen, absorb, mediate, help, and soften. According to the counselor, my role was the family "hero child," enlisted to patch up the leaking ship of our home, determined not to complain about it, and to be a good-enough girl to remain under the radar of parental concern. The guidance counselor, who was also the mother of one of my classmates, told me kindly that I could take refuge in her office when needed, and suggested that I try a meeting.

In spite of the diversity of our town and my naïve sense that addiction was a young person's problem, the meeting, held upstairs in a linoleum-floored and wood-paneled church rec room, was populated mostly by grandmotherly types. Many looked weary, like they'd lived through a century of Midwestern winters. They introduced themselves at the beginning of the meeting and had names like Doris and Shirley. *Surely, Shirley, you can't expect me to stay here,* I snickered to myself, surveying the scene. A few wore synthetic-blend cardigans clearly knitted by hand and at least two reached into tote bags and took out bulky knitting projects to work on while the meeting was in session. The paneled room smelled both musty and freshly oiled with Old English, a citrus-chemical odor that lingered in my nostrils and made me wrinkle my nose as I looked around, taking it in, my mouth pursed in a sweet little smile of friendly curiosity in case any of the ladies were looking at me.

After the reading of a few boilerplate introductory texts, the women raised their hands—sometimes interrupting tens of seconds of painfully uncomfortable silence, during which only the odd sniffle or squeak of a chair leg could be heard—and took turns sharing for a few minutes about things that seemed to me entirely unrelated to drugs or alcohol. The women (almost all were women, and all but a few were white) in the meeting were talking about decisions as minor as choosing not to call someone back immediately, saying no to an invitation to lunch, holding one's tongue rather than offering unsolicited input on the wedding of a grown child. *What the fuck does any of this have to do with anything?* I wondered. I had been told by the guidance counselor that Al-Anon meetings were a place where people could talk about what it's really like to have alcoholics and addicts in their lives, but in this room, I couldn't grasp what the common thread was. If what the women were saying could be grouped into any theme, I guess it would have been self-esteem? They generally seemed to feel at ease doing what they pleased in their rather uneventful-sounding lives and reporting on these events to the larger group. That was sweet, I guess. I imagined—with the flagrant ageism of a very young person—that these were women with little else to occupy their time. They must not have anything else to do, maybe it was fun for them just to get together and chat.

Were they married to alcoholics? The mothers or sisters or daughters of alcoholics? They scarcely mentioned their "qualifiers"—the people whose drinking got them into "the rooms" in the first place. Rather, they cycled through "shares" on a constellation of everyday behaviors that didn't sound that bad at all. At the end of the meeting, afraid one of them would try to talk to me, I made a beeline for the door.

The "scene at home" was so much more dramatic than anything these elderly women seemed to be living through. And it didn't even strike me as possible that they *had* lived through equally harrowing things and had through their efforts ended up being *this* okay, this calm and removed. Almost once per share, something was said that would send a ripple of tranquil laughter around the room, and a couple times an eruption of real laughter and enthusiastic nodding. I attended a few other meetings—because the culture of each meeting is slightly unique, newcomers are encouraged to try at least six different meetings before deciding whether the program is for them—but Al-Anon scared me off. I was too young, and things at home were too crazy. How could I raise my hand and say the words "heroin" or "crack"? I thought the mild-mannered knitters would fall off their chairs.

Years later, I would wish I'd been compelled by some wisdom spoken there, or had found a person to relate to, or a book to read. Instead, I left, wondering what the thing of it was, why it was so hard to draw a through line from a loved one's drinking to the nonsense these church ladies busied themselves with. At the time, I was into literature, music, and politics. I was a teenager honing my bookish sensibility and I was alienated by the simple language, slogans, and pat answers offered by the program. In fact, anytime I came into contact with what I then considered the self-help industrial complex, I was both drawn in and repelled. There was always something to relate to in the literature, usually descriptions of the kind of emotional chaos that becomes normal in alcoholic families, but much of the material felt generalized to the point of meaninglessness. And it wasn't hard to alienate me at the time. In the evenings, I read about anarchist uprisings and feminist installation art and the lyrics sheets inside the angry, antiwar, anticapitalist, anti-TV punk records I loved. Smack in the middle of adolescence, I was skeptical of anything for a mass audience, especially something as gentle as self-help.

chapter four

B ecause their marriage was dying or because my father was busy or detached or depressed or because I had grown dependent on the hit of intensity I experienced while worrying and meddling alongside my mother, I often played the role of another parent in our unfolding family saga. While still in high school, I remember sitting with my mother in the two cushioned chairs opposite my sister's therapist and discussing her case, her plan for recovery. Harrowing as that time was, it makes me laugh to think of us, this ersatz parental unit, showing up places like that without explanation. I must have looked like a child in adult drag. But in the world of our family, it made a kind of sense. The therapist, a soft-eyed Marisa Tomei–type with a no-nonsense New Jersey manner, squinted at us a bit when she asked me, "Do you think it's odd that you're here instead of your father?" I did not.

"Co-dependence originates in a tendency, particularly common among daughters in 'dysfunctional' families, to overcompensate for parental inadequacies by becoming parentified and by developing an excessive sensitivity to the needs of others," wrote clinical psychologist Janice Haaken in a 1990 paper called "A Critical Analysis of the Co-Dependent Construct." The thing Haaken doesn't expressly say is that the daughters in dysfunctional families are often overcompensating for their fathers' inadequacies in particular. Among the women I know who've dealt with a sibling's addiction, this is a common dynamic. Unable to match his wife's level of concern, Daddy drops (further) out of the picture and a daughter steps in. The care work of addiction is gendered and, as such, underrecognized.

I became parentified. It felt like a natural extension of a way I already was—a sensitive middle child who was always enlivened by being let in on the intricacies of human dramas, being invited to expound on peacekeeping strategies. And it felt useful—indeed, crucial—to the family. As the cycle of addiction-related drama replayed itself again and again, I gained enough experience to see my own behaviors differently, to understand that they were harmful or self-destructive. Occasionally I knew in the moment that I was doing something pointless—knew, for example, that accusing my sister of being high or telling her how much she was hurting our parents wasn't helpful, was maybe even cruel—but I didn't know how to correct myself.

Depression made a nest in my mind. I thought it must be that way for everyone—don't all teenagers cry every day?—but apparently it isn't. The racing fear that my sister would soon die, part of a Medusa's head of coiled anxieties, began to take over my emotional life. The *pit of snakes* was how I described to myself a feeling I now recognize as the beginning of a panic attack. It was a quavering combination of nausea, envy, fear, and rage, a coalescing of all the bad things I'd seen, and all those I could only imagine. The pit of snakes was titillation and trauma: drugs, sex, and death. A mental place where I'd see things in patterns and then notice the pattern beginning to move, revealing itself to be a darkly crawling lattice of bees or maggots or eels.

Years later, when my first baby was starting preschool, I told my mother that it hurt to think of him out in the world, experiencing all the tedium and specifically the humiliations of a life. *It's so uncomfortable loving someone this much,* I said. She knew the feeling I described, but encouraged me to enjoy this innocent iteration of it.

Watching them grow up is painful, but it's also wonderful. This is the sweetest time of their lives—enjoy it while he's little.

You're right, I said.

Little kids, little problems. Big kids, big problems, she said then, in the half-ominous, half-breezy manner she uses to dispense timeless wisdom.

By the time I was finishing high school, we had big problems. Grown-up problems. I still thought of my parents as young lovers—there had always been something easy and unencumbered about them—and the end of their love story came down on me with a crushing weight. The house had been sold. Poor Anya was consigned to live out the rest of high school alone, bouncing between our parents' apartments. Lucia was lost to drugs, living in Brooklyn with her boyfriend, Lorenzo, who was charming and handsome and also perhaps the worst possible thing: a drug addict with money. Maybe this was just what adolescence feels like. The storybook quality of our early childhood had been a fantasy, and the exposure of its artifice, of the many falsifications it entailed, was a heartbreak, a bubble bursting. A pin to the gathered, dumbly bobbing bunch of helium balloons that held my childhood beliefs about the essential goodness of the world. *Pop. Pop. Pop.*

I yearned to run. I did run on the soccer field until my legs shook and I was wobbly in my guts, then got a ride home in the crisp post-practice dusk from a senior with a driver's license and ate everything I could find. *Move a muscle, change a feeling,* my depressive, soccer playing father told me. He cheered me on from the sidelines and was visibly gladdened when I did well. By senior year, I was the soccer team captain. I was affable and social, but frequently overwhelmed by sadness. I loved my family—my heart, my home—so much, but the almost perverse closeness of our pack, part of our buoyant charm throughout my childhood, had come to feel suffocating. As high school ground to a close, I dreamed of small sunshine-less spaces that belonged entirely to me, the more booklined and bunker-like the better. I didn't like being seen. I just wanted cozy quiet: a fantasy of detachment from the webs of accountability in which I felt already puzzlingly ensnared. I began to tell myself that if I could get away and start my own life, I would be okay. So I balled up a dozen T-shirts, packed them in the powder-blue vintage suitcase from the thrift store on Route 73, and left.

· · ·

San Francisco had a darkness that was entirely unlike what I knew from the East Coast, maybe because my East Coast was circumscribed, as my parents had designed it. I was a child of the suburbs, carted into the city periodically for edification. In New York or Philadelphia, we passed through bad neighborhoods, but only on the way to better neighborhoods, to eat, see family, look at art. Or my father, a journalist who knew every square inch of New Jersey, led us on day trips to the Ironbound in Newark for paella or the back room of a Middle Eastern market in Paterson because they had the best hummus. On the East Coast, if you're in a bad situation or on a scary block, you know. Things look different, feel different. People regard you differently. Someone might ask you bluntly what you're doing there, whether maybe you're lost. But in California, everything was so pretty. The sky was bigger. Industrial expanses looked functional, not forgotten, as they did in Elizabeth or Linden or on Brooklyn's waterfront. Even decrepitude had a soft-hued beauty, the late-day sun pouring caramel light over powder-blue and milkshake-pink houses. Danger was illegible to me there—I couldn't read the streets. And the menace that dwelled there felt less criminal and more psychotic. San Francisco in the 1990s had a distinctly sinister Manson vibe, the lingering hangover of the far-gone hippie creeps who'd dropped too much acid. A small, bedraggled army clad in muted rainbow hues with pale eyes and leathery faces. Peace and love gone sour. San Francisco, Oakland, Berkeley, even Marin— these were places where you could meet someone, find yourself deep in conversation with them, and not realize for twenty minutes that they were raving mad. A person's absolute nuttiness was a revelation that dawned slowly, unreliably, and was all the scarier for it.

The city also felt freshly ravaged by AIDS, the animating terror of my youth. There were faces that bore the shadow of illness and grief and there was a traumatized quality to many places. The Castro, where I spent most of my time, was a cemetery of sorts, haunted by lives extinguished quickly, painfully, and senselessly. I worked among young men who had lost their pack.

When Rachel, Kat, and I landed in San Francisco, we were taken in by a beloved friend of my parents, who set us up in the living room of her house out in the foggy Avenues. On a block dominated by quaint, pastel-colored Doelger homes, hers—painted black with red trim—looked like a goth oasis. The perfect place to land. In the mornings, we pored over the classifieds in her bright salmon-colored kitchen and made phone calls, then drove around the city looking at apartments and smoothing ourselves fleetingly into presentability in order to twinkle and grin through twenty-minute interviews for retail and service jobs. Our city map was unfolded and folded back up a dozen times a day. We found a three-bedroom apartment on Fourteenth Street between Guerrero and Valencia that would cost us each four hundred dollars a month, and got two jobs apiece.

There were no meditation apps, no activated-charcoal water. To feel clean and alive we ate salads overflowing with sprouts, kidney beans, and avocado, drank sweet fruit smoothies, and took long walks, studying the cultural differences between this place and the place we'd come from—some of those differences were minute and debatable, and others stark enough to elaborate and expound upon for blocks. Our punk scene back home had grown slicker, more stylized and goth-leaning. Everyone wore black. But here, there was a touch of the circus in punks' style. In the gritty, candy-colored Mission, girls had a special kind of grime. They wore ill-fitting vintage pencil skirts, oversized sweatshirts, and cowboy boots that rode mid-calf, exposing half of their hairy legs. Their magenta hair was permanently matted. Some women wore muscle T-shirts and had mustaches and would buy you drinks if you hung around the Lexington looking like you had a hometown chip on your shoulder, some shit to work out. They wrote poetry and played punk folk music. We lived a few doors down from Red Dora's Bearded Lady, and I fell for butch girls and trans boys who had the swagger of the typical asshole guys I was drawn to. LIQUOR IN THE FRONT,

POKER IN THE REAR read the café's T-shirt, which bore the icons of nineties tattoo culture: flames and dice, dancing girls.

I developed fierce crushes. I wanted one of the bearded ladies to save me, even to break my heart. I thought: What if you could be with a hot tough guy whose creamy emotional middle when you bit down—whose heart—was that of a woman? What if I could play caretaker-starlet to a slick, white-T-shirt-clad macho man who wouldn't carry the unfortunate baggage of having been born a boy? It didn't happen—I must have been afraid. I seemed, however, to know already that the masculinity I was in thrall to was just a flimsy performance no matter the person's gender. You had to prop it up, though, act like it was real, in order to play your part and get what you wanted from it.

I was learning about casual sex. About casual*ness,* in general. That if you wanted to be seen as cool, you had to act cool, in the sense of being detached, unperturbed. I practiced it on the men who sought my attention. There was Miguel, the beautiful boy I worked with at the record shop, who flirted with me in the count-out room and left a note written on receipt paper in my jacket pocket that read, in art-school capital letters, *IF YOU LET ME, I WILL.* I acted nonchalant, never even acknowledged receipt of the message, though later, with a thick, shiny piece of packing tape, I affixed it to a page in my journal. I continued to play it cool around him, and we circled each other, the tension between us rising for a couple weeks, until one night around 2:00 A.M., our buzzer rang. The sound was so blaring it woke me and Kat, who emerged bleary-eyed from her bedroom. Her coffee shop shift in the Sunset started at six. Rachel came out of her room, too, although she was wide-awake, in peach velour short shorts, holding a calligraphy pen. *You're up?* I said, though she often stayed up nearly all night and slept in until the late morning. Some nights she worked at It's Tops, the twenty-four-hour diner, in a pink-and-black uniform dress with the name BONNIE— her waitress name—sewn above the breast. *I'm drawing a bird. Who goes there, do you suppose?* she asked, directing her chin toward the door and squinting one eye. *I have a feeling that's for me,* I said, heading toward the stairs. *If I'm not back in five, come down.* Rachel, who had been my protector since we met in the fourth grade, snorted and said, *Oh don't worry,* then retreated into her room. The building we lived in was set back from the street and to let someone in we had to walk from our doorway down a long alley to open the gate. I didn't even put shoes on, I just felt a momentary charge of gratitude for the good fortune of having fallen asleep in a cute yellow nightgown and padded barefoot down the alley, my feet loudly slapping the concrete. The meaty *thwap* echoed off the walls of the narrow passageway. I opened the door and there was Miguel, smiling bashfully in apology for the time of night or for his own state. He stumbled a bit just trying to stand still there, eyeing me glassily. I let him follow me inside. He tasted like cigarettes and tequila and fucked me like a freight train on the bare mattress in my closet-sized bedroom, whispering in my ear in Spanish. Afterward, we gulped tepid tap water from pint glasses.

During the day, everything was relaxed between us. Occasionally, his gaze lingered playfully, or he winked as he passed me in the tight aisles of compact discs, but mostly we acted like nothing had transpired between us. I savored the feeling of having a secret and knowing that the secret was sex. What good was sex, really, besides this, a place in my mind where I could store stealthily the footage from these cloak-and-dagger nights of noises, nests of hair and wetnesses, moments of looking, longing, release. Darkness. Myriad moles and holes, small sounds. The act itself was one thing—I think I enjoyed it. But the highlight reel I played back in my mind throughout the day was even sweeter to savor. Like the soreness in my body—this was the aftermath, the memory, the part of the experience that was mine alone. An unknowable, unlegislatable thing I had a right to. It felt hard-earned. This was what you got in exchange for the sleepless early morning hours lying next to someone you wished wasn't in your bed.

For a time, Miguel was a proper paramour, but we were not bound to each other. I had other less exciting, less mutual encounters, so I was also learning what it felt like to let something happen that you didn't want to happen or to be terribly embarrassed by someone you had slept with. There were sloppy one-nighters with people we didn't really know, who the girls and I would run into while eating breakfast on Sixteenth Street and—following the painfully stalled, stuttering exchange of chill pleasantries—laugh at. This tended to happen the morning after a night of drinking because every night was a night of drinking. The bloated, exposed, skin-crawling feeling of a bad hangover was worsened most strongly by one of these brunchtime run-ins, like the one with the guy we called Ballet Steve, a dancer friend of a friend of an acquaintance whom I'd gotten tanked with at the Kilowatt on cider that tasted like halfway-flat pear soda. In the cold light of day, he looked so much shorter, sounded so much more Canadian. I'd instinctively smiled when he saw us, but that drew him over, where he stood too long at our table, trying to find something to say after we'd traded initial observations about the weather. Did he feel that because we'd had sex earlier in the week, he owed me a lengthy conversation? Kat and I always strained for politeness. Rachel had chutzpah, and she never suffered fools.

This has been great, Steve, she said, as the waitress set down the extra maple syrup she'd asked for, *but we're going to continue on with our meal. Thanks for stopping to chat!* I chortled into my breakfast beer.

That's the guy?! I said, incredulous, once he was out of earshot.

That is the guy you brought home the other night, yes, said Kat.

He looked so much cuter then, I said wistfully. It was puzzling, this part of growing up. How odd it was that people just fucked each other, and then saw each other on the street or in a restaurant and had to pretend to care enough to say hello. But even though it was the flipside of the power I'd felt with Miguel, there was power in the Ballet Steves, too. It all gave me the sense that I was the architect of my own romantic destiny. I might make a few mistakes, but affection, desire, and sex were there, flowing forces in my midst. It was simply a matter of choosing a worthy mate.

I worked the first half of the day at the gift shop in the Mission, the kind of place stacked floor to ceiling with prayer candles and stickers and goofball novelty gifts and Día de los Muertos figurines.

The owner was an odd woman in her forties who'd decided to hire me almost immediately when she introduced herself and I remarked that her name was an anagram of mine. In San Francisco, that kind of thing is a sure sign—of what, I still don't fully know. The anagram lady ran a phone-sex hotline out of the back of the place. They didn't seem to stick to any regular kind of schedule. There were only two other employees who manned the front of the store, both lovely, druggy weirdos in their twenties or thirties or forties—it all looked the same to me—and we split the week evenly among us. When one of them relieved me at the end of a shift, they treated me with a tenderness I resented mildly, not understanding that I must have seemed to them like a child. On my days, but for the yelping of cats and the mewling and purring of the phone-sex operators whom I could sometimes hear when I went into the back to make a cup of tea or use the bathroom, the shop was quiet and it was mine to preside over. Having the run of a small, dark store, something akin to what my parents called a "head shop," was divine. I read, wrote letters to my East Coast friends and entries in my journal, and leaned for long hours on the glass display case, which held the kind of cheap, heavy silver jewelry toward which goths and hippies are both improbably drawn. Most important was that I controlled the stereo and piped into the dark shop whatever suited my mood. I'd spent high school cultivating a brassbound music snobbery almost macho in its deployment that only deepened once I worked at a record store. But at the shop there was only a CD player, so I stole stacks of soul and blues and alternative rock albums from Tower and carted them to the gift shop to play the next day. I lit incense and let the sounds envelop me as I indulged my passing moods. I never knew if the doughy guy with the dyed-black hair I saw scoring dope on the corner of Sixteenth and Guerrero really *was* Elliott Smith or whether I just wanted him to be Elliott Smith so badly because I was playing *Either/Or* nearly every day in the store and feeling my heart contort to accommodate the fresh depths of anguish and torment I heard in it. To think he was buying drugs just feet away while I smoked a Parliament in the doorway, half-sheltered from the slanting, sputtering rain, it was almost too much. I took it the way I took everything—as confirmation of the sadness of the world, a sign that I was built for sadness above all else.

That year, El Niño hit the Bay Area, bringing unexpected torrents, mudslides, and long, dark monochromatic days of rain. When I think back on that year, I remember the dark grey slab of sky like the too-low ceiling of a shitty apartment. Rain in awe-inspiring sheets and big, individuated cartoon teardrops and endless ambient drizzle, the mist that would spin my hair out into frizz and tell the truth about my Jewishness and my curls. I hated it for that. The gloom was tuned perfectly to the misery in me. It felt appropriately punishing to drag my ass uphill from one job to another in tight black pants with the cold, tinkling rain threatening my eyeliner, my bobby-pinned hairdo. Forty-three days of rain. We stayed inside, bored. Rachel's sister, Miriam, came to visit, and we made Valentines on the kitchen floor. Another one of our best friends, Miranda, came from the East Coast, and trapped inside, we played with makeup, tried on the prom dresses Kat had stolen from the vintage shop where she worked—stiff, tube-like cylinders of crinoline in pale lavender, pistachio-ice-cream green, and baby blue—and took Polaroids of one another. This was beauty to us—reclining on the cat-hair couch in stolen secondhand party dresses, drinking ruby-lipped from tall cans of beer, or better, a forty. Miranda was the most Kewpie-like of our crew. She was Greek and Irish by blood, but she looked elfin and Asiatic, and wore her hair pinned into two high Björk buns. We *oohed* and *ahhed* when she tried on the strapless white dress with the raised turquoise flowers that looked like dots of meringue. As the rain pelted the rooftop, I photographed her on the telephone, ordering takeout chow mein.

But then, like the big reveal after a makeover scene in a movie, there would come a sunny day. The beauty of San Francisco is in these windows of redemptive splendor, we learned, the days when the fog "burns off," as they say, and gives way to a piercing, almost perversely joyous sunshine. New Yorkers joke about being in an abusive relationship with the city. In San Francisco, I understood this. We were constantly being pummeled by clouds and rain, then promptly apologized to by sparkling sunshine. This is the thing the city does best: convinces you, through a blustery string of freezing, gunmetal-grey days, that life is shit, and then, when you least expect it and most need it, it seems to practically shatter open, revealing a crystalline brightness that pings light around, reflects it off of everything, and air-dries the pale, soaked buildings. It was a magic trick that got me every time. The grey doesn't usually give birth to the day until about noon, and back then, in the Mission, that was when the city—the parts we cared about, where the young people were— revved to life. Coffeehouse punks came out of their houses, and bartenders began squeezing lemons into pitchers of Bloody Mary mix. On our days off, we curled up in the precious patches of sunlight that streamed through Rachel's bedroom windows on the quilt that still smelled like her house in New Jersey. Even though it never, ever got truly hot, when the sun came out we put ice cubes into our coffee and smoked cigarettes out the window, then went to Dolores Park and kicked a soccer ball around.

. . .

K was a master of the art of mixtape seduction, and a couple weeks into our courtship he made me one that remained in heavy rotation until I lost it. But I kept the case, which was adorned with Japanese photo booth stickers in which it looked like a tiny K was suspended in a shiny, ink-black galaxy. One grey afternoon, he came to visit me at the head shop, jangling the bells on the door, and his sudden presence immediately shifted the energy of the small space, seemed to change the very structure of the cells in my body. Everything at attention. I had another hour or so left in my shift, and then a long break before I had to be at Tower. If he waited with me, maybe the sun would be out, we could walk around the corner for a watermelon agua fresca. *Yeah that sounds good,* he said as he walked around the display case, trespassing on my little employees-only perch, and kissing me decisively. *What should we do until then?* he asked and kissed me again, this time more firmly. This was what they meant by "butterflies." This was like a John Hughes movie. Slowly, aware of my back, my ass, my skirt, I padded over to the front door and locked it, turned the little OPEN sign around, and led him into the storeroom at the back of the shop, where we had quick, breathless sex atop a stack of boxes containing tissue-wrapped ceramic bookends in the shape of praying hands that I would unpack, smiling, the following day.

I was collecting experiences, as young people are meant to do, turning them over, layering them on top of one another, comparing them. But then, there was this. The feeling of my body stiffening as a man's large, tattooed hand (a *tattooed hand!* this was not yet commonplace in the nineties), the animal warmth of it, settled on my waist and then with a gentle movement of fingers coaxed me forward to be kissed. My life, it seemed, had finally begun.

It's hard to remember the quality of pleasure I felt during the actual sex. When I was younger, it was always hard to tell whether I was enjoying the experience or merely the sensation of being wanted, which at the time was almost everything. Like all the other adventurous activities in my life, sex brought about a vague heightening, a feeling of arousal that was pure nerves, the quivering of fear and uncertainty. It was the same feeling I got from punk rock, from seeing certain bands play live, the same wincing sense of naughtiness I'd felt that day in eighth grade when I bought a cassette by a band called Dayglo Abortions. The album was called *Feed Us a Fetus* and it had a picture of Nancy and Ronald Reagan smiling on the cover, sitting in front of a plate with a tiny bloody baby on it. I liked that heart-pounding, these small, private pushings of the envelope, moments when I thought to myself, *Am I allowed to be doing this?* And then felt vaguely ill from the high of realizing that yes, I could do it, I could in fact do whatever I wanted. Being with K always had this wild quality. The city itself did. Maybe my friends and I were just eighteen with time to kill and, once we'd clocked out, we had nothing to do—no homework, no soccer practice, no parents. The hours of freedom were like extra money burning a hole in our pockets. It made us itchy for trouble, our looming adulthood like a cold we had to feed. We poured in candy and cocktails and boys and drives to the beach and day trips spent praying the

little Honda would make it up steep, guardrail-less climbs. We grew
a tenderness for the particular Bay Area flavors of bad art that were
everywhere on earnest display, and we went to the big museums and
saw good art and to the Roxie theater when *Kurt & Courtney* came
out and the drag queens snaked around the crowd-control belts in
baby-doll dresses and fruit-punch lipstick. We smoked West Coast
weed, which came in fresh, moist clumps from which you could tear
a small piece to smoke as if ripping a bite from a hunk of bread. As
with all of the flora and the produce in California, it looked so
much greener, so much more alive than what we were used to back
home, and the high was so strong I occasionally had to lock myself
in the bathroom and look at myself in the mirror, feeling my face
and wondering at the greasy magnificence of my 3-D ugliness,
thinking, *Hang on, hang on, CALM DOWN, there must be an end
to this.* Thinking, *Is this fun? Am I having fun?* Things felt law-
less then, like you couldn't call for help. There was a chimerical excitement and some fear in that anticipation, that not knowing. Time
and darkness had a different quality, didn't they? Without cell-
phones, text messages, without a map? We went out for the night
and hoped for the best.

. . .

For all of his affection, there was also something adversarial in my
relationship with K. The flipside of his chivalry—which could make
me feel so regal and special, so much like a lady in the most encom-
passing, old-fashioned way—was chauvinism. He held the belief
that men and women were two distinct and opposing teams, that
they were fundamentally doomed to misunderstand and hurt each
other. This wasn't something unarticulated that I read into our dynamic. It was stated breezily but plainly, an anchoring tenet of his
worldview. When a friend called him late one night and said he'd
been cheated on by his girlfriend, K said tersely, *Well, that's what
you get for trusting a chick*—a line that landed cruelly on my teenage ears, somehow stunned me, even though I knew that men spoke
to each other this way about women, like we were an invading force

to be beaten back, like we were double agents. I lay on his mattress and watched his back as he listened to the guy's tale of woe. He turned to me after a couple minutes and made the bored *yada yada* motion with his hands, rolled his eyes back a bit to suggest to me that the conversation was tiresome, that he was trying to wrap it up and would be with me—a chick, who shouldn't be trusted—shortly. *Meet me tomorrow, I'll buy you an ice cream,* he told his friend, and I imagined the two sitting on a bench, laughing and commiserating about girls and their conniving, while they licked their scoops down to tight rounded masses, economically, the way boys do. I was jealous of his friend—that he would command K's attention, and hear his honest riffing about relationships, something I could never really get from him. I was jealous, too, in the nonspecific way I often was of men. Just that they were men, that their voices weren't lilting and full of question marks, that they seemed to move through space with so much more ease.

But I also felt for K—it wasn't his fault. He'd been raised this way. He bore the wounds of a boyhood spent being doted on by his mother and urged to toughen up by his father. K's dad was a first-generation Italian raised in Philadelphia during the Depression, who played minor league baseball and became a French horn player in the San Francisco Symphony, blending athleticism and cultural sophistication fairly seamlessly, although K would be the first to remind me that symphony musicians are like any other musicians and not exactly known for gentility. He was tall and handsome and affable with a mile-wide mean streak that the whole family knew to do their best to steer clear of. When his wrath came down, it was frightening. K was the favorite child, the beautiful first boy born to Italian Catholics—so, basically a small god—on whom his father's hopes were pinned. That meant that the pressure was on him to conform to rather narrow ideas about manhood. K was encouraged to cultivate physical strength through sports. Once, in elementary school, he found himself unable to fight a bully—he'd been told by his dad not to bother coming home unless the principal called to say he'd fought the kid, but K had only managed to hit the kid with his *Land of the Lost* lunchbox. So his father took him to a boxing gym in the Tenderloin and threw him into the ring so he could learn to fight with his hands. He got chewed right up that day, but he kept going back, until he was the one doing the chewing.

At an Italian bakery at the end of a date, he explained to me how mystified his parents had been when he discovered heavy metal, and then punk rock, in the eighties. He laughed as he described the horror on his father's face when he noticed a boot print on K's back after a show. His dad was in his sixties by the time K was a teenager; he had absolutely no point of reference for a mosh pit. "What the hell kinds of movies are you going to anyway?" he shouted. The generational rift between them became ever wider as K grew into a young man and his father began losing control over him.

Eventually, I had that moment every kid has, where you think you can beat up your dad, he said, smiling as he polished off our cannoli and licked powdered sugar from his fingertips.

Everyone has that moment? I asked incredulously. He nodded as he chewed.

Yeah, when you're sick of being pushed around and you think you're finally big enough to take on your old man? Everyone has it, he answered.

Oh, I said. A bookish girl with sisters. What did I know. *And what happened when you did that?* I asked.

I lunged at him and he cracked me in the face, broke my nose, he said, instinctively reaching for the bridge of it and running his thumb and forefinger over the place where it went slightly crooked.

I drew back in disgust. *Your own father broke your nose? I'm sorry but that's child abuse.* I shook my head. *That's horrible.*

Eh, K said, shrugging. *I had it coming.*

K continued boxing, then took door-guy jobs where he continued fighting, but only as a last resort, he said, when words wouldn't do the trick. More than fighting, he enjoyed the strategy involved in assessing other men, determining their threat level, managing their outbursts, leveling them only when necessary. He was very good at it. He did this scanning and evaluating wherever we went, and it made me feel safe, like a red carpet of protection being rolled out before me. After an adolescence spent confusedly navigating the murky waters of male attention, it was like having my own Secret Service.

Part of falling for K was falling for this origin story, the tale of a sweet boy who had a certain predilection for violence bred into him, beaten into him. He wasn't born like this, that story went, and it allowed me to believe that somewhere deep in there was a very gentle soul. The tender tough guy: that's a story so many women are charmed by. He had cultivated a stylized *Raging Bull* masculinity that found romance in the flare of a hot temper and the amorous apology afterward. But that was all reserved for someone special, and mostly, he was just playing the field. To him, girls were like trophies to collect. And you had to know how to get rid of the ones who were too needy, too clingy, too crazy, too slutty—it was a get-them-before-they-get-you mentality. He insisted that he was in search of "the one," but I think that was just a way to keep the ladies on their toes, forever vying for that position.

Still, the overwhelming sense I had about K was that he could see and understand me, that he understood everything. He seemed experienced above all. Maybe this was because he was older, or appeared so much more confident than me or any of the boys I had known, but also because he was somehow familiar. I read some continuity into K's nature—there was great overlap between his gregariousness, his anything-for-a-laugh humor, and the boisterousness on my mother's side of the family, and I was comforted by that. Into my rainy and disgruntled grunge nineties, he'd appeared in his khakis and bright white T-shirt, as if from *A Bronx Tale*–era East Coast. I thought about how to make him laugh, how I would retell the events of the day to him. Every song was about him. Onto a dollar-bin record I paint-markered "fifteen minutes with you / oh I wouldn't say no," a quote from a Smiths song, and gave it to him as a birthday card.

While K and I were involved, my little sister, Anya, came out to California to visit. With her two long blond braids and baby face, she looked too young to get into bars, so we drank and smoked pot at home and went for walks and out for burritos. We lay in the living room talking and crying about our parents' divorce and our sister's drug dramas, and I told her I was really and truly in love. We cried about that, too—just love, the idea of it, that I was grown enough to have found it. Was there anything higher to reach for in this world? *I know it sounds crazy,* I sniffled, *but I feel like my whole life has changed.*

·   ·   ·

Four months after I began falling for K—about eight months into our California life—the kitchen phone rang around midnight. It was Anya, her teeth chattering audibly.

Where are you? I said.

Home. Her voice quavered. *I'm—*

What is it? I asked. *Lucia,* I thought, as I drew a sharp breath. *Anya, what? Tell me.*

Lorenzo died tonight, she said. *He overdosed. He wasn't with Lucia, he wasn't at home, but she's freaking the fuck out. Mommy and Daddy just went into the city to get her.*

A bloom of fear spread, buckling my waist. They lived together, Lucia and Lorenzo. They were mad about each other. They intended to get married in just a month's time. I blinked and pictured him blue. Stiff. Not as I'd seen him last, shirtless and barefoot, tan and happy, taking a long drag off a cigarette in the Tenth Avenue apartment they'd recently moved out of. He was twenty-one.

So many times, I'd heard my parents admonish or plead with Lucia, reminding her all it takes is one bad batch, that this is life or death. Now, it was death, here to announce itself, to abruptly, irrevocably raise the stakes.

My father had picked my mother up in the black Nissan minivan he still drove, the family car we affectionately called the "dog-hair chariot," and my parents were driving from New Jersey to Brooklyn. My mother was afraid Lucia would kill herself in the interim. She'd looked into Anya's eyes as she and my father left the house, passed her the receiver, and said sternly, *Do not hang up this phone until you hear my voice on the other end.*

So you talked to Lucia the whole time? I asked.

She just cried, Anya said. *She was crying so much I couldn't understand her.*

You're alone there now? Are you okay?

Rebecca was sleeping over, she said, *but she called her mom and got picked up.*

You didn't want her to stay? I asked.

It seemed too weird, like . . . she trailed off. *I don't know. She would have stayed, I'm sure, but they're gonna come back with Lu soon and she's really fucked up.*

Anya's stoicism was chilling. Or was it numbness? She could have been in shock. She had been shielded from the worst of the family's problems, maybe she couldn't have seen this coming. Still, we didn't know any young people who had died. How could she be home alone, thinking about the fresh cadaver of Lucia's beloved Lorenzo and not feel terror in her bones? I thought often about that conversation my sisters must have had, a little bubble of screaming trauma, that forty minutes between the two of them, three thousand miles away from me. A sixteen-year-old looking for the words to pack the wound of her big sister's fresh grief.

I'll fly home, I said. *I'm coming home. I'll pack now and I'll be there as soon as I can. But stay on the phone with me now. I'll wait with you until they get home.*

No, it's okay, said Anya, her voice small but resolute. *I'm okay. I'll see you soon, I guess.*

. . .

In San Francisco, I sat stupefied in a lukewarm bath, the mint trim of the bathroom looking garish under the thin overhead light. Rachel and Kat sat on the floor just outside the tub and we all just looked at one another. When my parents returned home, they called me, and when we hung up, my father bought a bereavement-fare ticket for me, and called back with the details. The girls drove me to the airport and hugged me fiercely. *Call as often as you want*, Kat said, squeezing my hands one last time. *Call all the time.* Rachel held my face and kissed me on the mouth. *I love you and you're brave*, she said. In the airport in the early morning hours, everything was moving. The smell of cheap coffee filled the large, open space. I bought a newspaper and tried to do the crossword puzzle. I wrote in my journal about heroin, which had reached out like a claw, grabbed me from clear across the country, called me home. My idyll—the fantasy of remove that California represented—had been seized by it. Before leaving, I called K from a pay phone and told him I didn't know when, or if, I'd be back.

part 2

At home, it turned out that my parents had lost their minds. Fear and worry and grief had combined to form a temporary insanity that rendered them tender, ultra-present, and completely distracted at the same time. My dad hadn't moved back in, but he hadn't not moved back in. I don't remember where my mother's boyfriend was—had he been sent away? That wouldn't surprise me. Ours was the type of family that banished outsiders and closed ranks in the event of emergency. It seemed, for a period of weeks, that we were always all together. The original five. My parents on the phone, accessing their network of doctors, directors of programs and facilities, and others with cultural capital, connections, wisdom to share. Someone knew someone who knew someone. Jews are breathtaking to behold in a crisis. We had a leg up—whiteness, money to borrow, doctors to call—and still, drugs had proven indiscriminate. We operated as though they could take her at any moment.

In another house, far away, Lorenzo's family was busy with their own phone calls, except for flowers, a casket, a priest. There was no one left for them to worry over, nobody—no body—to save, and the guilt of this disparity, the narrow, twisted fork of fate by which someone else's child had been sold the bad batch, also fed my parents' madness.

It was April, and the San Francisco flora to which I'd grown accustomed—technicolor California wild roses and poppies, flowering vines in fuchsia, hot orange, and carmine red, crawling up cracked apricot stucco walls—all had been replaced. In New Jersey, everything looked like a *Sopranos* set and felt like childhood. Cement. Low skies pitching forward, spinning carousel-like. Intermittently, a timid scatter of crocus or daffodils quaintly teasing the dawning spring. There was familiarity in every route and pattern, like wallpaper memorized from a crib. It was there in the grand castle-like houses up on the hill and in the modest box-like ones at the bottom, made of red brick and aluminum siding in a limited array of muted breakfast hues: butter, oatmeal, coffee with cream.

We ordered takeout and cried. Drove in pairs to Watchung Plaza for twenty-ounce hazelnut coffees we greyed with skim milk, and sesame bagels with cream cheese. CVS on Valley Road for tissues, Tampax, Visine. Then returned to the fold and became again the five of us, in the bunker of our erstwhile family home. Every room had been beautified to my mother's elevated-rustic specifications, and I skulked around makeup-less in an old T-shirt and pajama bottoms, savoring it. For eight months, I had been living in the damply foreign paradise of Northern California, in an ever-changing climate that sent my internal thermostat spinning, and I still had not adjusted. No diurnal rhythm had been established in the chill of that twinkling elsewhere, a verdant city where Rachel, Kat, and I were totally free and making it on our own, pooling what we could earn and what we could steal from our six jobs.

Back home, I remembered what it felt like to not have to be responsible for myself. I'd missed this suburban safety. There was a neat stack of clean towels in the linen closet and an endlessly renewing store of string cheese and nonfat yogurt in the fridge. Big brown boxes of sourdough pretzels stood sentinel in the pantry. Even beneath the shroud of grief, everything felt abundant, paid for by someone else. It filled me with shame that I could enjoy the special, locked-down coziness of even tragic extenuating circumstances.

Times like these should be the inverse of holidays, but they feel an awful lot like holidays. I liked the forced closeness, the reliable swelling of feeling, hushed planning. Being altered by that sudden lurch into intimacy. I liked being among my people—a kind of "going to the mattresses." That was an old mafia phrase my mother had taught us as kids. I assumed she got it from *The Godfather*. It was what the mob bosses did when they were going to war against a rival family, when they needed to be out of sight and be able to keep an eye on one another. They would lie in wait someplace and strategize, ready themselves for action. I liked the extemporary, make-do domesticity evoked by the phrase, a family closeness that arose urgently, that was imbued with sudden purpose. We weren't going to war, but our clustering together in trauma could feel that way. It could make you feel cupped inside a hand.

I remembered the time a few years earlier—before she threw the party while my parents were out of town—when Lucia went to see a band in Pennsylvania with friends (and a twelve o'clock curfew) and never came home. I was in eighth grade at the time, Lucia a sophomore in high school. I woke in the morning to find my parents frantic, my mother looking somehow gaunt and haunted after the one lost night of sleep. My father was on the phone with the police. They'd already called hospitals in two states. No information, which could be good or bad. Even the breakfast dishes looked different. I sat at the table and joined in the worrying, telling my mother it was going to be all right. *You don't know that,* she said, her brow drawn up like a mime in exaggerated concern. Everything was all right in the sense that Lucia resurfaced. She had spent the night partying in a motel room with some friends, and my parents' relief that she was not found lying in the proverbial ditch superseded their anger, although I remember she was eventually punished. The feeling in the house that morning was a beginning. Up to that point, we'd been good girls.

Now my sister was in a catatonia of mourning—hours of quiet and then, from the bathtub, wailing. Spasms of crying during which she heaved and shook with shock, grief, withdrawal, and end-of-an-era panic. She'd seen Lorenzo as her soulmate and salvation: *I've met my match*, she told me, grinning, the first time she showed me his photograph. He looked like a rock 'n' roll singer, leaning back in a chair with aviator sunglasses on and a faded T-shirt so worn it had small holes around the neck. They'd rushed headlong and hot-blooded into love, partying together, moving in together, and getting engaged all within a little more than a year. That was the way in our family. Now he was gone.

My mother and father had a frenzied, under-slept look that was unmistakably middle-aged. They took turns sounding sane and insane. In the days following my return home, at the urging of a doctor, they took my sister to a rehab so she could detox and be monitored by professionals. But she was put into a padded cell, or some sort of fiercely surveilled ward for people who posed a danger to themselves, and when she was finally able to call home forty-eight hours later, she cried and begged to get out.

So they brought my sister home, somewhat defiantly. We would minister to her ourselves, heal her with love, keep her alive. No pressure. *I believe that she is suicidal,* my mom told me, *and until we can get her into a new treatment center, we have to watch her like a hawk.* I stayed up at night, writing in my journal as she slept. The living room was bathed in cool moonlight, the asphalt of the street velvet-smooth outside the window. The house smell: a sedentary comfort in its faint moisture. The threat of rain, new paint on old wood, East Coast in spring. The April showers that bring May flowers. I ate the sourdough pretzels. I kept watch. If my sister killed herself, it sure as hell wasn't going to happen because I got distracted. I was in the same room with her, or else I was peeking in on her or trailing her. I followed her everywhere—a regression to an earlier time, when I'd been the needy little one. Dealing with this version of her was a paradox. When caring for her as part of this triage team my parents had made us into, I felt like the big sister. It took only one withering look from her, one eye roll, and I could still be made small and superfluous, like I was getting in the way, too young to understand. *Get out of here!* she protested as she sat down to pee, reaching toward the bathroom door to shut me out. I edged my way in anyway and stood by the sink, waiting. *Jesus, are you fucking kidding me?* she sniped. *Can I please have some privacy?* I shook my head feebly, trying to stand my ground and offer a partial apology at once. I stayed put as the stream of urine slowed to a tinkling drip, and as she wiped, she groaned with annoyance. *Mommy told me to!* I said defensively, sounding like I was five, as she breezed past me on the way back to bed. These moments were mildly humiliating. I was a reluctant warden—it didn't feel like it was in my nature to be a spoilsport, or a rat. I still wanted my sister to love me, to think I was cool. But I also didn't want her to die. Especially not while I was in the house.

In the aftermath of Lorenzo's death, the full weight of Lucia's sickness laid heavy on the house. Her illness seemed newly unpredictable and now even more evil, and our household turned on the simple idea that she did not know what was best for her. The rest of us knew better how to heal her. My mother led the effort. I was her faithful deputy, just following orders.

Beneath my compliance, resentment stewed. Flashes of rage toward my parents had been a regular feature of my last few years at home—normal hormonal disturbances, I imagined, to which were added the strains of our situation. I was angry about their divorce, angry that they always seemed focused on either Lucia or themselves. I was especially mad about the thing I couldn't yet put into words: that I'd been told everything, let in on everything, that I'd been compulsorily enlisted in the parental ranks and was expected to carry out my duties with the equanimity, responsibility, and care of an adult. I was mad that I was so sensitive in the first place, trained in an empathy so granular and heartbreaking and Jewish, that my view on the family was so robust that I couldn't just be plain angry like a regular teenager. So inclined was I toward empathy and understanding that I didn't even know how I *really felt* about anything, whatever that even meant. I saw everything from everyone else's perspective and I felt bad and sad for us all.

But I also loved being seen as an adult, and felt defensive of my parents' choice to treat me like one. I was precocious, after all, and proud of it. When a therapist referred to my parents' oversharing and overreliance on me as a form of "emotional incest," I felt physically sick. *That phrase is disgusting and I don't want to use it,* I said.

.   .   .

At home in New Jersey, I noticed new books on the built-in shelf in the living room: *Courage to Change* and *The Language of Letting Go,* books of daily meditations on codependency.

Reading these? I asked my mother.

I'm trying to educate myself, she said.

Is it helping? I asked.

I don't know how people can let go when their children are in trouble, she said. *That's not ever going to make sense to me.*

I started reading the books, which were full of benedictions, creepily oversimplified descriptions of alcoholic family life, combined with some of the seemingly random material I'd been so alienated by in that first meeting full of grandmothers—weak analogies for struggle and surrender involving a dog or a long walk on a beach. Each entry was followed by a quote from a famous dead writer, movie star, or president. I found the books soothing and irritating in equal measure, but I was at least relieved to see it written that my intermittent rage was normal. "It is important to allow ourselves to feel—to accept—our anger toward family members without casting guilt or shame on ourselves. . . . Help me accept the potent emotions I may feel toward family members," I read in *The Language of Letting Go.* "Help me be grateful for the lesson they are teaching me."

chapter six

Both my parents acted like we were on the run from something, but my father's craziness didn't hum like my mother's. His energy has always been steady, his voice deep and reassuring. Rather, it seemed he was seized every once in a while by panic, but even that he expressed in his usual reasonable tone. His panic lived inside the things he said. About a day after my sister returned home from the psych ward, he met me in the kitchen as I poured a glass of lemonade and handed me a white plastic shopping bag from A&P that felt like it was full of long utensils. *Bury this in the backyard,* he said unceremoniously as I swallowed a warm, tangy sip of juice. I looked up into his eyes, suddenly confused, and terrified by his senselessness. *I'm sorry, what?* I asked.

Do something with this, he said, shaking his head. *I don't know—bury it in the backyard. It's the sharp objects. We're supposed to get all the sharp objects out of the house.*

Um, okay, I said. I took the bag and felt its contents, which were stretching the thin plastic. Their handles knocked together in my hands. *She's really gonna kill herself with tongs?* I asked. He didn't smile. The look he gave me was resigned. It was either "the doctor said to" or "your mother is making me do it" or "I don't know what the fuck I'm doing." It contained the same confusion I felt that we were living in this reality at all—our world, but flipped fully on its head—a place where someone might turn a kitchen knife on themselves. None of it made any sense. I don't remember what I did with that bag, but I can recall its weight in my hands. What would we cut with now? Or would we all be living like patients, picking halfheartedly through soups and puddings. Did we even own this many knives and pairs of scissors? I could feel the shape of the blades through the plastic, but the parcel felt also full of salad utensils, ladles. I wondered if the nail clippers had made it in. Or the old wood-handled barbecue fork with which my dad had speared our summer steaks.

Between the death and the funeral, there was a week. A funeral dress was procured from Macy's—something black, a widow's sheath, plucked from a circular rack of synthetic wool blends. Opaque black tights. Pumps. My parents drove into Brooklyn to begin to clean out Lucia and Lorenzo's apartment, a trip that so disturbed my mother that for the second round, I went in her stead. What had been so terrible? Shit she'd only seen in movies. Needles. Cigarette holes in the mattress. Blood on the wall. A roommate who looked her in the eye and said of my sister, with both menace and sympathy, "She's in real bad shape." Like she was a minor character from an episode of *Law & Order*, just some fucked-up chick who would soon die of an overdose.

To finish cleaning out the apartment, I went with my dad. I still enjoyed the quiet, upholstered warmth of the front seat of his minivan. I'd spent so many hours in his car, en route to soccer games, school functions, parties, and dates, comforted by the casual strength of his hands, the dry knuckles of his long fingers spread along the steering wheel. My dad knew every road, every vein and artery in the whole state, and he drove confidently, making intermittent conversation while the radio was on, and then turning it off to gently interview me. I'd told him secrets from that front seat, complained about my mother or my boyfriends. I'd cried into my lap, and he'd laid that big, dry hand on my knee. When we were kids, he drove a blue Volkswagen van, which felt big as an airplane, and to the beat of the gender-bending late seventies rock 'n' roll he loved, with the window rolled down, he tapped his left hand on the driver's side door, his wedding ring making a rhythmic knocking sound. I always felt safe inside his car, listening to that clunking reminder of my parents' marriage, which still seemed at that time unquestionable, fixed as the stars in the sky.

Lucia came with us to Brooklyn that day. She sat speechless, wrapped in one of our mother's oversized cardigan sweaters in the back seat as we gently lurched through stop-and-go traffic. A seeming world away in an ungentrified, unnamed pocket of the city, in the chilling vacancy of their bedroom, we gathered her boyfriend's clothes. A dead person's belongings seem both newly worthy of attention and also entirely devoid of meaning. I put his shoes into a garbage bag—they made a pointless, unwieldy weight not unlike that of a body—and dragged it down the stairs.

On the grey drive home, a meek voice drifted up from the back seat, Lucia, saying blankly, *I want a can of Coke and a Snickers bar.* My father told her to say it louder, he couldn't quite hear her, and she issued the request a second time. *I want a Coke*, she said dully at an awkwardly loud volume. *And a Snickers bar.* A strange, uncharacteristic desire that hung in the air. The sealed-in silence in the car grew even quieter as my father exited and pulled into a gas station. I closed my eyes while he went inside, and when he came back we drove on, windows up, listening to the rustle of the candy bar wrapper and the crack and fizz of the can opening. I imagined the weak enamel of my sister's fingernail bending back as she pulled up the tab of the soda. There was soft gulping. My dad and I glanced at each other, a mutual acknowledgment of the sound of my sister eating and drinking—a sign of life!—and I noticed his eyes were wetly shining. *What?* I asked.

What, Dad? my sister instinctively echoed from the back.

That's the first time you've said you wanted anything since Lorenzo died, he said, his face ashen. We had grown used to occasional tears from our mother—I felt her compunction about crying in front of me in particular was dwindling to near-nonexistence—but seeing our father's face hover on the precipice of emotion, a loss of control, held us momentarily frozen in the car. He was descended from a long line of female criers, but I'd almost never seen him cry, not even when his own mother—a staunchly sentimental woman, head of the Ministry of Weeping—died after a long battle with cancer. I wondered what it would sound like if he really let go, if he began to sob, an ungoverned sea lion–like wail from somewhere deep. I wondered about the stories of people who might have seen their fathers really cry, what would have to happen to make a dad cry like that.

I called K a couple times from the mustard-yellow kitchen, pulling the phone into the corner staircase up to my mom's bedroom and sitting on one carpeted step while I let it ring, but I couldn't reach him. Night in New Jersey was evening in California, and I guessed he was getting ready to head to work. I imagined him fixing his movie-star hair in the semi-frosted Art Deco rectangle of his bedroom mirror, devilishly raising an eyebrow as he met his gaze in the reflection. Could he see the vicious gleam in his own eye? A year before, he hadn't even existed to me. California itself had been nothing, a palm tree in my mind. A hundred music videos: the flat, faded belt of highway, shimmering with heat. Now it was a real place, my place, and in it somewhere was a pile of my clothes, worn underwear still nestled into hastily stripped-off tights, half-read books beneath a water glass dotted with my DNA. In it was the pack of cigarettes, matches neatly tucked into its cellophane, that I had looked for when I got off the plane but realized I'd forgotten to take from the green glass ashtray on the mantelpiece. In it somewhere, cracking jokes, was a boy who smelled always ready for a date, like mint chewing gum and Irish Spring and sickly floral pomade. The pain I felt at home with my family seemed to mean nothing if he didn't know about it, if it couldn't be refracted through him, through some kind of "us." Without that, I was only part of the "us" of my family. Was I supposed to endure them alone?

We had been together only four months, but I missed K terribly. From the kitchen table, I wrote him a letter, summoning my best penmanship, my easiest cool-girl tone, leveraging the small store of inside jokes we had by then amassed together. He didn't write back, but eventually, he called. My stomach leapt into my throat when I heard my mother say, *Nina—K on the phone for you,* as if it were the most normal thing in the world, maybe even mildly exasperating in its normalcy, like he called all the time or something. I loved her for making it sound regular and annoying like that. K and I spoke a few times in the weeks that followed, conversations I called "mildly strained" in my diary. It was my first time experiencing in a romantic context a feeling I would learn was an unremarkable part of life: it was the feeling of receding from a man's mind because you were not physically occupying the space in front of him. He wasn't unkind on the phone, but the softness he typically showed me was absent. I thought maybe he was watching a movie with the volume all the way down while we talked. Maybe the volume wasn't even all the way down. I remembered the vaguely animal way his face lit up when we were actually together and realized, helplessly, that there was no way to replicate that chemistry, to incite that interest, that desire. Three thousand miles away, I had no hope of holding his attention. Not with tales of our family drama, not with jokes. I wasn't *there,* where he was, wasn't among the girls who smoked and giggled outside the bar where he worked the door, wasn't a flesh-and-blood thing, whose smiling teeth could be seen sparkling under the streetlights, whose nervous shifting was plainly an invitation to be taken home and fucked.

It felt suddenly obvious that someone else, more likely many someone elses, were occupying the space of his real life. Who did I think I was, expecting some special treatment? And really, who was I again, a sad teenager who brought him used paperbacks? I was sick with love. I had never felt like this before. Each time after we hung up, I buried myself beneath an avalanche of self-recrimination. We weren't even dating exclusively. He was in his twenties and I was just a kid, my cheeks still flushed and dumpling-plump with youthful insecurity. In my absence, he was surely out with other girls, maybe even wining and dining a Real Grown-up Woman with a Real Job, someone poised and glamorous who threw her head back while she rode him. "Astride" was the word I always thought of when I pictured a woman on top, maybe because it sounded like Astroglide. She threw her head back while she was *astride* him, confidently experiencing the sexual pleasure to which she knew she was entitled.

What had I expected from him? Calling me back—the girl who sent him that stupid letter, not *the* girl who *got away* but just *a* girl who *went away* for an unspecified length of time and so must be dropped from the rolls, from his dance card, as he himself would have put it—felt like something he was just checking off a mental list. If, in his casual, low-effort, hot-guy kingdom, he made such lists at all.

.   .   .

I traveled back to San Francisco a couple months later and got back the head shop job. Tower Records was over. Lucia was at a residential treatment facility and sent letters. Rachel and Kat had been in close touch while I was gone and we reunited tearfully and happily. But it was hard for me to slide back into the life I'd pressed pause on in San Francisco. I had no experience doing such a thing, and the grief and worry I carried from home were near impossible to distract myself from. K picked me up from the airport and we spent my first night back together, but he was cagey. He'd been hard to pin down the whole time I'd been gone, and when we did manage to talk I never got the sense that he really cared what was going on with me. He always swung from affectionate to an almost frosty detachment. Now he was entirely frosty, making stilted conversation as though out of obligation, like I was an exchange student he was reluctantly hosting. Even his room felt different. I slept badly, unconsoled by being near him again and depressed at being unconsoled. I'd lain in bed in New Jersey for weeks imagining what it would be like to rest in the crook of his arm again, and now I was there, on his white T-shirt in the grey dark, watching a video play on his television, but it didn't feel like anything. Where had it gone? Had our connection been so readily extinguished by a little distance and time? That was disconcerting to me—I was in love. Equally upsetting was his seeming disinterest in the experience I'd just survived. Didn't this person who cared about me want to hear about what had just happened in my life? About Lucia's keening, my crazy parents, the apartment, Lorenzo's shoes, the feeling of springtime across the country in my homeland?

When he fell out of communication again for about a week, I grew sullen and stopped calling, too. I loafed around our apartment when I wasn't working, drinking Old Grand-Dad out of the bottle for the buzz and because it felt cool, and listening to the bands I'd discovered through the mixtape K had made me. I was filled with dread. Eventually, we met for a cup of coffee at a crepe place, though he didn't drink coffee, and while I gnawed on the end of a plastic stirrer, he told me cavalierly he'd gotten back together with his ex, Tammy. I'd seen a stack of photo booth pictures of the two of them in his room before; she looked beautiful in the flashbulb contrast. As soon as he said they'd gotten back together, I wondered whether Tammy had ever really departed the scene. They'd had a significant relationship. She was his age. Was she the mature older woman I'd imagined, the reason his attention sometimes dropped away entirely? I pictured her the way she appeared frozen in the black-and-white photo booth images: little pixie face, her perfect lipstick looking almost black, framing a rack of perfectly straight, sparkling white teeth. How did he know so many girls who were so pretty, all with shiny dark hair, straight bangs, and perfect makeup, perky *Seventeen* magazine faces? It was like he was living in a different San Francisco, one crawling with Bettie Pages.

K didn't say the words, "I'm sorry." He said, to fill the silence, *It's not like we're never going to speak again. I'm sure we'll see each other around.*

Yeah, I'm sure we will, I said. *So that's it? Really?* A waiter cleared plates of crepe scraps and wilted salad from the next table over, and I shrank from the feeling of exposure it gave me to be doing this in public, at an oily wooden table in full view of the crawling carnival of Haight Street.

Come on, what did you think was going to happen? he said. *I'm sure you've got other things going on, too. Isn't that your whole thing? Being a little minx, a man-eater?*

Was that true? Maybe it was. In trying to seem cool, trying not to be vulnerable and get my heart broken, had I given him the impression that I didn't care?

I'm not dating anyone else. I want to be with you, I said.

I'm not going to put myself in the way of that and get hurt, he said. *Face it, you have more killing to do, Pimentoloaf.*

More killing to do? I repeated slowly. *What the fuck is that supposed to mean?*

More hearts to break. You've got a lot to figure out, kiddo. And I know you have a lot of family stuff going on. But—he sat up a little straighter to deliver the kicker—*I know this much: you're going to be an amazing woman someday,* he told me. One final, patronizing flourish. My eyes narrowed in hurt, disbelief, and rage. So I wasn't even a woman yet. Or I was woman enough to have sex with, but not to take seriously. Me and my "family stuff," we were too complicated, but maybe *someday* we'd be cool.

.   .   .

I couldn't get comfortable in California after that. The rain had abated and summer was coming. That's what the sunshine suggested, although it was rarely warm and never hot, and the chill still crawled outward toward my fingertips from the moment I got out of bed in the morning. So, I started getting out of bed less. When I did, everywhere I went, I had a cardigan on, another sweater stashed in a bag, and a fleece-lined jacket tucked over my arm. There were more boys, more parties, more day trips, more nights out, but I was doleful, distant, awful to be around. I'd left my heart in New Jersey.

Every day for a couple months, I called and got an update from my mom. The phone call was a checkpoint I had to pass through in order to continue on with my day. She needed it, but I needed it, too. When I asked "How are you," she answered with a report on Lucia or her boyfriend, Jim, who was also intermittently in recovery. *No, how are you,* I wanted to say, but I thought the distinction would be lost on her.

The heartbreak I felt over K was the sort that never heals—it informs, instructs, shapes the remainder of one's romantic career.

He had assumed the kind of symbolic importance that endures, and it cast a shadow over my subsequent relationships. He was the original, the stencil that gets duplicated in the mimeograph machine. The string of men who followed were frequently referred to by Rachel and Kat as K wannabes. Guys with tattoos and dark, greased-back hair. For a long time, I didn't stray too far from that template.

After some time had passed, I didn't think of the real K as often, even though I always kept a jar of Tres Flores pomade among my toiletries and sometimes used it to slick back a tight ponytail. Those were days when the thick, floral, old-fashioned smell of him lingered around my head, and I felt swooning rushes of nostalgia. I found it romantic to keep a candle burning for him in that one small, secret way.

We were going back to the East Coast to start college, but I didn't stay to drive the U-Haul from California with Kat and Rachel— I felt the pull of home. I missed my family too much. Instead, I flew to Newark and my dad picked me up in the minivan.

chapter seven

After thirty days of inpatient rehab, Lucia moved to a halfway house and my mother and I drove three hours there on weekends to visit her. There was a fugitive quality to these missions. Me at the wheel of my mother's car, hugging the curves of the Eastern seaboard as walls of rock dripping with water streaked brownly by. She in the passenger's seat, dispensing our neurotic hippie snacks—rice cakes, raisins, Granny Smith apples—and adjusting the temperature and volume knobs. She bought Twizzlers when we stopped and peeled them apart, dividing them for us to share with her short, blunt nails as we talked, unobserved, for hours inside the capsule of the car. This was our private high. It wasn't like the interviews my father conducted with curious passivity from the driver's seat. This kind of talking was a Jewish mother-daughter bonding exercise. It was spirited discussion, disputation, with little breath taken between sentences. We excavated every possible reason for what had happened, every bit of family history that might have informed it, stretching back the couple generations we knew. We engaged in this genealogical gossip for a time—why was my father the way he was? Because of his parents, and their parents before them—and then we dropped the family and moved on to friends. Everyone's relationships, everyone's questionable choices. My mother was funny; we laughed a lot. We went through every character in our lives and dissected them, as though working through a phone book. No stone unturned. No life unexamined. Like armchair anthropologists, except in a car.

The halfway house was situated in a western Pennsylvania town that was swimming in heroin. We'd heard about a police raid on the news. Everything related to addiction feels Sisyphean but this seemed absurd. A relapse would take no planning at all. You could probably just walk out the front door to the curb and make it happen, if you even had to go that far. The inside was shabby, carpeted, decorated in the particularly sad style that could be called Mass-Market Feminine Hope. On battered dusty-rose couches sat sateen and floral pillows bordered by aggressive ruffles like the extravagant frills of certain fish fins. On the wall were the Twelve Steps, looking dire and joyless printed in bold black type on large white scrolls, and inspirational posters. A few women mingled in the kitchen, drawing slices of processed white bread from tall, generic loaves and slathering them with creamy peanut butter and industrial purple jelly. We knew from my sister that one of them had shot at her ex with a sawed-off shotgun, a fact that should not have been funny but that was so ridiculous it made me eject a loud sharp laugh when I first heard it. No, my mama's baby didn't belong there. At least that's what I could feel my mama thinking. I watched her register every detail, shift a bit in her shoes beneath the cheaply framed embroidered messages of self-love. But there we were. We signed Lucia out and drove to a Cheesecake Factory, where we picked the bits of fried noodles out of Chinese chicken salads and drank Diet Cokes with our sunglasses still on. *You look really good,* my mother told my sister, clutching her hand across the table, and a round of tears snaked down our cheeks from behind mammoth black mall frames. *You're doing this,* she said. *I see your hard work. I'm so proud of you. You are doing it.* It was an observation—Lucia did have that precious clear-eyed look, a look of healing—but it was also a command: oh—you *are* fucking doing this. There were only three outcomes: sobriety, a life lost to addiction, early death. We would not accept the second or third.

My mother says she never had the kind of moments of resignation that I later experienced with K, that she experienced with her own disappearing act of a boyfriend. Did she ever think of kicking my sister out, changing the locks, "detaching with love," as we were advised in Al-Anon? *It's different when it's your child,* she says when I call and ask her. I've heard her say this a million times.

There was never a single moment when you lost hope? I press.

No, she says. *Every day was a new day to turn the situation around. I remember walking through the neighborhood with her and Daddy and Sadie—our lumbering Labrador—and thinking "I want her to live. I want her to experience life." There was no other option. When you're a parent,* she says, *you start to hear—or you maybe pay more attention to—stories of children dying. In every town, or every school, there are a few of those tragic stories, and I just knew that I couldn't be one.* My mother told me that when Lucia's addiction was threatening her life, she would hear these stories and think, *I cannot be that mother. Someone else has to be that mother. Because I can't. I can't.*

No other option, except to keep trying, to try everything. Daily, she was sending this message outward, upward, a desperate, secular prayer. She held fast to that wild hope, my mother. That blind faith, that fortitude. It powered the purchasing of a pair of powder-pink fleece Gap pajamas that she sent with my sister to rehab. The fluffiness and the color—they looked like something you'd dress a new baby in. Did she realize it? Possibly. But the pajamas were a symbol, perhaps of new life, a new girl-baby who could be born, someone who could emerge from the fallout of this tragedy. They were a symbol also of my mother's tirelessness. She would smuggle coziness even into locked wards. She'd had my father bring big Greek salads to the hospital after having babies herself, a detail I always held on to because there was a lesson inside it, part of our family ethos: personal comfort trumps institutional rules.

chapter eight

n desperation, I returned to Al-Anon in college. My sisters and I were all living in New York City then. Anya and I would meet in Washington Square, eat a lunch of sautéed shiitake mushrooms, marinated seaweed, and steamed kabocha squash at a tiny macrobiotic café on University, and walk to a nearby meeting. Lucia, by then a widow of sorts, was intermittently doing well—which, by our family's standards, meant seeing a therapist and working some kind of part-time job. But then something would happen that made us question whether she was really okay. She would fail to return phone calls for many days, or say she would be somewhere and not show up. Once, she threw a party and Anya and I found a crackpipe in her bedroom. After that, we went to the Al-Anon meeting weekly at least four or five times in a row. Did we share at those meetings? I know we talked incessantly at the café beforehand, and afterward, standing on the street, unable to part. There was no texting, and we used email mostly for school. We weren't in touch throughout every day, so when we saw each other we were brimming. We talked tersely, like detectives, divulging our theories about whether Lucia was clean, whether she was okay, who had seen her or spoken to her last. We grew animated sharing our terror, and laughing darkly about our parents, especially our mother, whose life seemed organized around my sister's pain. We recited for each other Mommy's efforts to involve herself, inform herself, insert herself, all of which appeared pointless and occasionally pathetic. The puzzle and the pain of addiction had changed our parents and, above all, distracted them for years. Anya understood as no one else could how hard it was to feel overlooked.

"Recovery" didn't stick—the pursuit of it felt pointless, as I wasn't the one who needed help. This is a refrain I've since heard many times: *If only I could get these crazy alcoholics out of my life, everything would be fine.* And my life felt too busy to take care of myself. I was too interesting! There was too much to do. I did not see any of my behaviors as related to codependency: not my own daily self-medicating with alcohol, nor my failure to sleep, eat, or otherwise take care of my body; not my tendency to keep a half-dozen relationships with men afloat at one time; not my decision to add to my hour-long commute uptown to Columbia a nanny job in the East Village, a shift at the tutoring center, a volunteer gig facilitating a book club for homeless women in Midtown, or any number of social or familial obligations. I collected people and I seemed to find everywhere people who wanted—who seemed to need—to be collected by me, to be swept up in my current, to worship me and be worshipped by me, to take in my breathless apologies for not giving them more, for not allowing them unfettered round-the-clock access to me—of course that wasn't too much to ask, it's not that at all, it's just that everything's been *sooooo busy.* The word "no" was not in my vocabulary. "I'm sorry" was, and I often meant it, but mostly I felt sorry for myself. My notebooks and datebooks were a catalogue of perfectionism. My tiny handwriting looked like it belonged to a high-strung academic mouse. I showed up places on time, and I was cheerful always. But my anxiety was high, my bedroom looked forever freshly ransacked, and I was full of fear, shame, guilt, and toxic secrets. I'd happily let a day be derailed if someone needed to talk. People in codependency recovery use the word "insane" all the time. *I felt insane, I was insane, today the old insanity returned.* "The things I was doing to make people 'see the light' were insane," writes Melody Beattie in the *Codependents' Guide to the Twelve Steps*. It can sometimes sound dramatic. Aren't we all, after all, presenting one (false) face to the world and living as our real selves in private? But that is how it feels.

From the beginning I was intrigued by how it had come to be. What was this disease of misguided love, a disorder of knitting grandmothers that had felt like a tsunami in my family home? I was taking history and literature and philosophy courses and was starting to understand that nothing was static, monolithic. Every institution was made and remade by people, subject to the shifting forces of culture. Alcoholics Anonymous—like religion, like government, like college itself—was the product of human energies, forged as an idea and honed as a set of realities in particular times and places. I wanted to understand what forces had made it, and why they felt incongruent to our mess, to my life.

.　　.　　.

American women, as the gatekeepers of the so-called private sphere, have long been involved in crusades for moral reform. During the nineteenth century, in the period of large-scale Protestant religious revival known as the Second Great Awakening, concerns about improving social conditions and the moral fiber of society came to the fore. Women were particularly passionate about temperance.

Drinking was considered socially unacceptable for women, who at the time relied more heavily on patent medicines and other remedies (precursors to "Mother's little helper") to alleviate the physical and emotional aches and pains often dismissively grouped together as "female complaints." Men's drinking, however, was out of control. Images from the first half of the nineteenth-century show men enthusiastically knocking back liquor in dark wooden saloons, bodies littering the streets as they slept it off. Women relied on men for their livelihood, which explains why, as drinking increased, women grew embittered—and exhausted. At the time, alcohol consumption was very high, peaking in 1830 with a stunning average of 7.1 gallons of alcohol consumed per person per year. Beholden to men for their very survival, women were profoundly affected by men's drinking habits. They could not easily protect themselves from drunken or abusive husbands. Many expressed dissatisfaction with what they perceived as a morally lax and deviant culture around drinking, but they were specifically concerned with the law. The legal structure was designed to limit women's participation in business and industry, in their families and their towns. The temperance fight was a moral crusade, but also a bid for greater equality under the law. Women learned to agitate for broader rights and protections by learning about the legal system, but speaking in terms that a wide swath of the population could understand.

As historian Carol Mattingly argues in her 1998 book *Well-Tempered Women: Nineteenth-Century Temperance Rhetoric,* these women carefully calibrated their message so as not to alienate audiences. The mention of the broader platform of women's rights was often inserted casually, incidentally, nonthreateningly. By "carefully presenting their cause as an unselfish effort on behalf of suffering women and children," and by scrupulously maintaining the status quo, they made their way rather strategically into the major newspapers and halls of male power. Temperance orators referred often to a "new woman," but, Mattingly writes, this was not a radical new heroine. They "venerated women's connection with motherhood and the home, and they cherished their religious associations; at the same time, they argued for dress reform, for women's right to earn their own living and to be independent of men, and to women's right to equality generally." The "new woman" advanced by temperance women was seeking change within the framework of traditional femininity. Still, she was a precursor to the more progressive New Woman who would appear at the end of the century.

Temperance women's contributions are noted in women's history but are dwarfed by the more radical work of suffragists. The suffrage movement is thought to be the gauntlet in which politically engaged women honed their oratorical, leadership, and protest skills. In fact, the overlap between the temperance and suffrage movements was significant and complex. Mattingly writes that because many temperance women were rural, religious, and poor, the movement has been painted broadly as conservative, especially as compared with the suffrage movement. But, Mattingly argues, just because temperance women "nearly always presented non-traditional ideas in a manner carefully crafted to appeal to a widely diverse audience," that did not make the ideas conservative. Temperance orators may simply have been pragmatic about building the largest possible constituency.

In an 1852 speech to the New York State Women's Temperance Conference, Clarina Howard Nichols spoke to women's anguish, saying, "Woman is the greatest sufferer from intemperance . . . If intemperance did not invade our homes and tear them from over our heads; if it did not take from us our clothing, our bread, the means of our own self development, and for the training of our children in respectability and usefulness; if it did not take our babes from our bosoms, I would not stand here." The statement was met with resounding applause.

Some speakers encouraged divorce. Elizabeth Cady Stanton said, "Let no woman remain in the relation of wife with the confirmed drunkard. Let no drunkard be the father of her children." Stanton knew that alcoholics could be wily and good at giving apologies, but, she advised women, "Be not misled by any pledges, resolves, promises, prayers or tears. You can not rely on the word of a man who is, or has been, the victim of such an overwhelming appetite." The tone of such encouragement for divorce lends some historical context to the notion of "tough love" as it's been advised in substance abuse treatment. "Drunkenness is good ground for divorce," said Amelia Bloomer, "and every woman who is tied to a confirmed drunkard should sunder the ties; and if she do it not otherwise, the law should compel it, especially if she have children."

Bloomer, a suffragist, temperance activist, and editor for the first women's newspaper, *The Lily,* framed the issue as one of autonomy, saying in 1853 that women's "individuality must be recognized before the evils of intemperance can cease to exist. How absurd the idea—how degrading the idea that woman, before marriage, can enjoy freedom of thought, but afterward that she must endorse her husband's sentiments, be they good or bad. Call you not this slavery?"

Temperance was not strictly a women's concern. Men had

started associations like the Washingtonian Total Temperance Society, which was founded by six alcoholics and became one of the first fellowships to focus on treating the individual alcoholic. The under-recognized model for groups like these were Native American mutual aid societies, which had been operating to treat alcoholism since at least a century earlier. Women started the Martha Washingtonians, in one of the first efforts to distinguish the plight of the wives, mothers, sisters, aunts, and daughters of alcoholic men from the drinkers themselves. And into the early decades of the temperance movement, women began to forcefully articulate a distinctly female response to the scourge of alcohol.

In temperance rhetoric, women were often rendered as "angelic," the helpless victims of alcoholic husbands. From the beginning, temperance crusaders' speech "confirmed the worthy lineage" of all women and all mothers. This was in the context of a national discourse that feminized the nation, and saw women's procreative power as a source of national strength—to grow and fortify the republic. Early temperance advocates knew better than to foreground their anger. But they were arguably already formulating some of the tactical resources women would later draw on as they sought to find ways to live with the disease of alcoholism.

Their concerns were expressed mostly in the register of sorrow and needless suffering, but there are also traces of hopeful desperation, a try-anything approach that will be familiar to all codependents. Some women tried to leverage their sexual power, Lysistrata-style: a well-known photo from the temperance era shows a group of fetching girls carrying a sign that says LIPS THAT TOUCH LIQUOR SHALL NOT TOUCH OURS. Temperance pledges were a common tactic at the time. Some were drawn up by individual women and signed among family members. Others were signed in public meetings—there were whole ledgers full of signatures. An 1887 "Family Temperance Pledge" in the Library of Congress reads, "We, the undersigned Family of _____ Agree with each other that we will not Buy, Sell, or Use intoxicating Liquors as a beverage and will use our Best Endeavors to Curtail and Prevent the Sale and use of the Same by others."

Long before I learned of this phenomenon, I made K a temperance pledge, too. Not during a period when he was really strung out, but rather when he was newly sober and remorseful and I thought he'd be susceptible to the idea. I stood by the printer in my open-plan office, fiddling with a pen, completely visible, acting as if I was just waiting on a letter or other official document to be printed. No one needed to know I was really using company time to commit to paper this desperate prayer, a short paragraph followed by two blank spaces for our signatures. *I, K——S——, solemnly swear that I will not consume substances of any kind.* It went on, and included promises that he would not take money from me or "abuse my trust."

Did I really believe that if I caught him in a devoted mood, I could capture his motivation as if in a jar? Did I believe it would last?

After dinner later that night, he signed it, though, and I smiled as I took it, signed it myself, and pretended to notarize it by pounding my fist on the page—*thank you, sir, I believe it is customary to seal the agreement with a kiss*—and willing it to become reality.

chapter nine

When I came home from San Francisco, I started college in New York a few months later. Rachel and Kat were there, too, and we spent much of our time together pining for California, for palm trees and Mission burritos and bars and boys. When one of my roommates moved out, Rachel moved in and we painted the living room crimson. Then love appeared again, at a softball game the summer after my freshman year. I wore shorts and knee socks and my hair in braids—I was looking for it. Love's name was Randy, and he looked like a greaser with tattoos—a lot like K, in fact, except he loved me back. Rachel and I went to the softball game together. It was an informal beer-fueled gathering organized by Philadelphia punk rockers and followed by a house party. By the end of that night, I was in love with Randy, and Randy's best friend was in love with Rachel. We didn't go back to New York for a week. Instead, we became a foursome. We stayed in their hot, top-floor flat on Eleventh and Fitzwater, shopped for dinner while we waited for them to come home from their bike messenger jobs. We guzzled our weight in cheap beer and fucked within earshot of each other, stumbling out crease-faced and shameless in the morning for fried eggs and hair of the dog. When we finally made our way back to our New York apartment, it was with both boys in tow. They bummed around the city while we went to class. In the womb of our small, dark red living room, we passed around a bottle of Jack Daniel's, ate punch-red chunks of bodega watermelon, and talked about what we would do after summer ended. Rachel thought we should drop out of college and move to Philadelphia to be with the boys. My parents did not.

I considered dropping out—anything for love—but then I had an even better idea. I could do both things, have it all, live on the third floor of the grand, crumbling West Philly house that felt like a mansion, and still go to college three hours away. We moved out of the crimson apartment and to Philadelphia—the boys came up and helped us. I organized my schedule so that I was only taking classes on Tuesdays, Wednesdays, and Thursdays.

Without the crimson apartment, I had nowhere in New York to stay, but Lucia said I could crash with her. That year, my sophomore year in college, on Monday nights, I boarded a Greyhound bus to Port Authority, then traveled downtown on the A train to West Fourth Street, and hauled my duffel bag and a backpack full of books to Lucia's door. She lived on Thompson and Houston in a cozy, dark, ground-floor one bedroom.

Spending those three nights a week with my sister made me nervous. She had suggested the idea so easily and warmly, as though she couldn't foresee a single problem, and as grateful as I was for the offer, I also knew I'd be caught between wanting to respect her privacy and wanting (or being expected) to serve as an informant. Moreover, my love for her had grown complex, laced with anxiety. Our big sister/little sister dynamic had flipped, and it was hard for me to take anything from her, to rely on her in even a basic way. But I took her up on it and tried to be a gracious guest.

It was a window into her intimate life—I found that she still intimidated me in her complexity, her opacity, her self-containment. She walked around the apartment in lace thong underwear, sometimes also an open kimono, with a kind of tragi-glamorous city-girl nonchalance. In the counter-height fridge in the apartment, she kept Gatorade, which she chugged standing up in the middle of the night, and occasionally cheese or pâté. We slept next to each other in her double bed, with the radiator, which sent forth a scorching, tropical heat, hissing and clanging. In the winter, we foisted the heavy window up and kept it open with a dictionary in order for the sizzling hot air to be tempered by frigid outside air. That combination, the mingling of those two temperatures, had the effect it used to have when, coming home from family holiday dinners at my grandmother's house in Cranbury, New Jersey, we would pull back the sliding windows in the back seat of the Volkswagen van and snuggle under a blanket, to be carried by my father's expert driving and the soothing dynamics of my mother's voice back home to our beds.

I knew Lucia worked at a strip club—there were vinyl stilettos and stringy underthings in the closet—but we didn't talk much about it. We didn't talk about drugs, either. Sometimes she seemed sober, but more often she seemed lightly inebriated. For all the Twelve Step meetings she'd been to at rehab and in the halfway house, the program hadn't stuck. She was alienated by talk of God, by the idea of total abstinence.

Sometimes while I was staying with Lucia, our father drove into the city and Anya came and met us, too, and we went across the street to a small Italian restaurant for veal piccata and bowls of fresh gnocchi. Afterward, we all smoked a joint together in Lucia's living room and she made us laugh until we cried, doing an outrageously spot-on impersonation of the earnest mustachioed Italian waiter at the restaurant. She had taken a theater class on accents and dialects and could perfectly mimic practically any way of speaking. Watching Lucia make our dad laugh was deeply satisfying, especially when he was stoned and he really cracked up, started coughing from laughing so hard. I beamed and dissociated, watching us all. Occasionally, before bed, after Daddy and Anya were gone, Lucia and I took turns showering and shaving, then slathered on L'Oreal fake-tanning cream from the CVS on the corner and sat around talking while we waited for it to dry. At her place, Anya kept a special schmatte expressly for this purpose, but Lucia was more inclined toward nudity. She fell asleep with *BBC News* on the radio and twitched and stirred throughout the night, dreaming lavishly, desperately. By morning, she was sleeping so heavily I sometimes panicked trying to wake her up.

As I had for many years, I felt alternately close to her and miles away. I was so grateful to her for welcoming me, for sharing her home, and for being so nonjudgmental about my schedule, my many plans and obligations, and the term papers I wrote on her living room floor. But I was also wakeful and neurotic, a spy in the house of sisterly love, going through her purse while she showered, unfolding napkins and receipts, looking for clues, planning my reporting to Mommy, all with endless homework to do and a bus to catch. On Thursdays after class, I took the train back downtown to Port Authority, boarded the Philly-bound Greyhound, and rode in the dark back to Randy. I wasn't sure which direction was home—him, our friends, the rambling punk house where even the floorboards smelled faintly of beer, where we played music in the basement, baked, and threw parties. Or my sister with her stripper heels, Lou Reed on the stereo, half-smoked joints, anchovies and cornichons on crackers for dinner, the Gatorades she drank for cotton-mouth in the middle of the night. Maybe home was Butler Library, where I curled into a reading-room chair under the lemony glow of lamplight, letting my shoes fall to the carpet, and lost myself in Russian history.

A bus depot at night is always a site of small horrors. By the time the Greyhound pulled into the station on Thursday night and I'd exited and heaved my bag into Randy's truck, I was depleted, sad, and often confused. My sister didn't need me there, I'm not sure she even wanted me there, but leaving her alone—abandoning her to herself—left me feeling bereft. I pulled the door closed, kissed Randy hello, and cried. I didn't understand until later how much my weekly absence and its emotional toll on me were affecting my relationship with him. My punishing schedule seemed to me to be impossible to interrupt, somehow nonnegotiable. The sense that I had to take care of my sister—even though she was doing okay, even though she was the one doing me a favor—was also impossible to shake.

. . .

A few years later, in a different relationship, I canceled plans with my boyfriend when I got a call from my father saying Lucia had been evicted from her apartment and he was going to move her things out, could I come meet him? I brought my new boyfriend with me, and introduced him to my father on Thompson Street. My dad handed me a paper grocery bag full of Lucia's unopened mail and the two shook hands.

It's very nice to meet you, said my boyfriend.

And you, replied my father.

I wish it was under better circumstances! I said with a vexed smile. *But welcome to the family, I guess! Cleaning out Lucia's apartment is a pretty accurate introduction.*

I spoke the line so passive-aggressively, but I was genuinely both proud and ashamed of our drop-everything-for-one-another family. In that moment, I wondered why ours couldn't be more like normal families. Why couldn't my boyfriend meet my married parents around their wide suburban dining room table, where they would really listen to what he had to say, where they would merrily, wholesomely ask him about his job, about his own family? I wished that my parents would be more traditional, that my sister's drama would stop encroaching upon my life. That I would feel less called upon. But the craziness enlivened me and exhausted me both.

In her wildly successful 1985 classic about romantic codependency, *Women Who Love Too Much,* therapist Robin Norwood writes that women who have grown up in homes with addiction or other dysfunction "where the emotional burdens were too heavy and the responsibilities too great, for these women what feels good and what feels bad have become confused and entangled and finally one and the same." She goes on to describe the savior complex one female patient has experienced. It may sound healthy to be helpful, she says, but "while to have strength in a crisis is laudable," codependent women "*needed* crises in order to function. Without uproar, stress, or a desperate situation to manage, the buried childhood feelings of being emotionally overwhelmed would surface and become too threatening."

.　　.　　.

In the fall of 2001, Lucia moved down to Miami with her new boyfriend, Junior, who was also an addict and sometimes ludicrously high. My mother decided we should visit her. I don't remember whether she invited me or I offered to go. We billed these things to each other and ourselves as vacations of a sort, even when it was clear that the point could only be to check up on my sister. We went in the winter, just a few months after September 11.

There was no way my mother or I would get on an airplane. The option was not discussed. We'd taken car trips down to Florida a few times in my childhood to visit my grandmother and her second husband once they became snowbirds, and the route might have been comforting, but we both liked the idea of being brought there, being able to read and look out the window and talk unimpeded throughout the journey without maps or stops for gas, so we opted to take the train. I don't know what we were thinking—that it would be like a rickety but soulful journey from a nineteenth-century novel? Or something from a mid-century film? Did we think Cary Grant might walk through the train car and sit down to chat? The thirty-hour Amtrak trip began in Newark and felt doomed from the very first lurch out of the dim, domed station. The company in our car, a non-sleeper car because we thought we'd just nap sitting up, was ashen, grim. The bathrooms were disgusting. The snacks we'd packed were long gone by the time we reached Maryland, so we subsisted for the subsequent twenty-four hours on tiny bags of Lay's potato chips and Diet Pepsi from the concession stand. Somewhere in Georgia, we made an hours-long stop in a desolate rural train station because engineers had to tend to a problem on the track.

We arrived to find Lucia and Junior living in a motel. A ceiling fan above their queen-sized bed shook the room a bit with its whirring, like a small, constant earthquake. The place was close enough to the beach, but seemed dark, as maybe all interior spaces do when you're in a blazingly sunlit city. On the ground floor was a Cuban coffee stand where we each got a hot, superstrong café con leche to shake off the train trip. Lucia and Junior appeared tired, faded in the eyes, but tan and skinny. Lu's hair was bleached and pulled back in a small, high bun. She looked chic and beautiful as an off-duty model with her dark roots, a sprinkle of freckles over her nose and bronzed cheeks. She was clad throughout the trip in various diaphanous micro-garments of unknown provenance. Had she gotten all new clothes here? How could she afford them? I could have simply asked, but there was something intimidating about the way she held her secrets. Addicts are like celebrities or politicians in this way— the information they share is carefully controlled and you can never entirely trust it. In going along with whatever story they'd decided to spin about themselves, I always felt a little stupid, and resentful for it. I didn't appreciate the humiliation.

Junior had the kind of boisterous Brooklyn impresario energy that was always crackling and making connections. He worked in "nightlife" and had the kind of hustler energy that made "parties" happen at clubs. Maybe they got a cut of the door? We didn't know what they did for money. I thought Lucia was probably dancing at a strip club but I didn't want to ask or to say so to my mother and have to weather her reaction. They were living a kind of Studio 54 lifestyle, Lucia waking up after late nights with glitter in her hair and padding downstairs for a Cuban espresso in a stringy sundress and aviator sunglasses. *Your sister is the most beautiful woman I've ever seen,* Junior said to me multiple times on that trip, with an earnestness that was also a performance of earnestness. It was disarming, if slightly weird.

We looked at some art and watched motorcycles rumble along Ocean Drive in South Beach, and ate melting salads at an outdoor café table. We went to the beach and my mom took photos of me and Lucia sitting next to each other, looking as different as ever—me in a black tank top with a long curtain of black hair and red lipstick, her with her short, bleached hair in a baby-yellow baby-T with the sleeves cut off and glassy lip gloss. She'd had her nose done by then and looked enviably small-featured and pretty, less like one of us. One night we went to a rooftop bar—Junior knew the owner—that had beds instead of tables and drank mojitos as we lounged somewhat awkwardly on the flat, wide surface of one.

How long do you think you'll stay here? I asked Lucia.

We can go whenever you want, she shouted back over the dance beats.

No, I mean here here—Miami, I clarified, pointing at the floor but meaning the city, this whole creepy scene. She still didn't hear me.

I don't know! Whenever! she said again loudly, holding up her hands in a pantomime of flexibility.

My mother and I stayed in a hotel, where we would collapse at the end of the hot, humid days and put the television on mute and she would voice her concerns about Lucia. *She looks a little out of it. And he seems . . . do you think he's a little manic? But he was always like that, wasn't he? Do you think they're in really bad shape? He does love her.*

I absorbed her worry because I understood her worry—I, too, felt the frequent stab of concern for my sister, a paranoid feeling that was like emotional cramping. I had fully picked up my mother's habits—listening with extra intensity, looking for a long time into my sister's eyes to gauge their degree of bloodshot and to see whether they held some excess of pain or fear or regret.

.   .   .

A few months later, Lucia came home. My mother was so relieved. We drove to pick her up from the airport, me driving, as usual.

Can't park here, can't park here, can't park here, barked the post-9/11 cops as they shooed us harshly away from the arrivals door. Then Lucia emerged from a door behind us just as I began to drive away and around the entire airport again.

There she is! my mother shouted, but I was already in a moving lane of traffic. *Just pull over!*

I can't! I said. *I have to circle around.*

She's right there! Just pull over! Pull over right there. Look—there! she said.

Mom, I'm gonna get in a fucking accident! I said. *There's no-where to pull over! Jesus, she can wait two minutes for us to go around.*

We circled. I could feel my mother's alarm, her hackles raising. It was almost comical, her connection to Lucia, the desire to smooth even the most mundane rough edges of her day.

We had to circle the airport ONE TIME and Mommy got all Not Without My Daughter, I complained to Anya later, when we were all together celebrating Lucia's return.

Well, she was right there! my mother interjected. *You could have pulled over.*

It has always been like this, maybe because Lucia has always needed my mother most. Her appearance stops everything, redirects all maternal energy. Nothing can compete. It's still this way. It doesn't matter what we're talking about—if my mother and I are on the phone and Lucia calls, she has to take it. She announces it with sudden urgency, as though call-waiting is a loud alarm, cutting me off: *Lucia's on the other line I gotta take it but I love you so much I'll call you back okay call you right back okay love you bye okay bye.*

chapter ten

Some of the earliest conceptual material for what would become "codependency" came from a German-born psychologist named Karen Horney. In the first half of the twentieth century, the notion that some women had in fact deliberately—if unwittingly—*chosen* alcoholics to meet their own emotional needs was gaining ground. Throughout the 1930s and '40s, Horney challenged Freud when she elaborated a theory of "feminine psychology" that considered social factors in childhood—namely, inequality between girls and boys—to be more important for female development than the lack of a phallus. The compulsive predilection for control that came to be known as codependency was, according to Horney, an attempt to repair old wounds. In an essay titled "The Problem of Feminine Masochism," Horney argued that women the world over were socialized to overvalue the men in their lives, and that the masochistic tendencies many women exhibit are a result of this conditioning, not of "anatomical sex differences" ("penis envy," in Freudian terms). In a way, she was saying that codependency and womanhood are one and the same.

Freud, too, had seen masochism as a distinctly female trait, believing that women are naturally submissive and derive pleasure from self-harm or self-destruction. In a radical revision, Horney argued that Freud's notion of penis envy was symbolically useful but not actually true. What women long for is men's power and prestige. In a world where they are expected to serve men's power to the detriment of their own ambition, their frustration and aggression are turned inward and manifest as masochism.

But though this thinking may have informed the popular conception of codependency, the influence of psychoanalysis was not over. Codependency (or co-alcoholism) was first defined in the early years of Alcoholics Anonymous, when drunks got sober and still couldn't fully stitch their lives back together. The whiskey was gone, but the vitriol remained. Even off the sauce, alcoholics lost their jobs, watched their bitter wives peel out of the driveway, done with their shit once and for all. Or they continued to be mired in the same patterns and cycles, the same late-night arguments, the same dynamics with their mothers or children or friends. Alcoholics and their families realized that removing alcohol and "working" a twelve-step program weren't the only fixes. The disease had permeated the entire family system, and rebuilding what it had destroyed required more than a simple amends.

Alcoholics Anonymous was founded in Akron, Ohio, in 1935 by an alcoholic named Bill Wilson, known as Bill W., and Dr. Robert Smith, known as Dr. Bob. As early as 1936, while alcoholics did their thing in AA meetings, wives were gathering in adjacent rooms to discuss the traumatic impact of alcoholism in their homes. Family groups appeared around 1939, the same year the AA *Big Book* was published. It remains the fundamental text for the millions of adherents to the program. Chapter eight, "To Wives," lays out the codependent plight quite beautifully:

> Our loyalty and the desire that our husbands should hold up their heads and be like other men have begotten all sorts of predicaments. We have been unselfish and self-sacrificing. We have told innumerable lies to protect our pride and our husbands' reputations. We have prayed, we have begged, we have been patient. We have struck out viciously. We have run away. We have been hysterical. We have been

terror-stricken. We have sought sympathy. We have had retaliatory love affairs with other men.

Our homes have been battle-grounds many an evening. In the morning, we have kissed and made up. Our friends have counseled chucking the men, and we have done so with finality, only to be back in a little while hoping, always hoping. Our men have sworn great solemn oaths that they were through drinking forever. We believed them when no one else could or would. Then, in days, weeks, or months, a fresh outburst. . . .

There was never financial security. Positions were always in jeopardy or gone. An armored car could not have brought the pay envelopes home. The checking account melted like snow in June.

Sometimes there were other women. How heart-breaking was this discovery; how cruel to be told they understood our men as we did not!

The bill collectors, the sheriffs, the angry taxi drivers, the policemen, the bums, the pals, and even the ladies they sometimes brought home—our husbands thought we were so inhospitable. "Joy killer, nag, wet blanket"—that's what they said. Next day they would be themselves again and we would forgive and try to forget.

Like many passages in the *Big Book,* this one is a timeless depiction of the yo-yo-ing of codependent love, but it wasn't written by Bill's wife, Lois Wilson, the resident expert. Bill W. chose to write it himself, telling a dismayed Lois that he thought the prose should remain consistent throughout the text. It's presumptuous for a husband to write from the perspective of his wife, of "wives" in the first-person plural, about the unique pain of being lied to or cheated on. ("How heart-breaking was this discovery!" How would he know?) I wonder what Lois did with her displeasure, whether she told a friend or simply washed it with the dishwater down the drain. Another resentment.

By the late 1940s and early 1950s, an understanding of the particular affliction of the "alcoholic's wife" had come into focus. An early study from 1943 in the *Quarterly Journal of Studies on Alco-*

hol described the alcoholic's wife as "basically insecure," a woman who became resentful and aggressive as she experienced the disappointments associated with her husband's drinking and she began to use his drinking as a way to "prove him and keep him inadequate." Another writer cited in historian Lori Rotskoff's work on gender and alcohol wrote around the same time, "She knocks the props from under him at all turns, seemingly needing to keep him ineffectual so that she feels relatively strong and has external justification for her hostile impulses." Into the 1950s, psychiatrists with an interest in psychoanalysis continued to develop theories of the "neurotic" alcoholic's wife. A Texas caseworker named Thelma Whalen wrote of this type of wife in 1953: "Her personality was just as responsible for the making of this marriage as her husband's was; and in the sordid sequence of marital misery which follows, she is not an innocent bystander." Whalen even went on to create a typology of codependency, naming four personality types corresponding to alcoholics' wives: Suffering Susan, Controlling Catherine, Wavering Winnifred, and Punitive Polly.

In 1951, Lois Wilson cofounded Al-Anon, formalizing the existing network of support groups of families and friends of alcoholics. The joy she felt about her husband's sobriety had worn off. "I found myself losing my temper over trifles," she said, sitting beside Bill in an interview. "I then began to think of my own relation—to you, to myself, my inner self, and I saw that I was resentful that someone else had done something that I had wanted to do all my married life. My one purpose had been to sober you up. And then somebody came along and in two minutes did the job." She was resentful that they didn't have as much time together anymore now that Bill was busy with AA and inviting fellows to their house. "I love having a house full of drunks," she said, ". . . but I didn't feel I was needed any longer. . . . Then I realized that I too had to live by the Twelve Steps. It was just as important for me as it was for you. Not so obvious, perhaps, but just as important." Soon after its founding, Al-Anon developed its own literature and its own tools, all based on the Twelve Steps. Later, definitions of addiction and codependency broadened to become more inclusive and less obviously heteronormative and gender-specific, but importantly, the understanding of this role, which is co-constitutive of alcoholism, has its origins in romantic love. This could be among the reasons that Al-Anon did not initially draw me in. Though its materials are intended to be generalizable to all alcoholic situations, it was built with marriage in mind.

When Lucia was clean, I didn't resent her. I felt worry and suspicion—could I really trust it this time?—but mostly, I experienced an overwhelming sense of relief, a sense that I, too, would now survive. Lucia had often felt like an extension of me. We were close in age and had grown up entwined. In snapshots of our childhood, I was often lit up by laughter with her sitting slyly by my side, having just made a joke. Or I was relaxed into her—in one image, leaning my whole toddler body back against her as she sat in a rocking chair, her arms wrapped around me. While embracing, we were sharing a box of raisins. There were differences between my sisters and me, but they felt insignificant, especially in youth. We were but variations on a theme. There was Lucia, wild and unpredictable; and Anya, fierce and intense; and me, the median. So when she was sober it felt like *we* were sober, like we were going to make it after all. The resentment I felt was directed toward my parents for caring too much or too little, trying too hard or not enough, doing everything wrong.

But there was no such triangulated resentment with K—it was all directed straight at him. I was angry with him for obvious reasons when he was drinking or using, but, as with Lois Wilson, my rage barely moved during his sober periods. For a time, it lifted and I was elated to have him back, but before long, I found that the things I couldn't stand about him had merely shifted. Now he was distracted not by the rhythms of his own addiction, but by his phone lighting up every forty seconds with new messages from his sponsor. He left often for meetings and for coffee, endless cups of coffee, which gathered in clusters around the house and which he didn't like to throw out. He would reuse them, making himself a cup— strong, made with heaping scoops of the fancy brand I'd bought—as he left the house. *Can I take the car? It's for a meeting,* he'd say, keys already in hand. I couldn't exactly say no to a meeting. And I couldn't ask for more from him, could I? It was taking all he had to stay on the righteous path.

In relation to Lucia, my codependency was shot through with fear. But with K it seethed, a quiet fury that I strained to square with domesticity. I came to understand what has been called the "dilemma of the alcoholic marriage."

like discovering the ways my grandmother and I are alike. We both keep our Q-tips in a jam jar and eat smoked fish on crackers while standing in the kitchen. She makes a cucumber and tomato salad and I commend her for salting it liberally, as I would. When I pad around her small apartment, a little peckish, she asks if I want some sour cream as a snack. I do. I stand like a pelican while eating a few tablespoonfuls, on one leg with a foot balanced on the inside of my knee, and wonder if she did too, in nimbler years. We both own more tubes of lipstick than is reasonable, mostly corals and bright pinks that we enjoy trying on for each other, one after another, even though the matte ones leave a stain, thereby adulterating the subsequent color somewhat. We acknowledge even this to each other— *Here's this pink, but this isn't really what it looks like, there's still some of the other one underneath. Still!* she exclaims. *Gorgeous!* She likes mine so much I leave all but two behind for her, replacing her Revlon with Chanel, Cover Girl with Givenchy.

On the second morning of my visit, she lingers in the doorway of her geriatric bathroom, with its bright red EMERGENCY switch beside the toilet, and watches me apply winged liquid eyeliner. She can't wear it anymore because of Graves' disease, which has made her eyes more bulbous and sensitive, but around me, she enjoys remembering a more chic iteration of herself. *I never left the house without eye makeup,* she says. *Not one day in my life. I would die before I'd do that.*

Me too, I laugh. There is such comfort in these odd inheritances. The pleasure of continuity, maybe, or a connection to an era it's easy to think was much cooler than this one.

Now it is 2013, a number that sounds both futuristic and deeply uncool, and, running from gnawing confusion about whether to stay with K, I have come to visit and to continue the project of recording my grandmother's life. I set my iPhone on the kitchen table, from which she's cleared our breakfast bowls—hot oat bran cereal with salt—and tell her I'm beginning the recording. She knows that one motivation for this trip is that I want to capture her story in her own words, her own voice. *I don't know if it's so interesting,* she says, but once we start going, it's hard to stop her. This is for posterity, yes, for record-keeping, guarding the family narrative after she's gone. But she also rightfully intuits that a great deal of what I seek to understand is love.

One of the first questions I ask is how she kept her love, her marriage to my grandfather, intact. *It's not complicated,* she says. *I was crazy about him. Crazy! Of course, we fought, I used to threaten to move to California about once a week. Oh, how we used to fight. But he was the man for me.*

When they met, he was a bassist playing live on the radio nightly for WNEW in New York City. He lived with his brothers and one young cousin in an apartment on Brighton Fifth Street in Brooklyn. He was thirty-five and she was twenty-two, working with her sisters in a paint factory in Linden, New Jersey. She was ravishing. The family beauty.

The night they met, he told her she was going to be his wife. She thought he was nuts. They were married after just two weeks, by which point he'd already brought her six pairs of black-market silk stockings (their second date) and put a down payment on a Flatbush row house with new appliances (their third). *They call that stalking now, Nanny,* I say to her. But back then, it was romance. They had four children and were married for twenty-nine years, until he died.

Nanny's New York sounded impossibly grand. Was it really all brassy big band music, I wondered, giant pots of hot food cooked by blocky, bawdy, ugly women who didn't even care they were ugly? Boisterous parties and hushed street-corner gossip among glamorous young mothers zipping up fur coats against the chill, saying things like *Well, Henny, you know what I heard . . .*

Do you think he was faithful? I asked, taking a risk.

Oh, I don't know, she said. *He used to speak Yiddish with Tante Lottie and I could understand everything they said. She asked him once if he was fooling around—he came home at four and five o'clock every morning from playing music—and he said to her, "Are you kidding me? After Sylvia, I don't have the strength." That's a good thing, Ninaleh, if you're crazy like that. If you make them a little crazy, they don't have the strength.* We laughed and sipped our tea.

Nanny talked about her life a bit like it was a fairy tale, which in a sense, it was. Her own mother's life had been short and brutal. My great-grandmother came from Russia through Ellis Island to New York City as a teenager with her sister and young husband, but they both died shortly after in the flu pandemic of 1918, leaving my great-grandmother with a six-month-old baby boy. Alone with the baby, she went north to Canada, where she knew some family friends had settled, and there she met her next husband, my great-grandfather, a stern Orthodox Jew. They returned to New York. He raised the baby boy like his own, and they had three girls together and lived austerely in a cramped apartment in a tenement on the Lower East Side. While raising her son, my grandmother, and her two sisters, she worked in a sweatshop. On Sundays, she cooked and did the family washing by hand. By contrast, my grandmother's life, which came to include a car, a television, and a move out of the city to the suburbs of New Jersey, was charmed. And it wasn't only creature comforts, it also contained the sparkle of romance.

I grew up with the legacy of this love—loud, long holiday dinners, uncles barking jokes at one another, children being snatched as they ran howling past the table and smothered with kisses. *Get over here with that punim!* my grandmother would say from her seat as I bolted through the room, if she'd even managed to sit down for five minutes. That's a variant of the crazylove, too: *get over here.* It's like the words K so often texted in the early, urgent days of our affair, at the mere suggestion that I might be available for a few hours: *Get. Here.*

In other families, the answer to the question of how an elder kept a three-decades-long love alive might be "he was a good man" or "he always provided for us," maybe "he made me laugh." In my family, the answer is a sort of insanity. A man holds your interest because he's completely nuts: capricious, unpredictable, unsparing with affection and with everything else. Love is a party that lasts into the small hours of the night, a party you should probably leave but it's so fun you can't. Love is navigating together various forms of precariousness and prevailing not by establishing stability, but by evading debt and death, surviving to eat and drink and fuck at the end of it all.

Not all of the relationships in my family were like this. But these were the stories that stuck. The ones, I suppose, that I wanted. Safe love may be enough for some, but it seemed lesser in both quantity and quality. Obsessive, unhinged love was simply *more* love. A thrilling, if inconvenient, excess. Like a leak you try to contain by catching the water in a tin, but soon the tin overflows, soon the whole room is filled with tins, and still more pours down from the ceiling.

.   .   .

Anya liked to collect my grandmother's stories, too. On another visit a few years later, we meet there and stay two nights in the complex of apartments where my grandmother enjoys a form of dignified semi-independence. After the loud greeting, the frantic hugging and the kissing that leaves her lipstick traces on our hands and cheeks, we tell her we're going food shopping and walk from the complex through a massive parking lot to the supermarket in the strip mall next door, for something to cook for dinner so we don't have to eat in the common dining room on the ground floor, and for provisions for ourselves. Pretzels and flavored seltzers and the kosher chocolate bars filled with raspberry jelly that I love and Anya hates. Being around Nanny makes me want to eat very Jewishly.

Let's cook her something good, Anya says as we walk through the automated sliding doors and into the plastic-y chill of the massive supermarket. *Every time I talk to her, she's eating oat bran or, like, one fried egg, and the food downstairs in that place is awful.*

Let's make something easy but that she can't make anymore, like a roast chicken.

Yes, perfect! says Anya, clapping her hands together. *A big salad, too. Oh, I just want to feed her, you know what I mean? Let's watch her pick the chicken off the bones.* She raises her shoulders and eyebrows adorably in excitement and sets off into the islands of produce.

On the walk back to the apartment, I tell Anya that our grandmother seems to have let her guard down more in recent years.

Being on the other side of ninety has that effect on people, Anya says.

I'm still recording her stories, I say. *They're getting more real every time I visit.* Anya starts to do Nanny's voice, the thick Brooklyn accent, parroting her description of her wedding night. *I was a virgin, we were all virgins back then, but your grandfather*—she lowers her voice—*he was very gentle,* repeats Anya.

That's the tip of the iceberg, I say. *I think all the secrets are coming out.*

When we get back to the apartment with the groceries, I prepare the chicken while Anya pours wine and begins to roughly chop tomatoes, cucumbers, radishes, and parsley for a salad. My grandmother sits in a chair at the kitchen table, facing us, enthralled by our energy. She says she wants to call her friend Arlene to stop by and say hello.

She should see this beautiful meal you girls are cooking! she says.

You were going to tell us about your wedding, I remind her. We've heard the story so many times, but we ask for it anyway. The older she gets, the more we want to hear the stories because each telling has its own small differences. It's like tracing the same shape over and over, forcing here and there by repetition the slip of the pen, an errant line.

February fourteenth is Valentine's Day, she begins. *February fifteenth we were born.*

What? I say.

What! she repeats.

You said you were born.

No, not born, married! We were married February fifteenth. It wasn't very fancy, but it was full of love. Oh, I felt so sorry for the whole world, that's how I loved him.

Nanny didn't want a wedding—she had lost her mother recently and couldn't imagine having a party. And anyway, her Orthodox father did not approve. When she returned to his apartment to gather a few things for a honeymoon night away—specifically to borrow a nice new outfit from her also-newly-married sister—her father told her to pack all of her things and not to come back.

He doesn't understand what a nice Jewish man you married! said her mother-in-law, who hand-delivered an invitation to a meal at her place in Brighton Beach to celebrate the newlyweds. Her mother-in-law's apartment was full of music and booming voices and laughter that day, and the spread she'd prepared, well, you couldn't see an inch of the tablecloth underneath all those platters. Nanny's father reluctantly joined and took in the spectacle somberly, but because he kept kosher, he didn't eat a single bite.

Maybe because I had said out loud that all the secrets are coming out, or maybe because we *are* energized—by the smell of roasting chicken, the red wine Anya's opened that even Nanny is nursing out of a cheap-looking frosted wineglass (*I hate these glasses,* she says, after every other sip), Tony Bennett's smooth crooning coasting into the kitchen from the portable CD player—Nanny begins to talk in long uninterrupted memories, a monologue. This time, it isn't the well-worn tale of the nice serviceman she jilted when she met the bassist from Brighton Beach who swept her off her feet. Instead, she begins talking about the end of their marriage, the day, decades in, when my grandfather died.

You know, after the kids had grown up, you know how things slow down, it's not the same passion as in the beginning. But that day, I took a shower and was about to get dressed to go to the neighbor's house for a dinner party. Your grandfather was lying down to rest before getting dressed for the dinner. I sat down on the bed in my bathrobe and my hair was up in a towel. He was looking very tired, but handsome, he was going to get up and get dressed. Anyway, we made love that evening before going to the party, unexpectedly.

Anya is looking at me, her eyes wide. At that party, my grandfather felt a tightness in his chest and a wave of nausea. He collapsed there, on the neighbor's kitchen floor, and they called an ambulance. He died in the hospital later that night. My grandmother called my mother, who came from the city and tried to blow through the nurse's stand but was stopped because her father's body had already been taken to the morgue.

We never met our grandfather, but we grew up with the legendary tales about him. He was the son of symphony musicians and came from Alexandria, Egypt, to America when he was thirteen with his brothers and his mother, the one who always laid such a nice table. They lived together in Brighton Beach. All three of the boys were musicians, boisterous and funny. He'd led a lively life, an unusual life. (*He wasn't like other dads,* my mom once told me. *When other dads were getting home from the office, he was putting on a tuxedo to play a debutante ball in Larchmont.*)

I feel a serene awe, the feeling that comes over me when I hear a good love story, and I rest my hand on Nanny's and say, *After all those years, you had sex—made love, sorry—the day he died?*

That's the most romantic thing I've ever heard, Anya says, her eyes filling with tears.

Nanny does pick the chicken from the bones, and saves the carcass for us to use to make soup the next day. After dinner Anya and I clean the kitchen, leaving it spotless, we think. But when we get up in the morning, we see that Nanny has rewashed the roasting pan, from which I hadn't, apparently, managed to clean every crusty trace. Now it gleams almost tauntingly on the stove. She didn't even leave it in the drying rack beside the sink—everything she washed, she dried on the spot.

She washed it again, I say, shaking my head disbelievingly, holding the pan up to the light. *What is she thinking? She's almost a hundred years old! How the fuck does even she get things this clean?*

Anya comes over to inspect the surface of the pan, which is older than either of us but bears no sign of having ever been used.

You left bits behind! She had no choice, she had to clean the bits! she says in another perfect imitation of Nanny's heavy Brooklynese. Anya turns the pan over in her hands, closely inspecting its immaculate surface, shaking her head, too. *That's some fifties housewife shit,* she says.

My mother and father took longer than two weeks to marry, but not much. For them, it was two months. They met at The Bottom Line, a rock 'n' roll club in Greenwich Village, on a humid August night in 1976. Having lost her own father months earlier, my mother had spent the better part of the year shut in and grieving. But that night her little brother's band was playing a show and her friends coaxed her out. At the time, my father was casually seeing a woman named Moxie Mandelbaum, and my mother caught his eye in part because she looked like a prettier, sexier version of Moxie. The pickup line was characteristically direct. "You look like someone I'm dating, only better," he said. My mother hadn't even planned on going out that night, let alone falling in love. Like Nanny, she couldn't imagine throwing a party without her father alive to be there, so they eloped, married at City Hall with just one witness— a friend and *Rolling Stone* photographer, who captured them beaming as they got into a yellow cab, my mother looking casually stunning in her wedding dress, a belted haute-hippie summer frock the color of mushroom soup with a cream bohemian patterning—then retired to a room at the Plaza Hotel, from which they telephoned their parents to announce the nuptials.

I've always thought that the decade when your parents were in their twenties is the one that assumes the greatest significance in your mind. For me that is the seventies. I can picture its colors, I can smell it. I know its cultural artifacts and I long to have experienced its particular variants of cuisine, of concerts, of tourism. Though I don't have any of my own memories of that decade, I still feel betrayed by television shows that I don't think, in their costuming or their coloration, get it quite right. My seventies is the one in which my parents, bronzed to a deep summer tan, met in the Village in tight T-shirts and jeans. Or maybe my mother wore a calf-length denim A-line skirt. Some of the T-shirts even survived into our childhood: one for Baby Watson cheesecake, one for the band Sparks, one a bright green long-sleeve shirt, tight on my father, with the realistic image of a palm tree emblazoned on the front. One, which I still have, that is mustard yellow and bears a silkscreen of my father's smiling face—a birthday gift to him from my mom. I've thought fondly about her wearing that fan T-shirt, her being that big a fan of my dad, her long brown hair falling casually around the dollops of her bra-less breasts. After their non-wedding, they took a honeymoon to Greece, where they got even deeper tans. A few photographs survive from that trip. My parents look nut-brown and sultrily zombified by love, their green eyes glazed over with that gaunt, electrified early-relationship sex calm. As a child, I used to see frequently in friends' houses the iconic framed photos from their parents' weddings. The dad in a suit, the mom like a happy cream puff in frilly lace. There was the prom-style one, heads tilted in together, or the one of them dropping a knife together into the tall, tiered white cake, teeth flashing. We had none of these. In my parents' early photos, happy is not the word. Rather, they appear strung out on love, like they've been fucking for days and now are moving slyly, wolf-like, through the streets of a hot European city in search of food.

There was something wild and lustful in this love, something sensuous and frankly ethnic, which always seemed to me to counter the chilly, WASP-y love of movies and diamond commercials, of other families, with their big houses with wraparound porches. There might have been other things they did better, but we did this best: loved loudly and laughed.

I've also thought that when love reaches this tenor, we catch a glimpse of what a women's world could look like, a matriarchy. In *All About Love: New Visions*, bell hooks has written, "Men theorize about love, but women are more often love's practitioners." It is men who tend to put limits on love, she says, leaving women in a "constant state of yearning, wanting love but not receiving it." Swept up in a powerful, perhaps unpragmatic love, it can feel like a man has submitted to the women's way, entered the temple of women's love, which is abundant and wild, boundless.

Although it wasn't just the women who were lovestruck in my family. Even my father, for all his stoic silences, was prone from boyhood to a kind of mania around love. He told me that his first crush seized him in elementary school, long before he even knew what sex was. In bed at night, he imagined rescuing her from the ocean. She would plant a kiss on him in gratitude. At ten, he developed a crush on a girl named Sally Stone. He didn't know Sally, he just saw her get out of a car each morning when they dropped his sister off at school. He attended a boys' private school and wore a jacket and tie to class all day. When he found out Sally Stone's name, he began carrying a stone in his breast pocket. "Right next to my heart," he said. The two never even met.

Is this love or madness, or is love madness?

While in graduate school, I traveled to Russia one summer. I was supposed to be starting my doctoral research, but I spent most of my time there wandering. I took Russian language classes during the day, then walked for a couple miles, stopping at markets and bookstores, eventually descending on the long breezy escalators into the gorgeous metro and heading back to the apartment where I was staying. When I emerged at my stop, I bought a foil-wrapped block of ice cream, which I ate while perched on the windowsill, looking down on an evening soccer game. In the neighborhood where I was staying, I kept noticing apologies graffitied onto the sidewalks and walls. Walking down through the courtyard to the street one morning, I saw a message, in big, bright, royal blue lacquered lettering. KSENIA I'M SORRY. It was enormous, all-caps Cyrillic, and some letters had dripped, blood-like, nearly down to the ground. I felt my breath go out of me a bit, a jolt of excitement at standing before so large and bold a renunciation of propriety, of property. This wasn't like New York, where graffiti was everywhere. I walked on briskly, but it wasn't even another block before I spotted the next message, in the same hand, taking up three big sidewalk stones. KSYUSHENKA I LOVE YOU. And then a half block later, a bulbous, badly drawn heart with another one: KSYUSHA MY LITTLE STAR, and three long arrows—I imagined the remorseful lover, bent over in devotion, dragging the tip of a spray paint can along the avenue. The arrows led all the way to the corner, the metro entrance, where there was one final plea, this one in curlicued script, a schoolboy's best penmanship: KSYUSHA FORGIVE ME YOU ARE MY LOVE. I had no idea who she was, but I loved to imagine that she would see all this, whoever she was, teetering to the metro on stacked heels the way the girls did there, that someone had vandalized the city in her name. I wanted that. Was there a way to compel the grand gesture if it wasn't an apology for an equally grand mistake?

chapter twelve

My parents' marriage didn't reveal itself to be broken until it had already fallen apart. To me it looked like this: One day my parents were happy. Then, they spent a summer smoking and talking in hushed voices on the screened porch. Were they having a good time or a bad time? Lucia was living in a dorm in the city, twenty minutes away, but it felt much farther. She was hard to reach and when she came home she was exhausted and looked wan and sickly. Could they be talking about her all that time? All we knew was that anytime we walked by, they went silent. *Need something?* one of them would say upon noticing I was in earshot. An abrupt leap into geniality that made everything awkward.

I'm going to meet Emily for ice cream and to study. We have an English final this week, I said.

Okay, honey, said my mother but they were already back in conversation with each other. They talked and talked and smoked and smoked, and then they were done.

My father thought things were fine—*I thought we were happy,* he actually said, with a kind of wonder, as the ax came down—but my mother's dissatisfaction had been building for a good decade at least and it had finally found expression in the dreaded and tragically conventional form of another man. I've since learned that this is, if not common, then certainly not rare either. A Norwegian friend once called the man who plays this role in a woman's life the ferryman. The man who carries you out of your relationship. Some people know the ferryman is only a catalyst. Others try to stay with him. My mother tried to stay. She fell in love with what he'd shown her in herself; she mistook that vision of herself for him.

Jim was in my mother's work orbit. She ran an art nonprofit that put artists in underfunded city schools and he worked for a similar nonprofit nearby. Not because he was an artist but because he was the kind of well-meaning guy who threw himself into secular good works. He seemed smart and kind and solicitous and she found him cute. He *was* cute, after a fashion—cut from the same preppie cloth as my earnest, chiseled English teacher, and literary in the benign, mildly awed way of someone who still quotes the Wallace Stevens poems he read in college. I was the reader in our family, so he was always trying to connect with me over great works of literature and new books he thought might lend him some street cred. *Have you read Junot Díaz's* Drown? *Your mom and I really liked it*, he said. He could be funny—a punster, the type of guy who talks out loud while doing the crossword, who feels himself to always be operating in some capacity as entertainment. Her infatuation was beyond the scope of what I, the teenage child of my mother, a child newly adjusting to the dissolution of her parents' marriage, could possibly understand. But I was close enough to my mom (primed by so many hours of worrying over Lucia with her and talking about her marriage to my father) to be able to see her also as an independent adult, not just Mommy but a woman. A woman with needs. I accepted my mother's choice faster and with more ardor than either of my sisters, and I tried to be friendly to Jim. Yes, as a matter of fact, I had read *Drown*.

You're kind of a kiss-ass, said Anya.

No, I'm not! I said. *I'm just trying to be supportive of our mother.*

Well, "our mother" is acting like a teenager. Besides, he's annoying. He tries too hard.

He does try too hard, I agreed. *But he makes Mommy happy.*

I was a total kiss-ass. Or merely a codependent. Determined to appease, to be flexible and hide my true feelings, which came out when I was alone, writing frantically in my journal, or more rarely in snide remarks under my breath. But mostly I wrapped up my real feelings and buried them. If you do this long enough, you stop being able to tell what your real feelings even are.

My parents had crazylove—or at least started there. Over time, their marriage became something steady and reliable—at least to us, their children. But we were not aware of the tectonic shifting taking place beneath our feet. Maybe because of his age or his eagerness, Jim illuminated in an almost cartoonish way the things my mother lacked in her marriage: enthusiasm, playfulness, possibly the virility of youth. In that regard, Jim embodied our worst nightmare. He was closer in age to some of our boyfriends than to my mother. He was peppy, or maybe he was just nervous when he was invited into our home, the one our dad had lived in. Initially, Jim made my mom so happy it was almost sickening. Via the jitters of early love (perhaps also the anxieties of divorce), she shed as if by magic the ten pounds she'd been trying for a decade to lose (which she didn't need to lose; the same ten I'll be needlessly trying to lose until I die). She looked svelte and gorgeous. She started wearing dresses like the ones she'd worn when we were kids, long, chic, silky floral dresses that emerged from her closet like long-lost cousins. She began to look different to me, like a young person all grown up, rather than like an old person—a mom—which is how she'd looked before. Watching her fall for Jim, I kept realizing she was simply a woman. I wanted to be a big enough person to grant her that, to smooth the way for that, maybe even eventually celebrate it. My sisters were more guarded, or maybe simply more honest, as they always were. But I wanted to remain my mother's good girl—I embraced him.

I navigated cautiously my relationship with my father, who seemed more obviously crushed by their parting, even as he enthusiastically took up dating. Once, my dad revealed to me that in the days after he'd moved out and Jim had moved into our house, he would sometimes park across the street and just look at our house.

Jesus, I said. *Were you waiting for one of us to come out?* I asked. He wasn't. He was fantasizing about challenging Jim to a basketball game under the hoop in our driveway.

When it became clear that their marriage was really ending, my father took to bed. The low queen bed in the upstairs room. A glass of water beside it and a paperback facedown. The sheets had begun to smell like wilted cotton and bodies, that tactile-textile bedroom smell that hangs in the air and can be comforting in spring and summer. He was diagnosed with depression, and though he had always been mildly depressed, my sisters and I had never seen him like this, in an almost catatonic state, and when I sat on the edge of the bed to talk to him, mostly to announce my comings and goings, his face looked wan and actually hurt. It was frightening to see him like that—not a shell, like depressed people are so often described, but rather full with discomfort, with pains that seemed to shoot around his body like gas, forcing small adjustments as he lay there. *You're going to be okay,* my mother told him, dressed for a work event in a black sheath dress and heels, some artful glass-bead necklace dangling as she leaned over him. *I'll call in one hour and check on you. You're going to be all right.* How good the click of the pavement must have felt when she finally closed the door, strode away from the house, and headed Jim-ward to freedom.

Once, while my father was still living at the house, Jim called and asked to speak to my mom. Anya wasn't home, it was just me, my parents, and my Uncle Nick and Aunt Josie, who were staying with us for a while. *Jim for you,* said my dad, handing her the receiver. My mom took the call, then came back into the living room and said he'd been hurt, badly beaten up, and she needed to go get him. I watched the gravity, the implications, of the statement unfold across my father's face. She had to "go to him," she was saying, like a lovestruck girl in a movie.

Where is he? asked my father.

East Orange, said my mother.

You're not driving to East Orange alone at night. My father, always calm, now almost alarmingly so, stood and retrieved his keys from the entryway table. *Nick, go with your sister,* he said. I sat in the excruciating quiet with my dad and Aunt Josie that night, picking at a pizza.

Jim had a few gaps in his résumé, but we didn't know that yet. He said he'd spent a year in Portugal building houses, whatever that meant. He liked Mexican food and alt-country music—before long, my mother was eating tacos and listening to Cracker and Steve Earle. I even ran into the two of them at a concert once and couldn't decide whether to find it embarrassing or sweet. His age and boyish manner were mortifying. But my mother looking that happy? That charmed me.

The drinking problem was hard to hide. He could blow through a six-pack in a couple hours. Outside the convenience store where we bought our coffee and cigarettes in high school, I ran into him blind drunk one Friday night. This was after he'd moved into our house. My eyes widened in mortification when he stumbled over to talk to me.

Isn't that your mom's boyfriend? my friend Alexandra said as we walked back to her car, smacking our Parliaments into the palms of our hands to pack the tobacco.

Oh my god. Oh god, I thought. *Yeah, sort of,* I was answering her when the foghorn of his voice went off.

Heyyyyyy, Ninnna! he said too quickly, then blinked to let his brain catch up to his mouth. *Nee. Na.* Laughter. *I do know your name. Howzerrr night going?* he spat. I instinctively took a half step back, farther out of the arc of his arms, his warm breath.

Yeah, it's a nice night out, we're on our way to our friend's party. Are you driving tonight? I asked, like a cop.

Nah, I'mmm not driving, s'okay, he said. He raised his eyebrows with his eyes still closed as though he had an idea. *Could drive, but I'm got a buddy at McGuire's want to have a drink with. But I'll see you at home later, cool?*

Cool, cool, I said back, and we walked past him through the parking lot. *Is this my actual fucking life?* I said, settling my ass into the low seat and pulling closed the door of Alexandra's Honda Civic.

Jim's crack addiction revealed itself slowly. My poor mom didn't even know to think of crack. Once, he said he'd been jumped by some guys in Newark for no reason (love truly is blind if she bought this after the East Orange debacle) and came to work with bruises on his face. Then he took a couple "business trips" during which he was unreachable and following which he was pallid, ornery, and exhausted, his vocal cords burned out. She began asking the questions she was by then practiced at asking my sister and finally wrestled the truth out of him.

Jim was "fun." Though he sometimes affected a shy air (in a way I found completely disingenuous), his personality was big and goofy. He "got" all the cultural tidbits that my mother found amusing. He watched *The Daily Show,* which my father didn't find particularly funny. He was very much unlike my dad, whose evenness, unflappability, and obliviousness were sometimes maddening. My dad was a steady presence, but he wasn't always paying attention. In high school, Lucia once came down for breakfast with blue hair and he didn't even notice. The same happened when I pierced my nose myself. These were things we did perhaps only to get him to snap to, to yell, to give a shit. He never did—a testament to his open-mindedness but one that could leave us feeling unmoored.

My father always held a certain power as the man and the breadwinner. He was a big fish in his small pond. And he'd come from a family with more money and cultural capital than my mom's. My mother had a good education, but she'd been raised in the brash immigrant spirit of her parents' families. She never felt she fit into my father's more formal, high-achieving family. They were more aristocratic, and more inclined to conceal their Jewishness. At home, my mother was often trying to get his attention, and was frustrated that getting it was essential to getting certain things done. *I shouldn't have to go before the tribunal to buy the girls' tights,* she once said to him. "Going before the tribunal" was a phrase she often invoked when they were discussing money, and it stuck with me always. I was especially attuned to the paradox of her role—at once powerful and powerless, the director of all household energies and still beholden to my father for all official and financial decisions. During some of the worst chapters of Lucia's addiction, my mother had locked herself in the bathroom to cry over my father's inaction, his lack of urgency.

Once we knew about the crack, Jim was off and running. Disappearing for days, one time moving away to Utah for a year, spinning some bullshit yarn about needing more freedom on the way out the door. My mother wept. She broke out the acoustic guitar we hadn't seen since we were kids and began to write really good country songs in her bedroom. But he always came back and discovered that not even his absence, the sudden and cruel withdrawal of his love, had convinced my mother that he was wrong for her. There were apologies and promises. My mother did not feel the same level of panic as she did about Lucia, obviously, but she felt an echo of that panic, and all the enlivening, purpose-granting, and righteous feelings of duty and meaning that accompanied it. She felt responsible for him, and she did want to do everything she could to get him sober, to love him into being the man she knew he could be.

Her anguish over Jim's addiction was repellent to me. It looked like weakness. It was one thing to throw yourself into saving your own child, but this guy?

As with Lucia, she exerted control wherever she could, in the only places where she might have an effect. She worried that he was cold and bought him a winter coat. The worry seemed to obsess her. *So what if he's cold?* I thought. *Let him be cold, let him fucking freeze.*

But we'd spent so much time talking together about love and drugs by that point. Our bond, the one represented in snapshots of her holding me as a baby, had been supplanted by the need for survival. Now we were like friends. I could be sympathetic because I thought she was really in love.

Just as she had with my sister, my mother loaded up the car with CDs and rice cakes and made the three-hour drive to visit him in some rehab in Delaware every weekend. I didn't go with her on those trips.

In Al-Anon meetings, people say that they fell in love with a person's potential. *I did that thing we do,* they say, *and I fell for the person I knew he could become. I should have been able to see who he really was, and not expect that I could change him.* They say that they "went to the hardware store for milk"; in other words, they looked for something in a place where they should have known they'd never find it.

Jim left my mom after eight years. She'd just bought a new house, a small fixer-upper they planned to work on together while raising their new puppy. Instead he broke up with her on their moving day, with the truck idling outside. Then, some weeks later, before knocking over a liquor store and leaving town, Jim broke into that house and robbed my mother, took everything of value she owned. Any paltry heirlooms we might have one day inherited—our parents' gold wedding bands. A ring made from an Egyptian coin passed down from Nanny's mother. And one very valuable thing: an antique star sapphire and diamond ring my dad had surprised my mother with years earlier. We thought it might be languishing in a local pawnshop, but no one had it.

The house she fixed up herself with sweat and tears. The puppy she raised into a dutiful, soulful dog that became her partner and her Buddha. I was twenty-something then. Angry. In a touring band, riding around America in a van, getting drunk, and setting off fireworks. I still remember that I had my feet up on the dash when she called to tell me about the burglary. The sun shone brightly, my cellphone was hot in my hand.

That sick! Mother! Fucker!!! I yelled out the open window. *That twisted fucking fuck.*

I used to wait for him to get to the ninth step and have to make an amends to her. How long could that take? I wanted him to return, not to be with her, but to sit his ass down at the kitchen farm table with its Fiestaware fruit bowl and have to hear what it had been like for her, all that heartache and pain. But we never heard from him again.

·　　·　　·

More than a decade later, on a road trip from Oakland up to Portland with my mom and Lucia, I put on a playlist and a cover of the

Dido song "White Flag" came on. "I will go down with this ship," the Irish pop singer had crooned on the original single the summer of 2003, which was after a breakup with Jim. My mother listened to it over and over. "I won't put my hands up and surrender. There will be no white flag above my door. I'm in love, and always will be."

Now the car grew quiet. My mother took out her iPhone and set it to camera mode, then pressed the back button on my phone to start the song over again at the beginning, and positioned her camera toward the passing trees and sunset. For a few minutes, no one spoke, we just listened to this song we knew the meaning of, and watched our mother make a kind of music video of the lush foliage of I-5 passing by. The cover of the song is more steely than the Dido version. It is the best kind of cover, a cooler, lower-fi riff on the super-produced pop strains of the original. It is to the original as my mother is to that former version of herself. When the song ended, my mom turned the volume down and watched the video she'd just made, the whole song playing again and the screen lit up with the blue-violet of the sky, the streaking by of forest-green trees. Men miss these moments, I think. They so rarely stick around for the magic of women becoming themselves, or maybe we can only become ourselves in the spaces where they aren't. I looked in the rearview mirror and saw that, like me, Lucia was crying. *You're so cool, Mom,* she said.

chapter thirteen

Love is women's work. Or the work of love belongs to women. It falls to women. We punch out at work and punch in again at home—the second shift, the double bind. It is not only labor that is required at the workplace, nor simply domestic labor at home. In both places and everywhere in between there is another more ambiguous set of expectations—that we will bring a swirling emotional energy that sands down edges, that smooths and warms and nourishes. That we will be kind. That we will sow love.

Throughout history, women have grown tired of this work. In college, I became enthralled by Russian history, specifically the spasms of revolution and the new world order the Soviets had tried to usher in. One of my favorite Soviet propaganda posters depicts a kerchiefed, smiling woman opening the door of her dark domicile to let in the light of socialist utopia beneath the words DOWN WITH KITCHEN SLAVERY! A second woman is visible inside in the darkness doing the washing in a tub. Outside their door are buildings with the labels CLUB, NURSERY, CAFETERIA. I remember the first time I saw this poster. It was fuzzily projected onto a massive screen in the grey-dark of an art history lecture hall. The professor was a beautiful Dutch American scholar of Russian Constructivism who rode a motorcycle to campus. She had written about the design of Soviet dresses and cookie packaging. I wanted to be her. Once, as I smoked a cigarette before class, I saw her pull up in a leather jacket and floral dress, black boots to the knee. I watched as she took her helmet off, shaking loose a waist-length curtain of straight, chocolate hair. An image encoded as indelibly in my consciousness as any Titian or Botticelli.

. . .

Kitchen's closed, my grandmother used to say as she finally hung the dish towel on the oven and brought one large, commanding, dishpan hand down over the light switch to turn it off for the night. It meant don't ask for anything else to eat. Just hearing her utter that line made you feel a little hungry. She had four kids in five years. When her grandchildren slept over, she made Jell-O in sundae dishes and served it with a dollop of Cool Whip. I ate mine one miniscule bite at a time so it would last for an entire episode of *The Golden Girls* or *Empty Nest*. Sometimes she dispensed with dessert altogether, then later was forced by her own appetite to reconsider, and offered us each what she was having: one frozen marshmallow, the sole nightly treat she allowed herself in the diet-mad eighties. By nighttime, she seemed tired, her ankles bulging slightly in her nude hosiery socks.

Kitchen slavery, kitchen servitude. The perfect utility of "kitchen" as an adjective. Handy as a wooden spoon. In the early days of Al-Anon, women mostly made coffee and cake for their alcoholic husbands. An undated mid-century memo from an Akron AA describes the wives' group as a "non-alcoholic kitchen brigade" that "was allowed to wash dishes, make coffee, organize picnics, and things like that." (Allowed to wash dishes!) It was seen as a privilege of sorts to be welcomed into the fraternal organization. Wives were understood to be integral to the recovery process, but that didn't mean all the men wanted them in the program. Some were suspicious, thinking the women were gossiping about them, which they likely were. In the beginning, Al-Anon cofounder Lois Wilson writes, "Some of these groups were what we call 'coffee and cake' groups or AA auxiliaries. The wives did what came naturally to wives—

made the coffee and served the cake. If the AA's had a clubhouse, these wives groups hung the curtains and all that sort of thing. Any spiritual growth was just a side issue." As historian Lori Rotskoff has pointed out, AA literature has long characterized the contributions of Lois Wilson and Anne Smith, the founders of Al-Anon, "in domestic terms, focusing on the behind-the-scenes encouragement and gracious hospitality they displayed toward the alcoholic men in their lives." The work of restoring balance in the home, of achieving "emotional sobriety" as it was called, was to be shared by the recovering alcoholic and his wife, but women's spiritual growth in the program was rarely figured outside of the context of marriage or domestic and emotional labor.

chapter fourteen

The love myth I bought into was human-made, fallible. A modern invention. I couldn't see this. To me, love existed outside of time, space, or bank accounts. I believed in the idea of two lonely souls finding each other and finding completeness. Not exactly happily ever after—in fact, wasn't a little tumult the mark of true love? It was more like desperately ever after.

Lucia continued to swing between clean and not clean, okay and not okay, and my love for her felt unrequited. It had left me brokenhearted. In 2003, she was back in rehab. "Sweet Lucia," I wrote her in February on the stationery of the company where I worked, "It's Valentine's Day and crisp and cold and I'm wondering why Aron girls never have warm enough winter coats." Addressing her almost like a lover, I went on to tell her she had scared us with whatever behavior had landed her back in treatment, which now escapes my memory. "I feel lucky that you're alive, and I miss you so much. My thoughts are disjointed right now, at the end of this long work week (I sound like Daddy), but I just wanted to get in touch and tell you that I (still, always) love you, accept you, think of you constantly, and have hope in my heart for you. I know that if we want to repair our relationship, we have a lot of work ahead, but I'm still willing if you are. I want you back. I want you to want to come back, for your-

self and not for us." I told her I would be there the following weekend: "I want to see your face and hold your hand, if only for an hour
or two."

Two years later, I moved to Cambridge to get a master's degree
at Harvard. One October, in the orange light of a Cambridge bar, I
found one lonely soul, also drinking alone—a tawny, rangy, beautiful boy, twinkling with booze—and believed that he was the one for
me, that I'd been made complete. We were both involved with other
people—in fact, his girlfriend was on her way to meet him. But
sometimes there's nothing you can do, right? A bigger love sweeps in
like the rook on a chessboard and knocks over what was standing
there before. All's fair, et cetera. He told me he had seen me riding
my bike on campus and had been looking for me ever since. We
were talking and laughing when his girlfriend arrived at the bar.
Later, she stole his phone and erased my phone number and he had
to search every Nina in the university directory to find me again.
How I adore a story that begins this way, so long as I am the
searched-for party.

We fell into a perfectly transporting early love. One night, he
came over and never left. Throughout the winter, we drank from a
handle of whiskey in my cozy third-floor apartment. After dazed
afternoons in warm seminar rooms, I stopped at the market and
walked home happily in the cold, hands redly imprinted from the
weight of plastic shopping bags. I cooked heartily, enthusiastically.
We ate and talked and laughed and kissed, with sentences unfinished and meat in our teeth. In the middle of a December night,
amid feathery snow, we walked to a playground and shook the
swing set with our weight, competing to see who could go higher,
howling into the purply darkness, and then lay by the space heater
rubbing our feet together frantically to get warm. Under the covers
he kissed my whole body, lingering over my left side, the panel from
the bottom of my breast down to my lethally sharp hip bone. *This
sector is my favorite,* he said, his breath spilling warmly over my
skin. *What sector is that?* I giggled. Starting at my head, he began
counting out the zones of my body, districts of flesh he paused over
and marked with his mouth. *It's Sector Sixteen,* he said when he

landed back on the left side. At a bar with friends the following week, I went into the photo booth and lifted my shirt while the camera snapped four pictures. At home, I glued one into the middle of the Christmas card I'd been making for him. "*Happy Holidays from Sector 16*," I wrote.

I want a baby, I had said within the first couple weeks of our meeting. *You should know that I want a baby desperately—and soon. I love babies.* He fixed me in his gaze, this twenty-three-year-old, smiling confidently, breathing regularly, unafraid. *Let's have a baby, then*, he'd said.

We were young. We got a puppy. We drove across the country while the puppy tromped over our laps, napped in a pile of sweatshirts. Looking at him, at the dog's velveteen body, at the open stretch of American highway, I felt drunk with love.

part 3

chapter fifteen

We took I-40 across the country so we could stop in Oklahoma to visit his family, and in Arizona, where Rachel and her boyfriend were living in a rambling house with Tank, their Rottweiler. We could hear javelinas and coyotes at night. We spent a week with them, hiking, eating and drinking, playing cards, and then drove on. I have a vivid memory of driving west across the Arizona border at night, talking about love—how theirs looked and how we wanted ours to be. This early part of a relationship suited me well—its hopeful, almost boastful plan-making, the refining of a shared vision of love unhampered by reality.

We landed in California in a chilly South Berkeley apartment with a lapis-blue living room and a crimson-red dining room and figs and apples growing in the yard. He got a good job. I walked to and from graduate school and read anthropological theory by the fireplace. We had a miscarriage. The palette of our love grew more autumnal, cozy and blustery both. We got engaged, and found out I was pregnant again a few weeks before the wedding. My sisters laughed trying to hoist the zipper of my borrowed dress up over my body, which had been rail-thin weeks prior but was now rapidly swelling with the dividing and multiplying cells of new life. The spring after we married, I gave birth in the glow of our living room

while a record by The Cure played. Two nights and a day of low, bo-
vine bellowing, then I opened my eyes after one last squelching push
and saw an alien fallen to Earth, a creature who looked almost hi-
lariously like his giant father in miniature, and seemed already sage
and serene, with eyes the size of teaspoons.

What happened to us?

I wanted to believe that our love could transcend the usual marital clichés, that it might endure not just as weak embers but an enveloping flame, the way it had been in the beginning. It feels like a
part of writing this book should be revealing what happened, but I
still struggle to know what happened. Or we dissolved before either
of us could find out.

For starters: I couldn't outrun my own sadness. When we met, I
was only a year or so out of my first, truly debilitating bout of depression, during which, bedridden, I plucked my leg hair out one by
one with tweezers while watching the World Cup and crying. I was
halfway through my master's program then and had a research trip
to Ukraine planned, but I found I couldn't move. It had been Lucia
who intervened then, to tell me it was okay to take a break from
being a good student. It was okay to cancel my plans, she said, and
then she helped me cancel them. She brought Anya and a couple
bottles of wine over with her and I sat in quiet gratitude as their
energy brightened the apartment, as they called the airline, the funder
of my grant, and a therapist. I was diagnosed with depression—
both major depressive disorder and persistent depressive disorder,
or dysthymia. *So . . . I'm a little depressed all the time and sometimes really depressed?* I asked the therapist. *I suppose, yes,* she said
with a flat-lipped, squinting expression that seemed to say, "Must
you make it sound so depressing?"

Now, in California, I was medicated, but pooling all around me
like slick dark blood was the discovery that medication wasn't
enough. I was at the beginning of a PhD program, but I operated at a
remove from my intimidatingly smart and competitive classmates—
they called one another *colleagues,* as though we were already important. My husband was building his career and that was demanding,

consuming. He didn't quite know how to be with me in the pain of the miscarriage, a wound we patched up hastily with the engagement and then the baby. He didn't seem to notice how far I'd been carried after the birth of our son by the tides of postpartum depression and existential uncertainty. Or maybe he just didn't know what to do. I certainly didn't. Weren't we basically children? How had we expected to know anything at all?

When our son was a baby, my husband became a weekend sailor. He had often been gone for a night or two during the week on short business trips to New Mexico or Nevada. Then on Saturdays, he left for long stretches to race around the bay on his wealthy boss's cutter. When would he be back? *It depends on the wind,* he would say, a line I can now hear as Odyssean in its grandiosity. Why didn't I just say don't go? Because he'd worked all week? Because he made most of the money, and had "earned" it? Because I wanted him to be happy? Because I didn't know the word "no"? Why couldn't I be one of those bitchy wives who just says, *You've got to be kidding me, absolutely fucking not.* The kind who says, *We're ottoman shopping on Saturday, it's on your calendar.* Even the kind who says, *I can't do the whole day on my own.* I've always wondered what that feels like. But I was a different wifely species altogether: The kind who tells her husband to go, that it is fine, and then cries that she is lonely. Who wants her feelings to be intuited, not subject to the vulgarity of needing to be spoken.

The tears I cried in those early years—they seemed like a fairy-tale quantity. Would they fill a measuring cup, a gallon jug, a stockpot? I was Rapunzel or a seaweed-haired hag. It depended on the day, the rain, my mood, my meds, my milk. I say I was carried by tides, which implies helplessness, which is how I felt. I created the chaos I lived in, but I wasn't able to see that. Some days I could see it, but still felt there wasn't anything I could do.

All of my metaphors then were marine—shades of blue and shipwrecks. Fetuses I imagined were fish moving through the dark ocean of me as I leaned seasick over the bow. I was boundary-less, my marriage aqueous. A note from my diary while pregnant with my second child reads, "I am sharing my body with a moving, swimming creature, the curvature of whose back I can sometimes lay my hand against. It's uncomfortable, this pressure against the walls of me. I try to take a breath and make more space to share myself." In my diary, I wrote that this second saucer-eyed baby was an ocean liner turning herself around. She was a tiny whale. I wrote about my panic, fear, self-hatred, confusion. I wrote, "I want to make it to more solid ground, even if I have to paddle my way there like this, in humiliating desperation." One day I walked to Urgent Care and said with a dissociated calm that I was afraid I might hurt myself. The receptionist looked at my belly. I was sent straight back to be seen.

In one photograph from that time, my husband is standing alone on a boat on the black surface of the water, holding on to the mast, looking tall and commanding and handsome and entirely alone. Literally adrift.

"I want to SWIM," I wrote. "I want to feel the clogged, perfect quiet of underwater and feel this big belly (big body) FLOAT. I want to float I want to float I want to float." I was fucking drowning.

.   .   .

The hot, young, carefree love I had with my husband was transformed by marriage, babies, and the daily dulling of adulthood, forces I imagined working on our relationship the way a pair of hands acts on a piece of pottery as its spins on the wheel. Gentle pressure. Every day a new ridge, a narrowing. We had been together only a few years but daily life was already a struggle. The threads of hardship were all braided together. Who knows if they were correlated, causal, or all one thing. 1) I was depressed and anxious. 2) We both drank too much. 3) No matter what, the baby wouldn't sleep through the night. I was up with him at midnight, 1:00 A.M., 3:00 A.M., always up for the day by about 5:15, nuzzling his neck and watching the dog pee in the yard. *You have to sleep train!* people would tell us, as though we hadn't tried that yet. By 6:00, he'd had hot cereal and an episode of *Sesame Street* and sat bouncing in his ExerSaucer, a veritable command center of pointless toys, smacking its plastic tray, looking to me with his beautiful turquoise eyes for the day's direction, its activities and its zest. I was on my third cup of coffee by the time the sky brightened into dawn, my own eye sockets like dry, grainy pits in my pounding head. At 6:30, my husband got up with the alarm and smoked on the stoop first thing, in a shearling-lined coat, peering with disdain at another harsh, damp morning. When he'd kissed us goodbye and the engine turned over and he was gone to work, my stomach plummeted. I felt plunged into uncertainty as though alone in a falling elevator. I was ashamed to discover that I was a little bit afraid of the day and that made me feel a little afraid of myself. *Craaaaaazy.* I locked the door, drew a long breath, and turned to my son. *Me and you, baby,* I said, and he stomped his feet in recognition.

I had wanted a baby so badly. From the time I became a mother's helper at age twelve, or possibly before, naming and raising countless doll babies, snaking fabric Cabbage Patch doll legs into cotton outfits. In college, I worked as a nanny and found joy in the ardent, uncomplicated love I felt for those children, in the way complexity fell away when I only had to slice melon into chunks for them, tell them their drawings were lovely.

I'd feared falling into the kind of postpartum depression where I would feel nothing for my baby—or worse, I'd feel ill-will. But I never had that. I was madly, swooningly in love with my son in those hazy early days. That love arrived with him and was immediately incontestable, a blunt new fact like the sky being blue. In so many ways, babylove was better than any romance I'd ever felt. I danced him around the house like we were at a Victorian ball. I inhaled him and breathed his sweet milky breath. But I was still sad, maybe more sad. *The babylove should be totalizing,* I thought, *it should neutralize the sadness, all the other feelings.* That it didn't—that I still hated my body, feared for my career, worried I now lacked a common language with my husband—compounded the desolation. I felt confused, worried behind the scenes that I must be doing it wrong. Life had lost its previously recognizable shape. Nothing can prepare you for the formlessness of that time, which spreads like dough, traps you. As Rachel Cusk writes in *A Life's Work: On Be-*

coming a Mother, "The day lies ahead empty of landmarks, like a prairie, like an untraversable plain."

I had less patience for my husband now, but I would never show a lack of patience. That seemed uncouth, unkind, unladylike. I would store it away instead. Part of what had drawn me to him in the first place was that he was so much like me. A good boy who could be very, very bad, who was lured *just* enough into badness—into drinking, drugs, and misadventures—but who never fully turned his back on his responsibilities. No matter what had transpired the night before, he always made it to work in the morning. Clean-shaven, hair combed. It was the kind of balancing act I had perfected, too. It started in high school, while playing second-fiddle to Lucia, the genuine bad girl. I sometimes looked upon her missteps with pity. She acted out dramatically, which called attention to her, which got her into trouble with our parents, but it didn't have to be that way. Didn't she know that if you flew just under the radar, got good grades, and pretended you were okay, that you could get away with basically anything?

I learned to temper my own dark impulses, and finding my footing between two worlds became a kink of sorts. A secret. But now there was a baby and no leeway at all. Raising him could not be faked or phoned in. His life could not be set on autopilot.

.   .   .

What is the difference between me and a person who can live this life, who can coffee up and muscle through until the kids are school-age and she can get more sleep? Until there is more money to buy a house or take a family vacation? What is the difference between me and somebody who *stays* in a marriage—for ten years, twenty, fifty? I think about those mornings when I felt like a husk and wonder if I just had a bad attitude. A lack of patience. If I was simply immature, not a hard worker, a team player. Or if the darkly intertwined beanstalk of depression, drinking, and lack of sleep is insurmountable, attitude notwithstanding. Sleep deprivation is a form of torture, as new parents like to remind one another. Sometimes when people ask what happened to my marriage, I reply bluntly, *I didn't sleep for years, so I lost my mind*. I don't know why it feels good to say it that way, to drop a hint of mental instability like a small bomb, but it does. This is rare, though. Mostly, when asked, I perform a chipper little skit, collapsing a few years of anguish into a couple neat lines. *Oh, we just didn't know what we were getting into,* I say, as if anyone does. *You know, we get along better divorced than we did married!* I say, though I don't think that's even true, just a tidbit it seems a well-adjusted divorcée might offer up. I'm always surprised that people even inquire about divorce. Maybe they think I want to be asked? "Divorces and separation—that is the way to get attention," wrote Elizabeth Hardwick in *Sleepless Nights*. I do appreciate banter that gets honest quickly, but still, it's a peculiar feeling sitting at a playground and having someone pry into this particularly private corner. Besides, what do they think happened? Marriage happened. I always want to ask, *Isn't it much harder to keep one together than let one die?*

There remained throughout, of course, the counterweight of joy. There was laughter and warmth. Music. Hearts tacked to the front window in February. Attraction coursed between us, purring dependably like a sated cat. From across every room we smirked at each other, confirming it. Motherhood had made me an unequivocally better person, I thought, even as it unglued basic pieces of me. The days were very long, but buried in all of them, if I could be patient, was some momentary treasure or other. On weekends, we pushed the stroller to a coffee shop or drove up into the woods and rode a small steam train around as our son, in a toddler-sized version of the same shearling coat as my husband's, grunted with glee, and I thought, *Look at me! A mother!*

We were fixated on him. Our twosome had become a triangle. He made us laugh, especially as he learned to talk and began aping us, with that glint in his eye that kids get when they know they have your full attention. We'd censored our swear words, shortening the phrase "what the fuck" to become "what the f," which became, in our son's interpretation, "what the earth," a rhetorical question

I thought beautifully encompassed the enchanting, maddening mysteries of being alive. I was touched by the philosophical magnitude, the accidental profundity, of his every utterance. *What the earth?!* I still sometimes think when pissed off or puzzled.

My husband was handy and high energy. Before, in every place I'd ever rented, I'd prayed that nothing went wrong and avoided solving problems when they arose, but he made living in a house feel like it was simply a series of small, doable projects. He had an easy combination of luck, competence, and confidence that was almost annoying—he baked bread, he built things, smoked meat for eleven hours, enjoyed elaborate preparations for road trips and hikes. He decided casually to try his hand at growing marijuana and weeks later, our garage was filled with vigorously bursting, towering plants, one named for me and the rest for each of my girlfriends, our names Sharpied on masking tape on each of the big black buckets. *Claire is lookin' strong!* he'd say after checking on them. *But poor Miranda could really use some more light.* We harvested and trimmed the plants and gave the weed away in large mason jars like the chill Californians we were becoming.

We lived next door to good friends, a couple, one half of whom was a chef at a famous Berkeley restaurant. A few times a week, we brought the baby monitor over with us and laughed into the night over homemade cocktails and dinners made from the variegated Bay Area bounty I was learning about through her. Persimmons and puntarelle, chicories and little gems, meat and fish doused in thick sauces: chermoula, salsa verde, romesco made from the freshest peppers. I can still picture the quality of light in that kitchen next door, the smell of fresh thyme in the air, my pleasure at making my husband laugh as he swirled bourbon around in his glass. The flash of his perfect teeth. "May you always have what you want and want what you have" goes a common wedding toast in my family. The way I've always heard it is that having what you want is the easy part. It's wanting what you have that grows harder over time—that can require multiple, simultaneous tricks of the mind. At that time, I wanted what I had. A beautiful family, things to laugh about, the gathering rhythm of an everyday life that was not beset by hunger or poverty. I did feel far away from my own roots. I was making something new, I reasoned.

Our relationship was the simplest I'd ever had. And yet. "Never was there enough of what we thought we wanted," reads a line in AA's *Twelve Steps and Twelve Traditions*. Was I called by a darker force? Codependents grow accustomed to chaos and get bored and antsy when there isn't enough of it. They want to tend to a crisis, and with K's return came a familiar drumbeat—fear—to which I began to tap my toe. I'd been groomed to be a sort of social worker of the heart—did I need a needier case to work on? A purer dose of romance?

My husband had a math brain, efficient and unsentimental. He made a spreadsheet for our household budget. He mollified me before air travel by explaining in physics and engineering terms that the plane *wants* to fly. I laughed when he told me he believed that it was the role of scientists to chip away at a wall of objective truth. *But it was humans who came up with the notion of objectivity in the first place,* I said. When it came to certain philosophical matters, we had to agree to disagree. But I was impressed by the way he saw the world; it seemed like it could save a person a lot of time and heartache. I hoped it might rub off on me. For one Christmas early on, I bought him a volume of the letters of the physicist Richard Feynman. "*For my Fine Man,*" I inscribed it.

At times I found his rationality lacerating. Before the arrival of our first child, I enrolled us in a six-week birth class, and one evening each week we sat among other couples on the carpeted floor of a perinatal education center listening to a doula explain the miracle of life. In later weeks, as she described the dramatic viscera of the actual event—a catalogue of horrors: mucus plugs and bloody shows, perineal stretching—I even sat between my tall husband's splayed legs, leaning back into his large, warm, enveloping form, like a couple in a movie. I could feel his heartbeat in my back and I thought about the baby's heartbeat, the three of us, really, sitting like that, curved into one another like a shell, the healthy, hopeful pumping of our family's hearts. After the final class, we did not linger to exchange phone numbers, as some of the others did. We were first to push through the glass door into the moistened Berkeley evening, and we walked half a block to the car in a pleasant, pensive silence.

So, what did you think? I said, pulling the seatbelt over the taut torpedo of my belly.

Of that last one or the whole thing? he asked.

No, I mean the whole class, I said.

Ah, he said, sounding already slightly distracted as he pulled up to the curb and flicked the turn signal. *What did I think?* he repeated absently as he drove. *I think . . . that the entire class could have fit on one PowerPoint slide.*

Our son was born in spring, and by Mother's Day he was six weeks old, curled and wriggling in his plush muted clothing, still looking in-utero some days. I wondered what nod to mainstream domesticity my husband might ironically unveil to mark my first Mother's Day. A gift certificate for a facial or maybe a brunch of too-sweet waffles at the overcrowded French café on Shattuck Avenue. But he didn't do anything special that day.

You could have just written a card, I said teasingly, when I realized late in the day that no surprise was forthcoming.

Babe! I'm so sorry, he said. *I can't believe I didn't think of it.*

He apologized when things like this happened and I always knew he meant it. What's more, my mind scrambled to fill in the blanks for him—he was young! He was a man of good intentions. He knows I'm not that attached to holidays. Holidays are cheesy anyway. But somewhere in my heart, I kept the score.

.   .   .

I've met—collected—other mothers along the way who also bucked against the confines of their marriages, who in spite of seemingly stable circumstances found themselves all of a sudden feeling the same way I did, nested greyly inside the wifely paradox of solitude and suffocation. We usually become friends. We usually spend our first few coffee dates crawling out from behind the curated stories we've told, the display-case divorces we describe to the still-marrieds as though it was no big deal. We share our wonder at functioning unions (how do other people pull this off?) and our shame (why couldn't I?), and we talk about what it's really like dismantling the marital edifice brick by painful brick, to text with the ex, date, raise children in two houses, to face the heartbreaking existential questions we've forced them to ask far too early and for which we have only paltry or faltering answers. We talk also about the feeling of liberation that dawns as this unknown opens before us, a dark, starry highway leading who knows where. As Deborah Levy writes of her divorce in her memoir *The Cost of Living,* "Life falls apart. We try to get a grip and hold it together. And then we realize we don't want to hold it together." That terrifying and exciting feeling is a lot like the beginning of love. Maybe it's the beginning of finding out what loving oneself looks like.

The path out of a marriage is different for everyone, but for those who leave while their children are small, it is frequently lighted like the exit row of a crashing plane by the crazylove of someone new. One married friend became a dancer at a Portland strip club and ended up falling in love with a regular. She was drawn by the flexible schedule, and of course by the promise of fat stacks of cash, but I think also by the seductive idea of being, at least for a time, the opposite of Wife. A glittering novelty. One day she showed me the parallel Instagram account she maintained for her dancer persona, a parade of dimly lit images of her arched back, the curve of her waist and the skin beneath her belly button, her breathtaking yoga ass in a black mesh thong. In many of the photos, her long hair was visible in titillating tendrils, but in all of them she was faceless or headless. A suggestion of a girl. A rumor. This seemed like a particularly intoxicating freedom.

Even as I always nurtured a ferocious belief in a totalizing romantic ideal, a mate who would complete me and with whom life would be both wildly entertaining and eminently manageable, I lived in fear of becoming Wife. I wanted to be somebody's everything, but I was keenly aware of how quickly lust could depart the marital scene. (Why? It had not yet departed mine. Somehow it seemed smart to leave before that could happen.) Wife was all embers, none of the fire.

When I was young, I discovered Anne Sexton's poem "For My Lover, Returning to His Wife." I even heard a recording of Sexton reading it in her smoky New England drone, spreading resignation thickly over each line like butter on hot bread.

> She has always been there, my darling.
> She is, in fact, exquisite.
> Fireworks in the dull middle of February
> and as real as a cast-iron pot.

It goes on, as the lover laments being "momentary," ephemeral. The cast-iron pot stayed with me always, even as I unwrapped my own wedding-registry Le Creuset. In the poem, it's meant to conjure the solidity, the reliability of marriage. Such a pot will hold meal after meal. A vessel for sustenance, like the house itself, with a light kept on for a husband returning late. Like the wife, who carries and "sets forth" children, the substance of the family. Sexton writes that the wife's realness is what makes her "your have to have." Yet I've always seen this scenario the other way around, which may be why I made a better mistress than a wife. A mistress might be momentary, yes, but she is the true have to have, isn't she? The one that animates, lends that urgency that closes in on a person, makes a person ache. A wife is leftovers in the fridge. I couldn't bear to be that. A wife is my mother. A beautiful, dazzling, funny woman, smart as a whip, who made the babies and the pots of soup, and still was not enough. Still he lied and chased tail. Went after "littleneck clams out of season." Later in Sexton's poem, the mistress goes on to grant the lover the freedom to return to his wife: "I give you back your heart. I give you permission," she says—and we are meant, perhaps, to feel her loneliness. It's hard to be temporary. But even that gesture is an invocation of her own power. The ability to return a heart like a gift back to the store, carelessly, as though it simply doesn't fit.

Another poem, called "Wife," by Ada Límon, goes partly like this:

> Housewife
> fishwife, bad wife, good wife, what's
> the word for someone who stares long
> into the morning, unable to even fix tea
> some days, the kettle steaming over
> loud like a train whistle, she who cries
> in the mornings, she who tears a hole
> in the earth and cannot stop grieving
> the one who wants to love you
> but often isn't good at even that
> the one who doesn't want to be diminished
> by how much she wants to be yours.

I did not want to be diminished and so I was a failure at marriage. I could not bear to be the object of a forever gaze, of anything but a worshipful gaze. I thought I could become Wife, but I ended up feeling that there was no word for me, or I didn't want there to be a word for me. I went looking for answers, for solace, in the places where women's pain lives. I looked in self-help books and found pat, bounded answers—they've come up with a thousand different ways to say *Stay*. I listened to songs and I looked at art, my ear to the ground where the footsteps of the fiercest foremothers had walked, and these said *Run*. I ran.

chapter sixteen

K and I hadn't spoken in ten years when he found me on Facebook and tried to flatter me with a long message in which he said he'd been looking for me for a long time. He imagined I would by now have married Ian Svenonius, the dashing frontman of the Nation of Ulysses, my old favorite band. Had I been in the Bay Area all this time? Were we just going about our lives mere miles apart? Wasn't that rich. He wasn't looking to cause any trouble for me, he added—a sentiment I would laugh about later—but if I was open to having a cup of coffee, he'd love to see me. *I'm a year sober and living in Mompton,* he wrote with his signature breeziness, a casual self-mockery meant to disguise an abyss of self-loathing.

Mompton. I was charmed enough by the pun, I suppose, that I chose not to linger on the information it transmitted: he was thirty-nine and living with his mother. In fact, Mompton was Lafayette, a strip-mall suburb forty minutes from the city, where his mother ran a business and a small animal sanctuary out of her split-level home. She had a dog, cats, talking birds, and an enormous pig named Guido.

K and I did have coffee. I don't remember where. I told my husband we were going to, and he was unthreatened, even slightly uninterested. My depression had descended, and was a palpable presence in our lives, but it manifested mostly in sadness. Crying jags during which I wiped snot on my sleeves, then straightened up, sniffed loudly, and said, *I'm fine, I just need to get my shit together.* The force of that sadness was worrying, but it didn't seem destructive. We were happy enough.

K and I met on a busy street corner in front of a CVS, and I can still see the wide smile on his face when he first saw me approaching. I was a mirror, reflecting back the same grin. A moment of guardedness dropping away like a slip falling to reveal a frank and funny nakedness.

I'd chosen my outfit with great care and even solicited the input of Claire, my best California friend, and my mother, who was then living in Berkeley and carried the dozing baby around as I tried on half my clothes. I didn't mention the word "sobriety" to my mother then—why complicate things when this was only a quick coffee with an old flame.

It was just a T-shirt and jeans I was looking for, but the selection of the right combination felt enormously significant.

What are we going for here? Claire had asked as we sipped white wine at my dining room table a week earlier. *Is this like a "you really missed out" situation or more of an "I want you to want me but you can't have me" type thing?*

Those are different? I asked.

Yes, are you kidding?! she said. Her fashion sense was enviably refined. *You really missed out is a more demure look, like "I'm a mom now, you missed your chance, how dare you let your gaze linger." The second one is definitely hotter, maybe a plunging neckline*—she paused to laugh—*something just slightly more suggestive.*

That one, I said, laughing. *The second one. But nothing that makes him think he has a chance! I'm married, for fuck's sake. And fuck him, he broke my little teenage heart.*

We settled on a pair of Claire's perfectly faded black pants, and a worn, thin white shirt that showed just the faintest trace of my black bra underneath. For the oppressive Berkeley chill, I added an old denim jacket and wrapped Claire's most expensive scarf, a pale apricot piece of bohemiana embroidered in black, casually around me. The encounter was an opportunity to show K what he had missed out on, to let him look in for an hour at the pleasantly contained normative bubble that was my life—rented Craftsman on a quiet street, marriage to a tall, handsome man with a good job, slick black station wagon, and perfect cherubic son. I had no plans to reveal any chinks in my armor.

There were a number of memories of K to choose from—he had hurt me badly, and I'd been cycling through them all since he'd gotten back in touch—but the one powering me that day we met again was of his parting words to me when we'd broken off our relationship more than a decade earlier. *You're going to be an amazing woman someday,* he'd said. I'd been only eighteen, and still—or maybe especially because of the fact—that comment had enraged me. That feigned wistfulness beneath which lurked haughty condescension. *Going to be an amazing woman,* I laughed to myself. He'd been right, of course. I didn't know shit back then. But I was no longer a teenager—now I was a wife and mother and PhD student with plenty of heartbreak in my rearview mirror and the fresh memory of childbirth, that searing, spectacular loss of innocence, like an amulet in my pocket. I was tough, wise, and hotter than when he'd last seen me. *Just try me,* I thought.

I thought I knew exactly what I was getting into. I approached him prepared to do what exes do when they meet after much time has passed: take each other in with shining eyes, talk glancingly about what was, gesture playfully at what could have been, and double down on showing off what is. I remembered his charisma well, how disarming his looks and his jokes could be, but it didn't even occur to me that he might have the power to unzip the life I'd made and step inside. I didn't think I would let him. It didn't feel like there was room.

A few months into my "friendship" with K—the chaste, broad-daylight one that hadn't yet crossed over into infidelity, the friendship of a thousand sodas—I put my son down for a nap and hauled from the garage boxes of my possessions: zines, photographs, cassettes, journals, old show flyers. On the boxes was my husband's handwriting. He'd packed the last of the contents of our apartment while I was away in New York, and in his harried writing I thought I could read his annoyance at having had to be the one to do it. NINA: RANDOM SHIT, a cluster of boxes read, in the leaning, elementary-school penmanship of so many grown men. How righteous was the surge of anger I felt. *My journals are random shit? This is me!* I thought. *The me you thought you loved but who you don't want to acknowledge, the me who suddenly has no place in our you-centric universe!* But it wasn't his fault, nor his responsibility. The objects I thought were so important, that had once been most essentially me, proof of my creativity, my family history, my activism, the punk rock scene that had saved my life and nurtured me, I had left moldering in our dank garage. No metaphors were necessary.

When my husband got home from work the day I hauled the boxes out of the garage, our son was watching cartoons and I was sitting on the living room floor in the middle of a life raft made of unsteady stacks of my old things. He must have known trouble was brewing. He cracked a beer and ordered takeout while I sat refilling a juice glass with Bulleit Rye and communing with my teenage self, trying to remember something about who I'd been, who I wanted to be. I took photos of a few flyers to send to K, who I thought would get it. My heart bulged with longing. I sat in the living room and opened the boxes from my past and it felt like the real me was there. The one K had known, the one I was beginning to think he alone had the power to call forth, back into being.

I went to K's apartment, the one he'd moved into once he was back on his feet and could leave Mompton. I sat on his floor and looked through his records, a significantly smaller collection than he'd once had because he'd sold everything for dope so many times. It felt just like being in his room so many years ago. Now, on the eve of his fortieth birthday, he was still living the same way, a record spinning on the turntable on the floor, his bedroom door closed to the communal areas of the Richmond apartment he shared with some skinny musician. He went to the kitchen and returned with a bottle of water and two green apples and we sat on his bed and ate them. I was grateful for the distraction, the opportunity to hold something and to chew. The sourness made me salivate and made my mouth ache at the back, behind my molars. He got up briefly and changed the record, putting on something low and heavy that I had never heard before. He sat down with his legs crossed on his bed. *Crisscross applesauce,* I thought.

I want to show you something, he said, *but I'm afraid it will weird you out.*

It won't, I said.

How do you know? he asked.

Maybe it will, then, but I still want to see it.

He reached into his back pocket and pulled out his wallet, then opened the wallet and pinched his fingers around a small piece of paper, which he handed to me. It was a color copy of a photo booth picture of me, aged eighteen, with a chignon and sunglasses, biting the long end of a candy cane. It was one of a series that Rachel and I took at the end of high school, blowing all our cash on a dozen variations of sneers and pouts.

Holy shit, I said. I remembered giving it to him.

I've been carrying this in my wallet for thirteen years, he said, *much to the chagrin of a number of girlfriends.* He laughed quietly. I laughed back. I wanted to be that girl outside of time. That there were women he'd loved less—women who would be furious if they knew that he ended up with the girl in the picture—it gave me the electric feeling I was always chasing.

Well, I still have a jar of your pomade. It's in my medicine cabinet right now, I said. *I sometimes take it out and just huff it and think about you.*

Really? he asked.

Really, I said. *But that's not quite as creepy.*

It might be creepier, actually. So, the picture is creepy? he said.

No, I said. *The picture is—I can't believe you have that. The picture is incredibly romantic.*

By the end of the day, I had kissed a man who was not my husband. Some weeks later, I had sex with him. In the hours we couldn't see each other, we texted incessantly. I don't know how the average person survives the period of limerence, that chemical insanity of early love, in the age of text messaging. How we avoid crashing our cars, walking into walls or out of open windows. I remember certain bath times or dinner hours when my husband was working late that I spent wholly distracted by the heat of the phone in my hand. The only problem then was that I couldn't text fast enough, couldn't possibly say all that I wanted to say to K. Our high-stakes love also came to involve a lot of down time. How many hours of my life were spent waiting for him to text back? I carried out minute acts of housework or personal grooming in the time spent waiting. Surveying split ends. I peered at myself. Sometimes, I was doing too many other things, replying one-handed while getting dressed or opening a yogurt or wiping a child. So many tiny pauses stitched into my every movement. Literally everything I did was interrupted by him. And our texts, which we joked were being read by some rapt phone-company employee somewhere— if you added them together on ticker tape, they could stretch around the globe nine times or something like that. It almost freaked me out how much we had to say to each other, how much we were willing to peck out painstakingly throughout the day. It was *a lot*. It reminded me of the notebooks my girlfriends and I passed to one another in junior high and high school where we recorded all our gossip and longing, all our bubbly mental overflow. K and I similarly verified our reality—our individual lives and the great caper that was our relationship—by passing details back and forth. We were building our narrative and keeping each other company. It felt compulsive, but it also meant I was low-level fluttering all the time. I got to flutter. I was enlivened by the insistence of this new relationship, the sense of its irrepressibility.

. . .

I had brought a new man into our lives but I couldn't let my husband go. I wasn't ready to; I loved him. I didn't want to leave my life behind, it was just that when I was with K, that life fell completely away. It was as if none of it had ever happened, as though I hadn't already sworn myself to my husband. Time flattened, there was only now, a string of nows, an urgency both insistent and soothing, or maybe soothing in its insistence. To placate my new lover, I had to pretend I didn't care about my husband's feelings, but I was plagued by guilt. Every day I wept in shame and anguish, but I still continued on the path I was on. I felt sorry for my husband, who had to live in the humiliation and confusion of our dissolving marriage. I felt sorry for K, to whom I had pledged my undying devotion and who was waiting for me to free myself from my marriage. Mostly, I felt sorry for myself, for having to lead a double life, to metabolize my husband's pain, my child's confusion, my lover's anger. It didn't seem fair—I was only trying to be happy. Life just kept happening to me in such unfortunate ways. I was a victim of love, and felt further victimized by not wanting to hurt anyone's feelings.

The people-pleaser's divorce is a nightmare not because it's dramatic, but because it can scarcely get off the ground. It can scarcely be decided whether it is in fact happening at all, whether it should. I felt so uncertain about whether I was doing the right thing, about what any right thing was, ever—whether I had a right to happiness, a right to inconvenience others, to bring pain and heartache upon them. Another regularly circulated truism of codependency is that we don't know how we feel. We don't know how to access that thing people call a "gut feeling." Because the bonds that feel closest in our lives were forged in chaos and caretaking, we don't know how to access that inner truth that is meant to guide us through our lives, keep us out of danger, direct us toward well-being. And even if we can locate a feeling, we often can't express it. *I never, ever, ever, EVER just say what I mean*, a young man once memorably said at an Al-Anon meeting. Rather, we seek the outcome we desire through blaming, manipulating, or controlling others, or simply through inaction.

.   .   .

Was I saving my life or throwing it away? I ran to CVS for Huggies GoodNites and a bottle of Smirnoff and took selfies sitting in the parking lot, trying to locate myself in the blurry, murky darkness. Looking at the shameful curve of my nose, which always seemed enlarged by the camera, unless it really just was that big, my still-luscious mouth, uneven teeth. I snapped photo after photo, scatter-shot attempts to reclaim something, find something, come up with something to say about who I was and who I wanted to be. Like all girls, like everyone, I wanted to be known and seen, but I couldn't hold still long enough, stay open enough, to let it happen. I began to feel that it simply wasn't possible within my semi-suburban, het-eronormative marriage. But it hardly seemed likely that K and I were going to reimagine traditional gender roles together. Wouldn't I simply be leaving to take care of him?

．　．　．　．

Both my husband and K hated me intermittently. They grew frus-trated with my promises and my indecision. They decided to get together. To size each other up, or to talk, or maybe so that my husband could pass the baton? I didn't know why they wanted to meet and it made me sick with fear to think about the two of them alone together, but I had forfeited any right to object by causing these circumstances in the first place.

They agreed to meet one weeknight on a street near campus in Berkeley. I was at home with our son. I let him fall asleep on our bed and lay a knit blanket over his sweetly splayed form, over the dark blue pajamas dotted with spaceships and aliens. The dog jumped up, too, and, bordered by their heavy breathing, I halfheartedly watched a movie on my laptop. How could I possibly focus know-ing K and my husband were—what? Driving around together? Sit-ting on neighboring barstools comparing notes? I texted Claire at ten o'clock, then eleven-thirty.

still no word? she texted at midnight.

nothing, I wrote back.

think they're fighting?

i think they're drunk

oh they're absolutely drunk

i just imagined them doing karaoke . . . ?

ha that actually seems like a real possibility. are you okay?

i don't know what i am, I wrote.

My husband stumbled in in the middle of the night, dropping his keys noisily as he bumped into the tall dresser in our cramped bedroom. *Hi,* I said, waking up, remembering suddenly in my body the grinding anxiety of the previous night. *Are you okay?* I asked. I could hear the slur in his voice before he even spoke; just the way he opened his mouth was drunk. *I'm fine,* he said, with sarcastic you-should-see-the-other-guy emphasis on the word "I'm."

What about K? Is he alive? I asked.

He is alive, my husband said, taking off his T-shirt and arranging his body over our sleeping son to pick him up as gently as possible and carry him to his crib. *But—he is in jail,* he added as he scooped up the limp toddler and headed across the hall.

Seriously? I asked. In bed, I covered my face with both hands.

He came back into the room and snickered. *Yeah, seriously.*

They'd gotten very drunk very quickly and taken a walk together while drinking more. When they paused to take a piss, a cop drove by. My husband threw a beer bottle at the police car. The cop ran their licenses and K, who had failed to appear in court for some prior traffic infraction, was taken in.

Like into the back of the cop car and everything? I asked.

Yeah. Quite an end to the evening, he said. *I told him I'd get him tomorrow. It was my fault.*

What did you guys talk about that whole time? I pressed.

Everything, he answered. *A lot of things. You, obviously. That we should probably both leave you.*

In the morning, my husband got up and dressed, groaning through the initial encounter with his hangover. I heard the familiar sequence of toilet flushing, shower running, and coffee brewing that ushered him into the morning, and then his phone buzzed in the kitchen and he checked the message and laughed. The boisterousness of the sound erupted into the dull morning. I walked in to find him smiling, engrossed in crafting a reply to whoever had just cracked him up.

Who's that? I asked.

It's K, he said. *I guess they gave him his phone back. I'm going to pick him up and take him to the train.*

What did he say? I asked.

It says, "Wear something pretty. Daddy's had a long night," my husband said, cracking a broad smile again, the slightly deranged, irreverent, recognizable smile of a person who'd fallen under K's spell.

chapter seventeen

We tried some more, my husband and I. We went to a couples' therapist who made us sit at a tiny table and act out our childhood traumas with dolls. It was imperative, he said, that we understand that healing our marriage was contingent upon revealing to each other the wounds of our youth. After the session, we sat in my husband's truck and laughed about how much more traumatic the therapy had been than anything either of us had experienced as children. *That one doll with the crazy eyes,* he said. *I will never be able to unsee that.* We found a different couples' therapist, who told us we were too much in the habit of using gallows humor to deal with our situation and perhaps we should take it more seriously. *This is, uh, no-nonsense stuff, guys,* he said, in that stern-but-kind counselor tone. *It's pretty grim what you're going through.* I wanted to ask him: *Are you trying to scare us into staying together?* My husband and I were used to having fun together, it was what we did best, but even we found it strange that we sometimes caught a case of irrepressible church laughter while our marriage was falling apart. The therapist was probably right to chastise us, and it did bond us—perhaps that was his aim—because it made us feel like kids getting into trouble together. When we quickly sketched our personal biographies for him, the same therapist suggested that I was trying to exert control over the central scene of powerlessness in my youth—my sister's heroin addiction—by falling for a heroin addict and hoping I could fix him. My husband thought he might be onto something. I found the suggestion patently absurd.

I left these sessions feeling stigmatized, pathologized. I protested to my husband that the therapist didn't know enough about me to make these proclamations. But surely I also wanted to squirm away from the subtext of all that he was saying, which was that a healthy person would likely try to resuscitate a true, deep love that feels lost. A codependent like me—and here, I mean codependent in the sense of a manipulative martyr, a selfish, wounded victim, a pungently simmering pot of gnarled, gristly ham hock resentments about to boil over—simply casts that love aside in favor of a new love. And then looks upon that new love, that new external source of validation, thinking maybe *this* is the one that will heal me, fix me, fill me up. "[O]ur wanting to love, our yearning for love, our loving itself becomes an *addiction*," Robin Norwood writes in *Women Who Love Too Much*.

It began to feel like K was ruining my life. I tried to swear him off. I did swear him off, went for weeks without seeing him or even texting, collecting my would-be messages to him in a single document, soothing myself by telling myself I would soon be able to email him the choppy, aphoristic pages, a digest of my worries, my every thought. I looked at his social media and wondered whether certain posts were coded messages to me. I pictured him picturing me looking.

In the midst of this, trying to be a normal couple, my husband and I and our son went to visit friends in L.A. and on that trip I got pregnant—I could feel it happening. I googled "Can you feel yourself getting pregnant?" and found the same answer the Internet gives for any number of women's health concerns: basically that some women say they can feel it, but they're probably crazy.

I wasn't crazy. While my son was at preschool, I took a test and greeted again the ghostly pink stain of a plus sign.

Hello, life.

First came panic, a pulsing *NO-NO-NO* that chased itself around inside my body like a strobe light. Before I could think any more, I threw on a sweater and walked out the door and around our neighborhood, heart racing, humming quietly the way I do on an airplane. A low, almost imperceptible sound to ground me, remind me that I am alive, I am real, I will be okay. The sun beamed down through the latticework of leaves and made shadowed patterns on the sidewalk squares and I stepped on each one.

This couldn't be happening now. But it was happening. Of course it was happening. Was there any way it could be K's? The timing made that impossible, and cancer had left him sterile. But what if he wasn't really sterile? What if I was forgetting something? What if I had this baby and *then* it turned out that it—*it!* he, she, a whole squalling person—was K's? I wouldn't survive that, the humiliation. I'd have to end myself, Karenina-style. Maybe that's what I should do anyway. But no: my son.

At the thought of him, at the thought of another one like him—siblings! my heart exploded—there was joy. There is nothing in the world I love the way I love babies. Their gummy mouths and kicking feet, their early Buddha calmness, the brilliantly complex alien wiring of their thread-thin veins, which you can even see inside their heads. I thought of a sleeping newborn's head tipped back into my palm, thought about it waking up, its extraterrestrial eyes boring hypnotically into mine, and I wanted so badly to be in that heart-melding dyad again. Yes—I would have a pregnancy. Maybe this was the universe intervening to make my decision for me, to yank me out of perpetual questioning and put me back where I belonged, in a body that wasn't flooded with selfish, contradictory desires but was merely a vessel, devoted to the care of another, carrying innocent life safely, snugly into the world. I would keep it. *We* would keep it. Maybe I could make good—become good—after all.

I learned that K was dating a new woman now that we were "broken up"—a phrase that meant nothing, seeing as I was married. I wished it meant something. I wished I could give him and my husband and my son all what they needed and that they could simply love me. *How much could K possibly love me anyway if he had already taken up with someone else,* I thought, a small blonde whose online presence I also compulsively researched in the hopes of seeing her clothes, her apartment, of understanding the precise nature of their attraction, of glimpsing in the background the toe of his sneaker. It started on social media, but ended up, as these things do, in related Google searches and other sundry cyber ghettos. A link to a link to a link to a link; it went on and on. I tumbled down dark virtual holes and came to in others' electronic neighborhoods, friends of friends of friends of the girlfriend. Clusters, galaxies, all the people she knew, their abundant, cheerful thumbnail worlds somehow there to be both apprehended and misconstrued. I hopped miserably from link to link to link, uncovering something and nothing. She was like the rest of us. The rest of us were like the rest of us. We were nothingness—what were we? Breasts, legs, and thighs. Ten billion pictures of other women's manicures traveling through fiber optic cable at the bottoms of the oceans.

.   .   .

Pregnant, I recommitted to my marriage. Then one day, in a Target parking lot, my husband told me he'd slept with one of my closest friends. My body went numb. He had confessed to a retaliatory act of infidelity a couple months prior, an event I let him wave away as just a vengeful, drunken error, which was what he claimed it was. I thought I deserved it so much that I'd mostly nodded through the conversation, accepting it as obvious punishment. I should be punished.

Now, it hit me like a cannonball to the gut that it had been with her. I asked him and he nodded. The information settled on me with an almost satisfying weight. I had never been betrayed like this before. I had actually spent a fair amount of time discussing his first infidelity with this friend—how I felt about it, what it meant, all the while not knowing that she was the other party. How small and stupid I was.

Are you at least in love? Do you have *to be together? Because that's the only explanation I can understand,* I said. *Then, I suppose, I would have to understand.*

No, he said, *no. We were very, very drunk,* he added, as though it helped.

I could see that it pained my husband to say all this. I still recalled frequently the revulsion I'd felt in the moment he found out about K. Maybe there was something useful, something productive, in him feeling it, too. Would this neutralize things? An eye for an eye? Would he, too, settle into the discovery that you could love someone deeply and still betray them, and would it prompt him to actually, finally forgive me?

I'd always imagined that darting nerves would accompany such a revelation, that I'd want to slither out of my skin in a moment like this, but I felt dumb and heavy in my seat. Motionless. I don't remember what I said. I marvel at the way my memory has been gently scrubbed in places. The blankness seems like an act of evolutionary benevolence ensuring there are things to which we can never return. This is one. I try to recall the words that were spoken and there is simply nothing there. I remember that my hands, draped limply over my knees, grew clammy. I wasn't showing yet but I had gotten immediately bigger around the middle—I'd "popped," as the motherhood books distressingly put it—and was doing that makeshift maternity jeans trick, wearing my pants unbuttoned with a hair elastic threaded through the buttonhole and around the button. As my husband, shaking a bit, revealed the details he was willing to, I thought about the triangle of skin above my underwear, the panel of stretch-marked flesh that was exposed by my open fly and soon would stretch farther to harbor this poor child, to nurture her, that she might be healthily born—lucky girl—to reckless, degenerate parents who fucked each other's friends. I thought about the unmarred sweep of my friend's body and wondered where he'd lingered. It was not a mother's body. It was not like my body, like Sector Sixteen, once smooth and tan as coffee with cream, which now looked like it had sustained mortar fire.

The obvious thing to do in such a situation was drink—a long anesthetic dip in a salty swimming pool of vodka martinis sounded like the only remedy—but I could not imperil the baby, my little houseguest, with whom I felt in that moment a burgeoning sense of collusion. *There are two of us and only one of him, this stupid fucking idiot,* I thought, as I laid a hand on my belly. We were symbiotic.

So desperate was I for something to take the edge off that I started going to AA meetings and got a sponsor. My home group was a roomful of middle-aged lesbians who showed me a kindness so disarmingly pure that it made me cry each time I saw them. They nodded sagely as I spoke. They told me they had been there. I read from the *Big Book* about piecing the family back together in the aftermath of alcoholic disasters.

During this time, I went to Al-Anon meetings, too. At one of the only good ones, K's girlfriend was there, holding court. She looked right through me. I felt like a girl in the school cafeteria with nowhere to sit and never went back. I found another Berkeley meeting, smaller, with a more hushed and well-heeled crowd but there, too, I felt out of place. I don't know exactly why. Either because I thought everyone else was more together than I was, or because I didn't really want to get better yet, or both.

.　　.　　.

At least I was no longer the only bad one in our household. I sampled the dual smugness of being sober and having recently been wronged and found it was a potent brew. I arose exhausted but with righteous vigor.

Pregnancy was a trap, a curse, and also the greatest gift. A protective measure that ensured I stayed rested, well-fed, that I always in some sense had company. "I feel alone, but I am never truly alone, as I grow this cantaloupe of a person," I wrote in my diary. My son, beached on my body—his possession, his island—talked incessantly of the baby in Mommy's belly, what we would name it, how he would love it and play with it, how he would be *gennnntle,* he whispered, and wouldn't jump on Mommy so much because there was, he said, pointing conspiratorially, tapping at the globe of me, *a teeny tiny baby in there.*

Rachel was visiting when we found out the baby was a girl. It was a sunny day. She came with us to the appointment in a dreary one-story medical building on Telegraph. Days like that, with beloved company in the house, my husband and I allowed ourselves a vacation from the pain we'd caused each other. We casually had coffee together in the morning as though nothing was amiss. We held hands, and grabbed Rachel's hands, too, in the darkened examining room, and the three of us cried at the cantering of the impossible little heartbeat, the intergalactic whooshing of the ultrasound.

By autumn, I was a house. At the secondhand store I bought swaths of black cotton and a black wool cape, the only garment I felt I could hide in. On a website, I read about pregnant women getting dry eyes, but I cried in the bathrooms of university buildings and in the library stacks. I bought a French twist the size of my forearm at KingPin Donuts on Durant and cried in my car while eating it. I started making a lavender cardigan for the baby, and I cried knitting and purling in front of the television. Pining for New York one day, I found the recipe for Veselka's cabbage soup and ate it in the middle of the night. It was briny and marbled with beef fat and tasted so sweet and sour, so Jewish, conjured so precisely the smell of my grandmother's bustling house at the holidays that it, too, brought tears to my eyes.

The day before Rosh Hashanah, I squeezed my fat ass into a small blue plastic chair at my son's preschool, dipped apples in honey for a sweet new year, and sang songs as he leaned, somehow both shyly and proudly, against my knees in his brown corduroys and a construction-paper crown. *Ooh, yummy! What a good baker you are*, I said as I nibbled the salty stone-like hunk of challah he had made himself, and he threw his arms around my neck. *Did you ever make challah in your class, Mommy?* he asked. *I'm sure I did, but it wasn't this delicious*, I said, kissing him on the head.

I looked around the classroom, its every inch plastered with multi-colored finger paintings and collages, flags from the nation of childhood. Nearly every other kid had both their parents there and I wondered at the luxury of that, wondered why it seemed no one really had to work in Berkeley, whether the moms had pressured the dads or if they showed up of their own volition. I wondered if people liked doing things like this and whether they should, whether I should. I wondered about the state of others' marriages—my favorite pastime, right up there with looking into strangers' lit windows at night.

My husband only rarely materialized at events like this. *Tell him sorry I'm not there and to have fun!* he'd text from the office. I hated having to brave these things alone, having to hold it all—the nerves, sweat, smiling, my son's feelings and my own, but I didn't demand my husband's presence. Would I feel better if he were there? Would I be better off with a nebbish like these husbands, a guy who'd record the sing-along on his phone and refill my paper cup of grape juice? Any time critical or angry feelings toward my husband crept up, I quickly corrected them, the way an anorexic snaps a rubber band against her skin to stop herself from feeling hungry. It was the same with my parents and sisters. *Why isn't he here?* I thought. And then immediately: *He has to work! It's not necessary for him to interrupt his day when I can just be here. He has a real job, it's not graduate school.*

My husband's benign neglect reminded me of my father. What was especially similar was the way I let him off the hook. It wasn't quite his fault. After all, it wasn't like he was purposely letting me down. It was simply that he never thought of me in the first place.

After the celebration, I fled to my car, dreading more small talk, dodging other moms as though there'd been a bomb scare. *Mommy will be back to pick you up in a couple hours,* I told my son. I should have been preparing for my oral exams, writing long literature reviews demonstrating my mastery over fields of anthropology. Instead, I drove around Berkeley looking for the emptiest parking lots and sat in my car listening to music and reading, sometimes taking driver's-seat selfies, the worst kind.

My pregnancy with my son had been chronicled by my mother. We drove cross-country together when I was seven months along and she'd photographed me leaning back and laughing on a motel bed in Indiana. When we got to California, we walked the dog at Albany Bulb, a landfill-turned-peninsula, and she took photos of me looking large and glowing and happy with the dog's leash hanging around my neck and big, bug-eye Target sunglasses. But this surprise pregnancy hadn't been documented at all. At this point, no one loved me enough to capture it, I thought. *This child will think she was deposited by the stork!* I laughed to my husband, instead of saying, *Will you take some photos of me?* I tried to remedy the situation myself with my new iPhone and its Hipstamatic app, which overexposed me glamorously, blew out my fine lines and dark circles, made my hair look obscenely shiny. An entirely false image. But there was no angle that would accommodate the fullness of my body, that could believably replicate the easy joy of the same body sitting in the same car or on the same furniture just three years prior.

My husband and I moved between loving, civil, and openly hostile. I worried that the fetus was a sponge soaking up my worry and confusion. Was sadness blood-borne? Could my emotional waffling make her schizophrenic? It would probably make her depressed. How would she greet the world? I imagined her emerging weakly, already cynical, emitting a halfhearted *wah*.

Seeking ever-bigger adventures, like a Kennedy, my husband bought a motorcycle. *Promise me you won't ride it drunk,* I said, in a feeble attempt to set a boundary. Weeks passed. Then, he rode it drunk and got into an accident. He wasn't badly injured but he had scared himself, or shown himself something, a capacity. He decided to try to stop drinking and to move out temporarily. As Berkeley grew darker and rainier, he moved duffel bags into a furnished sublet. I nested. I avoided people and stayed in with my son and my belly and the dog. My mother-in-law came to watch my son so we could see the couples' therapist again—now that I was sober and carrying the first granddaughter in a family of boys, I felt newly worthy of her love. My husband's face looked suddenly new after days apart, and each time I saw him I had to spend a few moments reorienting myself to it. Were we staying together? the therapist asked. Would my husband move back in? How would we protect my sobriety? *We don't know anything,* I said. Still, it felt like maybe things were getting better. The impending birth, at the least, would bring change. I was growing heavier and would soon burst, and something would be washed away.

At the time, I was a teaching assistant for an introductory women's studies class, an undergraduate survey course that drew mostly underclassmen whose faces looked childlike. My graduate advisers had reacted calmly to the news that I was pregnant with my first child. Having a baby while pursuing a PhD was certainly not encouraged, but it was done occasionally. A baby was a sweet accessory and it was understood that an ambitious woman could stay the course if she so chose. Many professors had one odd child who skulked around the department on days off from elementary school. But when I began to show with a second pregnancy just a few years later, their eyes went dead. No one needed to say a word: I knew what they were thinking, or thought I did. That I should have at least waited until I had passed my qualifying exams, done my fieldwork, or begun work on the dissertation. Unless you had a wife, two children was simply not done. In academic terms, I was a goner.

I stood in front of my discussion section that December, talking passionately about material constraints to women's equality, the social construction of the role of motherhood. The irony of teaching about the struggle from inside what then felt like the prison of my obscenely pregnant body was not lost on me. By the last day of the semester, when I took a seat at one of the desks in the classroom to proctor the exam, I could just barely fit.

.   .   .

My daughter was two weeks early and barreled into the world so fast that the midwife couldn't even get there in time. When we called, she was at a holiday party in Sebastopol, an hour and a half away, and had to talk loudly over the festive din.

She says it's probably a false alarm and to try a bath? my husband repeated gingerly to me, angling the phone away from his mouth to relay her words.

NO! No bath! I shouted loud enough for her to hear. *It's not like that!* The contractions were already only a few minutes apart and I buried my face in a pillow when they rolled violently through my body. *Kill me, kill me, kill me,* I thought, imagining my vertebrae like train tracks beneath this hurtling wagon of agony. The hippie childbirth guides I'd read urged women to think about a contraction as a "rush," an intense sensation rather than a closing or shrinking. I couldn't ever manage that, but momentarily, I was able to conjure a blankness, the vision of a nothingness changing color. Two-dimensional space, pink, then peach, orange, red. The semester had ended only two days prior. I thought momentarily of the stack of final papers I still had left to grade, but then the spreading stain of pain arrived again and emptied me of thought. Even in its brutality, there was something welcome about it. I suppose if life feels like it's falling apart, that brain-blasting pain is, among other things, a reprieve.

My mother had planned to stay through the birth—it was the reason for her visit. She had by then witnessed the births of my son and two of Anya's babies and had proven herself to be an ideal attendant: confident, wise, soothing, intuitive. I wanted her by my side, holding my hand, smoothing sweaty strands of hair behind my ear, and I was relieved when she told me she'd come stay for the weeks surrounding my due date to be sure not to miss the main event. But Lucia had told me that, impressed as she was by my commitment to home birth, if "shit starts going down," she was going to gracefully make her exit and stay at a nearby hotel. *I just don't think I can handle that,* she said. *Is that okay? I'll come back once she's born, of course.* I told her I completely understood, that there was no pressure to stay and observe, and anyway, we were still a couple weeks away from the due date. But then it happened, and there was no time. Lucia and my mother had only arrived in California the day before, and all of a sudden, I was in the middle of labor, howling into my pillow, feeling the pressure of the baby bearing down on me like a dropping watermelon, the momentum of the event picking up, reaching a kind of emergency pitch. There was nowhere to go in the thousand-square-foot house—we were trapped, it seemed, as if on a ship. Lucia came into my bedroom, her eyes wide.

I'm sorry, I said between contractions. We stared at each other, eyes round with fear. Her long hair, dyed dark, fell past her shoulders. She looked like me.

What are you sorry for?! she said.

You said you didn't want to be here for this part! I cried guiltily.

Lucia smiled and put her hands on my shoulders. *Well,* she shrugged. *I'm here.* We both laughed and our eyes welled. *Do you need anything?* she asked. *What, do we boil water or something?*

In the oncoming wave of another contraction, I began to lose her, to lose the contours of the room itself, but I was afraid to miss the chance to thank her for staying cool. *Lu, thank you!* I grunted as she backed out of the room, leaving my husband and me to tend to our deranged nativity scene, which looked like something from another century.

The whole thing was over within a couple hours. My daughter was delivered by my husband in the narrow bathroom of our rented house, right into the chaos of our crumbling marriage, while the dog whined and the Christmas tree twinkled and the two-year-old slept. Everything but terror, hope, and the fiery burn of birth fell away as I braced against the sink and pushed her into his open palms. He looked right into my eyes, his giant hands open like he was waiting for a football, and said, *It's okay. It's okay.*

No one was looking at a clock when our daughter emerged sometime around midnight, so we'll never know her true birthday— a pretty good origin story for a wild girl. We became unwitting homesteaders that night, crying, laughing, looking for kitchen scissors to cut the cord. We were deliriously empowered, happy and free. My mother brought me cereal in bed and Lucia, stupefied by the scene, took a mop to the bloodied floor.

By the time the midwife arrived and weighed our daughter in a fish scale, the long, clay-red soles of her brand-new baby feet sticking out the sides, she was nearly an hour old. In my mind I said a prayer for the feeling I had then to last—not just the serenity of the finish line, but this communion. Family love. Did I really need any more than this homespun joy, the life I had right in front of me? How arrogant that I'd thought there could possibly be more. I'd said a version of this prayer so many times—take away my selfishness; my darkness; show me how to do this; let this be enough—but I didn't even know who or what I was praying to.

The next day, I pulled Lucia aside and asked if she would do me a favor. *Anything,* she said. I handed her K's phone number on a slip of paper. *Just tell him I had the baby,* I said. *Please. Tell him I'm okay.* She took the paper quietly and nodded.

chapter eighteen

"Good morning, destroyer of men's souls," temperance crusader Carrie Nation reportedly said when greeting bartenders. At the turn of the twentieth century, thirty-five years before the founding of AA, the severe, six-foot-tall Nation, desperate to wake the country to the "dreadful curse of liquor," began taking a hatchet to the oiled oak bar tops of popular Kansas saloons. She had tried peaceful marching, and made impassioned appeals to lawmakers to curb the illegal drinking in the state, but those had scarcely yielded results.

Nation was intimately acquainted with the private miseries of alcoholism. Her first husband, a physician named Charles Gloyd, suffered from the disease. Gloyd fought in the Union army, and Nation fell in love with him because he was expressive and passionate and represented to her a radical departure from the culture of her conservative family. Gloyd wrote her breathless letters, citing the instantaneous and undeniable attraction he'd felt when they first met. He couldn't wait to be married, for then "our deep, pure love may gush unrestrained from life to life and heart to heart." The couple wed in 1867 but the brief marriage was a bitter disappointment. Nation's husband was unaffectionate, remote, and, she would later write in her autobiography, "not . . . the lover I expected."

Gloyd drank himself to death in 1869 when their child was not yet a year old.

Carrie went on to marry David Nation, a journalist, lawyer, and minister who was almost twenty years her senior. In addition to running a hotel, she began working as the head of a local chapter of the Women's Christian Temperance Union (WCTU) in Medicine Lodge, Kansas, and praying about how best to help the cause. She buttressed her WCTU work by singing hymns and playing a portable organ outside saloons. Soon, she claimed she was called by God to go to the nearby town of Kiowa and destroy a saloon. Over the next decade, Nation would endure beatings and arrests and do numerous stints in jail. She and her supporters, mostly women calling themselves the Home Defenders Army, would destroy more than one hundred saloons throughout Kansas, forcing the state to better enforce its liquor laws. She called the bar smashings "hatchetations" because a hatchet was her weapon of choice, and she proudly affected a fearsome public image. "I will make all hell howl," she promised from inside a Wichita jail cell.

Nation was a particularly radical representation of the temperance movement sweeping the country. The way women articulated their intolerance had mostly been constrained by the conventions of Christianity and traditional femininity. Men, too, had lamented the effects of alcohol. An 1853 tract on "Martha Washingtonianism" by Lorenzo Dow Johnson opens with an anonymous quote that speaks to the stunning impact of drinking on women's lives: "Alcohol, the foe of humanity, is the demon curse of the domestic sphere, the murderer of countless thousands of wives and mothers—that which has robbed woman of her beauty, her comforts, her rights, her health, her home, her reason, her life. The tears woman has shed, would form a river; the groans she has uttered, collected and concentrated, would be louder than the earthquake's terrific sound."

Sadness and grief were acceptable, but there was little space in American society for public expressions of female anger. Arguably, however, at the heart of the temperance spirit was a rage that dare not speak its name, and Carrie Nation gave voice to it. "I represent the distracted, suffering, loving motherhood of the World," Nation would later write, "who, becoming aroused with a righteous fury rebelled at this torture." The torture was living with alcoholic men, and these lines contain the whole of the codependent experience—the one foisted upon a woman with few means of escape. Distraction, suffering, and a love that feels futile. These are the ingredients that combine to produce fury. I thought of my email drafts to K: the boiling frenzy of anger I felt typing *fuck you fuck you fuck you fuck you fuck you.*

. . .

Nation became an easy target for derision because, unlike so many of her contemporaries, she was unable to square her anger with the expectations of traditional femininity. The same year she committed her first "hatchetation," Edison Studios released a short single-reel comedic film called *Why Mr. Nation Wants a Divorce.* In it, a character playing Nation's husband is left to care for the house and children by himself. When his wife, Carrie, returns at day's end she finds him relaxing with a single drink. Her response? She throws Mr. Nation over her knee and sternly administers a spanking. Many accounts during this era, including an entire genre of temperance fiction, dramatized the damage wrought by alcoholism. But this short film flips the typical script, suggesting that it is perhaps radical temperance women, not alcoholic men, who bring ruin upon the family. The film illustrates the way that Nation was regarded by many; as "half-mad," in the words of documentarian Ken Burns, "a figure of fun, even ridicule."

Nation earned folkloric stature. To this day, bars post signs reading ALL NATIONS WELCOME, EXCEPT CARRIE. Eventually, her husband left her on the grounds of desertion. She went on to edit a temperance paper called *The Smasher's Mail,* bankrolling her activities by selling pins in the shape of hatchets.

It was easy for men to characterize temperance crusaders as killjoys—they were literally threatening the saloon, where men went for entertainment and fun, and where they were able to maintain a boundary between their free public lives and their private lives, which took place at home. But in spite of her reputation, Nation was a complicated woman. And if we broaden our focus beyond her hatchetations, she might be credited with inventing the approach that Al-Anon would later call "tough love." In many ways, Carrie Nation was an early proponent and symbol of "tough love," the cool-but-caring detachment and air of moral superiority. As she stood outside a Topeka saloon, she urged the men inside, "Boys, boys, come and let me in. Your mother would like to talk to you. . . . I'm not mad at you, boys. I'm not hating you a bit, even when I come around with my hatchet."

In the Al-Anon literature a few decades later, encouragements not to nag or show anger were reframed through the idiom of powerlessness. Anger was pointless because the more elemental reckoning required of recovering codependents is with our powerlessness to change the alcoholic in our lives. Nagging, too, was but a futile attempt to control that which we cannot control. "Each of us is responsible to himself and for himself," reads the introduction to the 1967 book *The Dilemma of the Alcoholic Marriage*. Instead, the emphasis was on individuality, personal responsibility, and love.

chapter nineteen

I n 1956, German American psychoanalyst and sociologist Erich Fromm wrote *The Art of Loving*, which took off from the idea that people don't interrogate the subject of love, that "hardly anyone thinks there is anything that needs to be learned about love." He didn't mean that people didn't find love compelling—he acknowledged that they tumble into it as though it will bring them salvation—but that they did not conceive of it as an area of study, something they could acquire skills around and improve at. Fromm challenged the idea of falling in love, writing that this "type of love is by its very nature not lasting. The two persons become well acquainted, their intimacy loses more and more its miraculous character, until their antagonism, their disappointments, their mutual boredom kill whatever is left of the initial excitement. Yet, in the beginning they do not know all this: in fact, they take the intensity of the infatuation, this being 'crazy' about each other, for proof of the intensity of their love, while it may only prove the degree of their preceding loneliness."

Is love a meritocracy? Do some people excel because they cultivate a talent for it, because they practice a set of exercises and improve over time? Fromm thought so. He outlined a theory of love as a skill that could be mastered like any other and stated that "love is an action, the practice of a human power, which can be practiced only in freedom and never as the result of a compulsion. Love is an activity, not a passive affect; it is a 'standing in,' not a 'falling for.'"

I heard something similar echoed by a therapist—one in a string of withholding, mildly disapproving motherly types I selected over the course of a few years after my husband and I split, perhaps to punish me back into goodness. This particular mother/doctor, wearing (if not clutching) actual pearls, urged me repeatedly to shift my focus away from the breathless declamations of love I found so romantic—what were those but words—and look instead at actions. My own and those of the people whom I said I loved, those who claimed to love me back. What had they done for me lately, she was asking. *Love is an action verb,* she said. It sounded like a line you'd find on the marketing materials of a weekend marriage-saving seminar, but I repeated it like a mantra for a period of days to see whether I thought it was true, whether it might help me if it was.

I understood this basic premise—that healthy love inheres in the repeated carrying out of various duties. But when I thought about love-the-action-verb, I could only think of the steady, daily, repetitive motions of parenthood. The over-and-over-ness of it all, like a movie montage—the sticky rip of diaper tabs, the rhythmic industrial squeeze of the breast pump. Those were things I liked even when bored and exhausted because they were done in service to the highest form of love. I thought of my own mother's hands buttering innumerable towering slices of cinnamon toast, gathering hundreds of pigtails and weaving thousands of braids. That was surely a "standing in" love. Loving as doing. But wasn't it also a "falling for," the wildest falling for? In the moments when I wasn't mechanically completing the menial assignments of motherhood, wasn't the pulsing, radiating love I felt precisely a "passive affect," in Fromm's words, one I often observed dumbly as it crashed over me? I felt conquered, annexed by that love.

If that therapist were to prescribe a healthy relationship for me, I suspected she might appreciate one studded by a few grand gestures—well-timed, not wholly impractical. Not the skywriting-scale stuff you see in the movies—in real life, that degree of earnestness is something to be suspicious of. She would want me to find a mate who might whisk me away on a trip, present me unexpectedly with a nice gift. Reasonable surprises. Instagrammable surprises. But at the center of the love the mother/doctor wanted me to covet was a man content to play a long game—undaunted by commitment or by the mundane, ready to embark upon the *Groundhog Day* slog of life. I pictured a kind-eyed, clean-cut man, a tall catalogue model in a nice sweater, his face gently etched with crow's feet, the markings of a lifetime of smoldering warmth. Like my husband, except paying more attention. With this type of person, I should make patterns on the surface of my days and in so doing discover that healthy romantic love could be like babylove—this was what she was saying. It, too, involved tasks and activities repeated over time until they'd worn a groove into everyday life. And the groove itself was a form of romance. The groove was devotion.

What had people done for me that had truly made me feel loved? she had asked me at the next session. I thought about the time K, with a beatific, postcoital smile, wrote I LOVE U in my menstrual blood on his bedroom wall, just above his bed, dipping his middle finger lingeringly into me like a quill into an inkpot as I watched and laughed and my eyes went wide as teacups. Was that gesture a doing or merely a saying? Was it an action verb? Was it empty, or was it a promise? Watching him do it gave me the feeling I'd always understood to be love—something low, rumbling, a little bit evil, a little revolting. Some sick and special secret wizardry that fouls you up with its unexpectedness, its brazenness. You can't wear a groove into everyday life with moments like these—they are by their nature strange and singular. I didn't mention this incident to the therapist—I rarely talked to her about sex, and I found it tragic to play the rebellious teenager trying to shock a grown-up—but I thought about it all day, how wonderfully cracked open and raw that had made me feel. That fear and wonder. Into the computer program I'd purchased to use as a diary, I typed a cube of questions, the same kind I was always typing. Wasn't love a hideaway. Bordered by darkness. A place of dissonance and therefore revelation. "Love that is compatible with bill-paying, child-rearing, with cleaning out a garage?" I asked incredulously. But but but. "Isn't the real thing supposed to get in your way a little bit?"

One of the earliest stirrings of curiosity about men that I ever felt was for Lord Licorice, the Victorian villain of the Candy Land board, who in my memory stood slightly bent in a skintight, dark red costume, devilishly twirling his mustache. I must have been about six. Looking already toward a cartoon goth for subterranean messages of lust. "Be careful," read his description in the instructions, "he may try to block your way along the path with his icky, sticky licorice!"

I wanted to find an explanatory framework that would enable me to be more comfortable with this period of painful flux. That would distract me from a simpler explanation, that perhaps I was just brazenly selfish—amid the aches and strains of normal life, I went looking for something shiny and new. Tore up the page I was on and started fresh. Maybe what I failed at was just working. Trying. Practicing Fromm's skill-building regimen and earning over time the insignia of a love expert, a love colonel. A lieutenant of love, practiced in the art of the everyday, in weathering loneliness, shouldering time and quiet, washing and rewashing the cast-iron pot.

chapter twenty

The end of a marriage takes on its own momentum. It was happening even as we were discussing whether it should happen. Even as we were experimenting with honesty, clarity, and remorse. I thought about my parents with their cigarettes on the screen porch.

The spectacular birth of our daughter was our finale, the last moment of deep, intentional, loving partnership. Out with a bang. I recovered from the birth quickly—I was so guilty, I didn't feel entitled to any special dispensation anyway, it was just a baby, I was fine—and we set about disassembling our shared life.

I rented an apartment for a couple months, the basement of a North Berkeley house a few blocks from the home I'd shared with my husband. It was not a nice place, but it was my space, the first space I felt I could be in freely with K. When he knocked on the door that first night, I opened it and we stood embracing silently in the doorway for what felt like an hour. The kids were asleep—my son in the extra bedroom and my daughter, so small she couldn't even roll over yet, on the taut floral sheets on my bed at the center of a fort made of couch cushions. The living room, which the front door opened into, was dotted with cardboard boxes and trash bags filled with clothing. K smelled my hair and kissed my head while I cried against his jacket. *All I want in the entire world is to make you happy,* he finally said. He opened his bag and took out a smaller plastic bag, inside which were two matching pairs of athletic shorts and kneesocks. I could picture the American Apparel on Haight Street where he'd stopped when he got off work. *Team outfits,* he said. *Put these on and meet me on the couch.* In the bathroom, I dried my eyes and blew my nose while I peed, then changed into the sporty ensemble and emerged to find K on the couch in the same garb, leaning on one elbow like a 1970s centerfold and eyeing me intensely. I lay down next to him, laughing.

You look great in a pair of kneesocks, Pimentoloaf, he said, shaking his head.

Thank you for this gift, I laughed.

Well, we're a team now, he said.

On my phone, I took a picture of our intertwined legs in the matching shorts and socks, and we kissed and cried until the baby woke up.

The next day was the day he overdosed with his friend Will and came home bleary and quiet with the electrodes stuck to him. I was speechless for hours as we lay with the sleeping baby in our bed. Then tears began streaming down my face. I didn't erupt, didn't wail, just calmly begged.

Baby, please don't do this, I said, *you can't do this now. Please, please don't die now. I need you, we need you. This life—*I gestured to the unpacked room—*is just beginning and I don't want to do it all alone.* He laid his big hand on my head and brought my fingers to his lips to kiss them.

I'm so sorry, he said. *I promise I won't die again.*

.   .   .

I wanted to make him happy, too. I dropped out of the doctoral program, defeated and exhausted. Did I even drop out? I just stopped going. No one cared. I got a job as a researcher and writer at a branding agency in downtown San Francisco and went to work in a fog. I was back to drinking again, but I was exercising restraint, drinking moderately and only when the kids were asleep. I brought home vanilla vodka and a big can of pineapple juice, the kind they used to pour from at snack in elementary school, the kind you have to start with the triangle end of a bottle opener. I poured the vanilla vodka—only $9.99—over ice, filling the glass by about three quarters before topping it off with the pineapple juice. Sometimes I threw in a maraschino cherry from a jar that had stood so long on the liquor store shelf its white lid had collected a fine layer of silvery dust. A low-rent piña colada. I brought home weed and its many cousins, herbaceous and fruity taffies and gummies and chews and suckers that were then newly and readily available. I wanted to get fucked up, and to be fucked up with K, but I also wanted to be the cool girlfriend who gets him fucked up. The nurse who breaks out the fentanyl lollipops. Not like the real junkie girlfriends, who had vied like vermin for his drugs, who might have stolen his morning shot and fucked up his whole day. I wasn't one of those. I was a mom. I wanted to be his good time, but when I couldn't, I would at least protect his good time. Arrange for it, facilitate it, create the conditions for him to enjoy himself.

The baby was too young to be away from me at all, so even when my son spent time with his father, she remained with me, strapped to me in the supermarket and Sephora, at cafés and in bookstores and to Claire's apartment and to the playground again and again, an already all-knowing appendage who issued side-eye from any number of fabric baby carriers and who learned to laugh within the first six weeks, a boisterous chirp that activated the devastating dimple in her right cheek. She was on my body the entire time I unpacked in the apartment, and then again a few months later when I packed to move into the next place. When K held her she looked especially small. One morning, I called in sick and we dropped my son off for preschool and went to a diner with the baby, still in her yellow-and-white footie pajamas with her kewpie tendrils swirling messily about her head. K held her and let her play with a spoon as I drank my coffee. She smashed it against his cheekbones and his nose and he put on a face of exaggerated concern and grabbed it back and when she giggled crazily, he kissed her neck and the insides of her open, reaching hands. *What are you gonna do about it?* he teased her. She looked at him with adoration and wonder, waiting to see what he'd do next, the same way I did.

chapter twenty-one

"'I love you' is always a quotation," writes Jeanette Winterson on the first page of *Written on the Body*, the bible of love books, the Buddha at the center of my shrine to erotic obsession, to infidelity justified by temporary insanity. She's right: "I love you" is a citation, a reference to one's past, to the entire past, to history. "I love you" is both singular and iterative. It denotes millennia of humans clamoring for meaning, for immortality: a symphony in one note.

As our love came into full, mad flower, I searched for solace in Winterson and elsewhere, steadying myself through others' tales of desperate love, stories I realized I'd been collecting rather compulsively my entire life. My love arsenal was comprised of hundreds of songs, novels, and films, and falling for K offered an opportunity—or an excuse—to go back through them all, sewing all the while the tapestry of our story, which was every bit as exhilarating, and as tragic, as any I'd collected, as any that came before. This was something I'd always done, a way of grounding myself, situating my narrative among others I'd learned and loved. It was, perhaps, also a way of elevating us.

After all, a keen, literary attention to detail had formed the bedrock of my desiring life. My sense of romance was informed by the idea of a man hyper-attuned to specificity, a man in a reverie over the clasp of a woman's necklace, the gather of her stockings at her ankles. "In the corner, in a trenchcoat, her hair gleaming, sits a silent girl with a face like a bird . . ." writes James Salter in *A Sport and a Pastime*, ". . . One of those hard little faces, the bones close beneath it. A passionate face. The face of a girl who might move to the city."

It seemed to me at the time that technology had destroyed certain forms not merely of romance, but of interest, curiosity, that a certain kind of fixatedness was dead. On the train, people looked at their phones. They collapsed their biographies into personal ads and used computers to find dates. They ordered books one at a time from warehouses controlled by robots. With the entire human catalogue of pornographic images and acts freely available on the Internet, it sometimes seemed there was nothing left to imagine, and no one really minded.

But in K's obsession with me, there was a charmingly outmoded fixatedness that I cherished, a fine-grained attention to the minutiae of me so intense it was almost frightening.

In the laser beam of his gaze, I came radiantly alive. Suddenly, strangely, unmistakably, I was legible. An open book. His love invited me to perform every femininity I could possibly want, every character I'd ever read, every starlet I'd ever wanted to be. He could see it all. He *wanted* it all, every inch of me, every word, urge, hormone, every costume change. I felt how I've always wanted to— I was safe and beautiful, pinned like a butterfly, still containing mysteries in my diaphanous wings. I was a looker, a hooker, a tired, middle-aged professional coming home to make stir-fry and make her husband listen to her yammer on about the day. I was a teenager with cramps. I was a frontierswoman hanging the washing on the line, squinting against a gust of prairie wind. I was a mob wife, clad in black lace with lipstick the color of blood, making his dinner. I was a worthwhile object of obsession. I was no one special and didn't care because I was with him.

. . . .

I loved him like a dog. When he described dopesickness as a totalizing, almost existential feeling of dread, I thought it didn't sound that different from the way I felt when things were bad with us, or when I couldn't reach him, or when he said he was going to leave me. I obsessed over him the way he obsessed over getting high.

But a totalizing love is not a safe love. When he was gone, I thought I would die.

When I imagined him dying, I thought I would never love again.

In the book *Desire/Love*, Lauren Berlant writes that "the love plots that saturate the public sphere are central vehicles for reproducing normative or 'generic' femininity." This does not mean that the love itself feels generic; rather, she goes on, the delusion of singularity is part and parcel of the form itself: "[T]he heteronormative love plot is at its most ideological when it produces subjects who believe that their love story expresses their true, nuanced, and unique feelings, their own personal destiny." To Berlant, this is akin to the capitalist commodity obscuring the relations that animate its production. Love and the proliferation of narratives about love's uniqueness are used to reproduce the traditional form of normative femininity. And women remain love's gatekeepers, as "the institutions and ideologies of romantic/familial love declare woman/ women to be the arbiters, sources, managers, agents, and victims of intimacy" to such an extent that we do not realize we are unwittingly perpetuating the same cycles, the same expectations and forms.

Was this what my grandmother had fallen for? And my mother? Does all romantic love entrap you with the certainty of its own singularity and then reveal itself to be a myth designed to obscure your captivity?

.   .   .

As a girl, I lived in thrall to a certain mousy, WASP-y beauty that devastated me, blank pale fair faces that were canvases onto which any idea or fantasy could be projected. I loved and hated these tabulae rasae, and the love and hate were heads and tails of the same coin: envy. Gazing into slick, high-contrast fashion spreads, I recall feeling actually ill with longing, a sense of dread that I would have to live out the rest of my life—a flat, undifferentiated forever—looking like me. I kept it to myself. I thought the shame of self-hatred, of hopeless aspiration, should be concealed. Even more crass than wanting something so badly was acknowledging it out loud, or worse, pinning models' pictures to your bedroom mirror the way some girls I knew did. "Thinspiration," these collections of images are called now. But I was thin. More than the dainty bird-cage of ribs and arms, more than thigh gap, I coveted small, proportional faces with little non-Semitic noses, adorable, freckle-strewn noses, and straight, Wheat Thins–colored hair. "Ethnic" was the word most frequently used to describe me—that was still okay to say, people seemed to love to say it—or sometimes "exotic." My sisters had, in my eyes, been granted a softer beauty, but I looked severe. My hair was thick and black, my eyes heavily lidded, my nose large and crooked. Sometime around the beginning of high school, a grown man told me I looked like the actress Rossy de Palma, one of Almodóvar's muses. This was before the Internet, so I couldn't look her up, I just remembered her name and felt gleeful thinking I resembled a European movie star. When I finally saw her—a striking, cubist painting of a woman (whom I've since come to love)—in a film still from the movie *Kika,* I came home and cried into my pillowcase.

My sisters and I just wanted to not be ourselves. To be half-girl, half-chipmunk, as everyone else seemed to be. Winnie Cooper. Kelly Kapowski. We were growing up in the mallrat eighties, in the valley of Jennifers and Stephanies, amid that lanky, white, neon-clad beauty. I had petite, porcelained friends with fine hair the color of butter, their ponytails the width of my pinky, and I wanted to be them so bad I couldn't sleep. My mother didn't exactly help to minimize our sense of difference. Once, I made friends with a girl whose large Mormon family had just moved from Utah. She was the eldest of five and dressed like a sister-wife. Her long, ash-blond hair matched that of her other siblings and to school she wore it tied back with an actual ribbon, like Laura Ingalls Wilder. When I told my mom I'd been invited to the new girl's house, she glanced up from preparing dinner. "The Mormons don't like the Jews," she said.

So strong was the desire to shape-shift that on Sundays, when our dad took us to do the "big shop," a grocery run meant to last the whole week, at the Grand Union on Route 1, we forced him to call us by different names. Not Lucia, Nina, and Anya, three little Gilda Radners screaming down the aisles in patterned leggings. We became Heather, Hillary, and Holly. Christians in our town loved that kind of alliterative flourish. Many families we knew had successive children with the same initials, as though they were populating a file cabinet. *Nina, will you get the English muffins?* my dad would say, and Lucia would shoot him a look, widening her eyes with impatience. *Oh, sorry, right,* he corrected. Ever-dutiful, our father, the man who let us apply full makeup to his face while he watched Celtics games, dipping his head side to side to see the screen but never objecting, who let himself be ridden like a bull in the living room. He didn't even crack a smile. *Hillary. The English muffins, please.*

It was the nose, but just as serious was the hair—our frizziness, newly awakened by mood-destabilizing hormones that seemed all the more powerful for arriving in triplicate, was just coming into full blossom. The day of the seventh-grade dance, I spent an hour trying to gel one recalcitrant section into straight "bangs," which resulted in one hardened baton of hair shooting straight out from my forehead, and ended up having to wash out the gel, leaning my head down under the bathroom tap to loosen the crust encasing the hair, making it extra poofy afterward. I could feel the air move through the "bangs"—not yet fully dry and growing like a Chia Pet—as I passed through the school entrance, into the area just outside the auditorium, that differently scented, faintly rank, carpeted enclosure that glowed at night like a circle of hell.

We were ten, twelve, and fourteen when our mother told us she had used a regular old iron to straighten her friends' hair in the sixties, to create those classic, waist-length hippie curtains. One girl would just bend over with her head on an ironing board, and the other would take the heavy appliance to her locks like they were kitchen linens. That night—literally within minutes of absorbing this learning—my sisters and I went down to the basement and tried it. The iron felt so heavy it soon made our arms hurt and we burned each other here and there trying to get as close as possible to the root, moaning *owwww!* through clenched teeth and laughing as the nicks of heat made little hyphens of melted skin. But it was a miracle. *Jew-be-gone!* The desire for conformity was a burning one. We heat-styled it right into the cuticle, and had straight hair from that day forward.

Still, I was not comfortable in my own skin. I knew I had good qualities, and my family imparted a vague sense of cultural and intellectual superiority over others, but I was still insecure, mostly about my appearance, and was always on guard against the encroachment of cheerleader types. From an aesthetic standpoint, I felt that it was a kind of sacrifice for a boy to be with me. I developed a theory, based on some evidence, that after dating me, men would always retreat someplace safer, more conventional. That sounds silly, as it posits that I might be a "dangerous" choice. I was not at all dangerous, but I was perhaps an acquired taste. From within a relationship I would imagine its aftermath, conjuring with startling specificity the image of the girl who would come after me. She always looked the same in my mind. She would possess a tidy, elfin symmetry. She would look clean. She would have breasts—not enormous, but of noticeable heft. They would look respectably sensual, sensually respectable, maybe even just the slightest bit disproportionate to her tapered bottom half, so as to be describable as big, or biggish. She would seem, with her somewhat bleached countenance, untethered to any particular history. Milky and fair, with hair and eyes the color of weak tea. She could be from any century, almost any country in the north of the world. Once I'd had a few significant relationships, I had a data set to prove that this was true, to demonstrate that I was but a stop—between Emilys, en route to a Kim, Kate, Sarah. I was a detour, or a diversion.

Be yourself! screeched the proto-girl-power messaging around me. But locked in a prison of youthful self-doubt, I could only half-heartedly get there. Certain relationships with friends or with boys, especially those to whom I felt genetically inferior, would bring out a strong conformist impulse. I'd depart from my usual black attire to don cream and white, to wear blue jeans and running sneakers to class. This almost always left me feeling off—light-colored clothing, especially, felt disingenuous, a wrong note in a chord. It would be many years before I would go the other direction: the opposite of blond. Before I understood fully the value of leaning into the shtick you were born for. Full-tilt me was crooked-faced, stormy, and dark. A slutty, sloppy Modigliani in sunglasses. Those were the phases when I stopped trying for Petal, Coral, Blush, Punch, and my makeup was called Chocolate Cherry, Vixen, Garnet, Merlot, Sable, Raven, Blood. But then I'd swing all the way back. It was fun, sometimes, playing the vivacious Jewess to Gentile men. I was never sure which me was the "real" me anyway.

My marriage had been a blondward swing. My relationship with K was the pendulum swinging way back, as in an election cycle. Back to teenage-hood, back to punk rock, to dyed hair and tattoos. Back to that almost-year in San Francisco, when I'd felt finally, fleetingly free.

chapter twenty-two

Later, when K and I were broken up, a new mom friend would say to me, somewhat judgmentally, *Weren't you put off by the fact that he had a drug problem?* We were two martinis in, at a downtown San Francisco bar, careening toward revealing the darkest parts of our lives, as two people who find themselves cheers-ing at dusk will. Squeezed in between suits with pints, amid the happy hour din, I gingerly confessed that I was not especially put off by that fact. The truth was, everyone I knew seemed touched by addiction or at least dwelled within its larger circle of influence. After my experience with my sister, I believed I would never allow heroin back into my life—about that, I had thought I was resolute—but I was otherwise tolerant of the daily dance between individuals and the substances they chose to mitigate or obliterate life's aches and pains. I did that dance myself.

Alcohol consumption was low in my typical Jewish family. In our WASP-y town, drinking was the province of *them,* the G&T set with their rolling bar carts, those with big houses and small noses, who played tennis and golf and observed cocktail hour. On my grandmother's liquor shelf, above mustard jars full of whole walnuts, wheat germ, and golden raisins, sat a sticky bottle of slivovitz from behind the Iron Curtain—two-thirds full—and a tall bottle of

Kosher cherry wishniak someone brought back from Israel. No one ever touched them. At holidays, there was Manischewitz. My grandmother's third husband might drink a couple sips of scotch during the coffee course. And into her signature marble cake, she upended a bottle of Harveys Bristol Creme Sherry. But drinking for social lubrication? It simply did not happen.

Growing up, my father drank a Heineken a night. The sea-glass green of the sweating bottle and the cereal taste of it on his bedtime breath were gentle hallmarks of those childhood evenings, but it was all perfectly benign. Everything in moderation, he taught us. My mother had a glass of white zinfandel or a wine cooler here and there. In our youth, it was marijuana that was abundant and rarely hidden from view. The majority of adults in my midst, though gregarious and complicated, were gentle souls and they were Boomers. Weed was always moving around, exchanging hands, being rolled up and lit. Someone grew it, sold it, bought it from another family member. Some used it more habitually, more recklessly than others, but it only made them a little fuzzier, friendlier. It didn't seem to have life-destroying power. My parents and their siblings and friends were a fairly merry band, who loved us kids and never lost their tempers. When I began dating, I marveled at the sight of boyfriends' parents who got sloshed at family dinners and holidays. *At least have the decency to get stoned instead of drunk,* I thought. It was entertaining, but also so embarrassing, and worse, frightening. When grown-ups drank, something came loose. I found it wild and insane to see a mother coming unhooked from the evening in that way, departing the dock of the domicile to drift glassily on a sea of Tanqueray.

But as soon as adulthood arrived, I sought that very sensation with gusto. Once I left home, I entered a long period of heavy drinking, and every single one of my friends was the same. They were writers and musicians who drank in torment and ecstasy as they tried to create meaningful works of art. They worked in restaurants and bars and took shots behind the counter. Or they worked in the dark administrative corners of nonprofits or under fluorescent lights in cubicles, and they drank to blow off steam. We drank to go out, to be out, to be seen, to kill time, and we drank to fuck. We drank to find the nerve to do any of the things we wanted to, and we drank to dull the disappointment of doing those things, of realizing that so many of life's imagined high points were in fact mediocre. We drank to meet guys and we met guys for drinks, and we drank because he called or because he didn't or because he said he would but he hadn't yet. We drank because we knew the bartender, or to get to know him. Because we'd gotten off early, or worked late. We drank because the company was paying. It was open bar, last call, First Friday, happy hour, brunch. As an AA old-timer once said, *I only drank on special occasions, like the grand opening of a pack of cigarettes*. We drank and dreamed of drinking other drinks—in Moscow or Paris, on trains and planes, toasting our glamour and success. We drank because we had read the books and seen the movies where they drank this way and now we wanted our turn. As Sarah Hepola writes of her move to New York City in her memoir *Blackout,* "I wanted my own stories, and I understood drinking to be the gasoline of all adventure." Not some sparkly accessory, but gasoline. The liquid powering all pleasure and excitement, without which you simply couldn't *go*. And the one most combustible if you weren't careful. Still, "the best evenings were the ones you might regret," she writes.

Part of drinking was recovering from drinking and there was such bonding to be done on the gallows of a hangover. I loved the indulgent, misery-soaked relationships I forged in the crucible of booze, especially in New York, which felt built for drinking. I went out nightly while working my first office job after college. The collective sigh as a group of rumpled co-workers slunk into a dark booth at the end of the day allowed me to play satisfyingly at a weariness I hadn't yet earned. I invited friends out to meet me, or I walked from Broadway to the East Village and met up with them and the night began to lose its outline. I even liked the Gchat text box that popped up the next morning, a few minutes after I sat down at my desk with a withering iced coffee, that said *I WANT TO DIE.* A fellow hungover traveler, ready to dissect the previous night and commiserate about its aftermath: that was real company,

I thought. I had come to see light alcoholism as normal human behavior, and as compared with other drugs, alcohol certainly wasn't the worst thing to be hooked on. I always had my experience with my sister in my back pocket. I could pull it out and remember its extremity, remember that there were needles and tears and track marks and death, for god's sake, and these—these glasses, here on this bar, catching the twinkling light, these were just drinks! They were no big deal.

I believed addiction was a spectrum and we were all on it somewhere. Those who weren't on it at all? Those who slept at healthy intervals, ate at normal times, and had sound romantic judgment? Those people didn't tend to stay in my life for long. They seemed boring.

K also had a sympathetic story. He came to heroin the way so many people do now—through a prescription for OxyContin, which he was given while fighting cancer. He was about thirty then. It was his second time getting cancer, and he was fairly convinced by this fate that his wasn't going to be a long life anyway, so perhaps he went at the pills with gusto. At the time, he had a DJ night at a San Francisco bar, and spinning records, hearing his favorite syrupy, druggy singles blasting loudly into the darkness on Oxys, was particularly magical. He fell in love with that feeling. At the urging of some of his seedier friends not to "waste them," he began shooting the pills almost immediately. Within a couple weeks, he was buying heroin on the street and had become that most unsavory statistic: an IV drug user.

Sobriety is often read (mistakenly, I think) as asceticism, the halting of a certain vividness, of wildness and creativity. But it's also a new lease on life, a new lens through which to see the world. Possibilities open up. I've thought a lot about why I wasn't scared off by K's history with drugs, which would be a sure deal-breaker for so many people I know, especially mothers. But the life of a sober ex-junkie struck me as perhaps the most meaningful life there was. One had defied death and triumphed. I could squint and see sobriety as a harbinger of relapse, instability, or death, yes, but I chose not to. Sobriety charmed me.

When he first reentered my life, I didn't know the particulars of K's story. What drug, for how long, how many people he had fucked over, how much damage he'd done. I heard it the way I wanted to: he was in process. Overhauling. Getting his shit together. In a chapter of the AA *Big Book*, the program's architects are careful to specify that "elimination of our drinking is but a beginning." Admitting powerlessness over alcohol is only the first step. "A much more important demonstration of our principles lies before us in our respective homes, occupations and affairs," it says. The labor required in order to perform these repairs is described as "strenuous" and considered a lifelong undertaking. There is something exciting about catching a person—a man—engaged in strenuous personal labor, seemingly on the precipice of leading an unprecedentedly principled life. Something appealing about getting to pull up a front-row seat.

This, too, is gendered, of course. It is hard to imagine a man excited by the discovery that a woman is in early sobriety—that she's living at home, taking stock of some of her more unsavory life choices, watching some of her old favorite movies again, and eating her mother's cooking. The kind of self-awareness sobriety demands is something we tend to expect from women as a default. Women, particularly now, are likely to frame their entire lives as a journey toward self-actualization. Sober or not, it scarcely strikes us as a big deal for a woman to be building toward living her "best life." It's also gendered because our cultural view of female addicts has long been dim, to say the least. Women with substance dependencies are largely seen as failures at the other roles our culture enlists them to play. The catalogue of tormented genius alcoholic men is large. But apart from a few famously sharp-tongued "harpies" like Tallulah Bankhead and Dorothy Parker (few were mothers), no corollary exists for women.

The kind of self-reflection that Twelve Step recovery entails necessitates pressing pause on various entitlements, which is rare for a man. There is a kernel of apology, a spirit of genuflection running through the entire process of inventorying resentments and fears, defects and harms done. And finding a man engaged in that kind of forensic sifting: it can have an aphrodisiac effect. Sober people also know something of sacrifice. Not just weathering the cycle of punishing hangovers—unending payments for excessive self-indulgence—but the real sacrifice to give up all that granted them confidence, to move through the world in a new kind of vulnerability. K's sobriety carried with it the promise of self-awareness, openness, willingness to change, and importantly, willingness to work. Or so it seemed. I remembered Jim, my mom's boyfriend, whose bouts of sobriety were accompanied by Herculean outings into pick-up basketball, Southwestern cooking, IKEA furniture–building. He used to turn the dining room chairs upside down and rest them on the table in one swift janitorial motion, then set about scrubbing the floor with a maniacal intensity.

I have often thought of myself, tragically, as a sucker for chaos. But seen from this angle, perhaps it wasn't chaos exactly, but the redemptive promise that chaos held. The seed of a future stability that would be hard-won and deeply rewarding, in which I would play a vital, singular role. Maybe Lucia's survival, which had felt so unlikely for so long, imparted the belief that in all wild careening, there is the possibility that things can be calmed, steadied, righted. It took me all of my youth and a significant portion of adulthood to realize that sometimes when people are careening, it's best to get out of their way.

chapter twenty-three

O nce the baby is one—old enough to be away from me and my breasts—the week is bisected and its two halves are wrenched apart. My husband gets one and I get one. We have both moved again, into more permanent apartments, and we parent our tiny humans mostly in solitude, a few blocks away from each other. The sadness is indescribable. I wonder every day at the ever-blooming swells of this particular pain, which is revelatory, downright psychedelic in its complexity, its nonstop novelty.

I feel I have extended the hardship of the early years of parenting by creating a situation in which I must do most of it all alone, and with the knowledge that I am persona non grata among my in-laws and some of our friends. Sometimes K is there and sometimes he helps. Often, it's a help simply that he is wild and entertaining. The juxtaposition on the sofa of my children's open faces, soft curls, and bright clothing against his hulking, weather-beaten form amuses me. He is willing to really play with kids and dogs—the kind of grown-up I like best—to get down on the floor and make silly noises, humiliate himself to entertain others. He makes the kids laugh until they can't breathe, their gaspingest, most contagious laughter, giving them jostling piggyback rides and giving voices to their battered army of stuffed animals and figurines, making vampire fangs out of green beans. He learns the name of every Beanie Boo, and he is treasured like a mascot or a zany uncle, but not what I need him to be: reliable. The man of the house. Even just another adult of the house. Instead, his is another swirling energy I must corral when it's time to set the table or get the kids into the bath. He is one of them. In time, I see that K is beginning to fall in love with the kids, and sometimes I think, *If he won't stay clean for me, he might for them.* I try hard to create the conditions for him to experience a transcendent happiness, a feeling of familial love and coziness worth rearranging his chemistry for. Settling in to the new apartment, I line one long wall with white IKEA bookshelves and take three nights to fill them with my impressive, curated collection, Instagramming the result. Inside that tiny frame, my life looks so neat. I try to make this new spot a proper home, even though it's in a terrible neighborhood and we hear gunshots almost every day. One day I arrive home to find our street cordoned off, cops gathered around a corpse, and I see a brief flash of the body, a vermilion smear against a pale blue T-shirt, as I round the corner. I think about movie murders I've seen where the killer plunges a knife into the victim's middle and yanks upward. I wonder if that's what I've just seen. I don't know what I've seen, but the red of it, the raw meat of it, lingers in my memory. Sometimes the cops knock on my door after something like this has happened, presumably to ask whether we know anything. I never answer.

Inside, music. Lively when I'm cooking, to fight the rain, or on a Saturday morning to shake the sleep out and face the day. Quiet after the kids have gone to sleep, when I stop going back and forth to the freezer and just bring the whole bottle to the coffee table to more readily replenish my martini. Well, "martini"—a short juice glass of vodka with olive juice and three olives. I'd long ago dispensed with the vermouth, with any ceremony at all, and just made them swiftly and salty as seawater, lipstick scalloping the edge of my glass with each briny sip. Like we did all those years ago, K and I spend hours lying on the couch listening to and bonding over music, trash-talking, comparing the catalogues in our heads. Combined, it feels like we know every song ever sung. We talk about the band we might start someday, one of those bands that's just a solemn-looking married couple in tight black clothing staring blankly into the camera. Never caught smiling on film.

On the weekend, I drag the kids to the farmers' market and fill out the week's cheap supermarket haul with a few vivid bunches of organic produce. Cabochon ruby–like radishes, dirty matte-golden beets, and stout Mutsu apples the color of fading celery. Once home, I set out fresh flowers and put the fruit in a jadeite bowl. A jam jar of garden growth even adorns the chartreuse kids' table where I serve them their oatmeal. K and I found it on the street on a walk one day and brought it home and cleaned it. Eventually, I found some used toddler-sized chairs to go around it. We call it the Tiny Table Café. It sits right in front of the tall bookcases and is visible from the kitchen. When the kids are eating or coloring there, with the cluster of mismatched picture frames hanging just to their left, my son with his mop of sandy hair, my daughter just growing out of babyhood and into teetering toddlerhood, they look like they could be in a Scandinavian design magazine. I think to myself that maybe motherhood is just this, creating these frames, the little vistas you can take in that look like pictures from magazines, like any of a number of images that could be filed under familial happiness. They reflect back to you that you're doing it—doing *something*—right. In my case, these scenes are like a momentary vacation from the actual circumstances of my current life. Children, clean and clad in brightly striped clothing, snacking on slices of organic plum. My son drawing happy gel-pen houses, the flourishing clump of smiley-faced flowers beneath a fat yellow sun. To counter the creeping worry that I am a no-good person, I must collect a lot of these images, postage-stamp moments I can gaze upon and think, *I can't be fucking up that bad. Can I?*

I find a new Al-Anon meeting where I don't see anyone I know and I try to attend it regularly, although I rarely find it as comforting as I'd like to. I give other women in the meeting my phone number and try to make friends, to form the kind of easy, bubbly community other people in there seem to have. It strikes me that everyone in the meetings seems healthier than I am—no one speaks of living with an active addict—but then I think that's probably my victim complex talking anyway and that's why I'm there in the first place. I pull the old books of daily meditations off my shelves and vow to at least read these, even if I don't make it to meetings, and to try to absorb their teachings. I know that I suffer from what these books would call "distorted thinking," an overinflated sense of my own capacity to change people and a hopeless, helpless anger when I can't. I know that K's drinking and using take up too much space in my consciousness and that I must find a way to make myself both bigger and more humble, to get "right-sized," as they say in the rooms, in relation to him and to love. I don't know how to do it for myself, but I have to do it for my kids.

Every day, there is the pulsing awareness that their father and I have broken the snow globe of their childhood, let its glittering contents, all our intentions and hopes, seep into the floorboards. But still—or maybe because of this—I want things to be nice. Safe. Snug. Pretty. The strength, the tenderness of this desire is so poignant it sweeps in with force, makes my knees buckle as I stir pasta at the stove, sprinkle cinnamon into the two small plastic dishes of rice pudding. They want to be with me, on me, at every single moment, and I am forever picking them up and putting them down, patting their heads and smoothing their cheeks, kissing and kissing and kissing them while they squeal, clenching my teeth to manage the urge to consume them whole. I learn that this feeling has a name: cute aggression. It's the intensity we feel when we look at babies or puppies or other adorable living things. The cute aggression I feel toward my babies is overwhelming, and mixed with my depression it sometimes alarms me. I am too animal—weighty and earthbound. I lumber around and want to eat my young.

Thinking of my husband doing this same thing, trying to make a home, but alone, as a young man, devastates me. That sensation also sweeps insistently in and threatens to topple me. Like those plastic giraffe toys we had as kids—you would press a button on the flat bottom of its pedestal and the stiff giraffe would simply fall apart, collapse suddenly at its string joints. I'll think of my husband and grimace for a second, feel my face contort into almost-tears,

my body go briefly limp, and then I'll swallow the emotion and resume the task at hand. I am such a raw nerve that parenting alone—
just the idea of it, that anyone has done it ever, has ever been
widowed or abandoned or merely bored—feels like the saddest possible thing. The quietest thing. The Cheerios and the wipes and
toys, a dozen handheld train cars, a chasm of hours between Saturday afternoon and Saturday evening. Coming home from the playground and opening the door into the cool darkness of the
apartment, time spreading barely forward, slowly as spilled honey
on the tabletop. The days are long but the years are short, they say
about these early years of parenting. (Who says? My mother, for
one. But she always seemed so happy doing this work, happier than
I could hope to be. *Weren't you ever bored?* I ask her. *Bored?* She
seems to think that isn't the right word. *No, no, I don't think I was
bored.*) Thinking about adults putting on a happy face for children,
or worse, being unable to put on the happy face, is devastating.
That we maintain this dishonesty with them, that we must. I have a
longing to protect the kids from coming into some consciousness
of the fact that taking care of them is difficult. I always imagined
that keeping that fact from them was an essential part of good
mothering. But parenting an infant and toddler alone is so depleting
that I find it difficult not to let them in on the dirty secret that they
are a challenge, that this is really fucking hard. There is much levity
in our home, but it is shadowed by my sharp sighs, performances of
my own oppression. I become the martyr mother who invokes her
own ceaseless labor in order to extract sympathy, puttering around,
muttering under her breath, refusing to take a load off or stop nar-
rating her list of tasks. K's presence exacerbates this impulse. I want
him to see how hard my life is, how much easier he could make it,
how unjust it is that he won't. I have this idea that he is a bad man
who is stealing my time and energy—that is meant to be a feminist
reading of what's happening, but the truth is I don't conceptualize
my time as mine in the first place. He can't steal something that I
don't consider my own.

Over coffee, an Al-Anon friend tells me that she thinks she's
growing healthy enough in the program to leave her alcoholic mar-

riage. She no longer fears being single or living alone—she is ready. *But*, she wonders aloud, half-joking, *now how will he see me suffer?* If a codependent falls in a forest and there's no alcoholic around to hear her . . .

Separation, which almost always marks the beginning of a divorce, is a liminal space. Order dissolves and categories become malleable, subject to redefinition, to new meaning. Everything is makeshift, jury-rigged, partial. Everything is changing. Simply dropping the kids off feels too traumatic to do quickly, so we hang around for a while when we do it, wallowing like buffalo in each other's apartments, looking around at newly acquired objects, following the action slowly, at some remove—in order, I suppose, to acknowledge our status as a guest, a trespasser, and to mark the transfer of power, signal that the other parent is now the one chiefly on duty. We are reticent, not wanting to carve out too definitively this new experience of our failed love, our post-relationship friendship. Are we friends? Who knows. We are friendly, sometimes very, then abruptly not. My parents always described their own divorce as amicable, and something about even that word sounded defensive to me, like *who asked for an adjective?* But now I find myself doing the same thing, even if only to myself. I feel the need to prove to myself that we are capable of kindness and grace in the midst of the mess we've made. *See, we get along,* I think, standing in his apartment watching him pack the kids' bag. One of us laughs at the other's joke. *It's going to be okay,* I think. *We can do this!*

K has promised so many times that this is the beginning of our life together, that he will care for me as no one has before, but in reality, family life grates on him, and he breaks from it often, sometimes on short notice. *Won't be home for dinner,* he texts at five o'clock. *See u later tho. Can't wait to see your beautiful face.* If my face is so beautiful, come home for dinner, I want to say, but I don't. He comes and goes as he pleases and I do the heavy lifting, literal and figurative, at home. I should get, by now, that the way things are is the way they're going to be, but I'm still scandalized daily by his selfishness and his nonparticipation. *Don't you want us?* I thunder inside each day. *Don't you want this life?* Occasionally he gets so angry he gathers his things and leaves, saying something cruel and slamming the door on the way out. I turn away from the kids so they won't see my face, their pathetic mother's eyelashes fluttering in pained surprise. (Why am I still surprised?) A small panic beats its wings in my chest as I think about the damage these moments must be doing to them. My parents never, ever did things like this. Not in our loving, liberal household, where anger was considered crass.

K mostly lives with us, but when he's drinking a lot or doing too many drugs, I tell him he can't come around, that I don't want him near the kids if he's fucked up. *Every adult is fucked up,* he says. *Not like you,* I counter. He is always quick to point out in an argument that my husband and I are also heavy drinkers, that we haven't been perfect parents, that he is no different. The shame I carry about my nightly alcohol consumption is bad enough that I entertain this point whenever he makes it. I'm aware that I could be better, could always be better, that I have fucked everything up beyond repair in some fundamental and essential and life-shaping way for my children and that that can never be denied. At the same time, I can't see my sauvignon blanc or even my nighttime vodka the same way I see heroin. The sweating glass I refill while waiting on the chicken to roast, chopping fresh herbs for the salad. I mean, come on. I can't see my own pencil-skirted professional reality, my ex-husband's demanding nine-to-five job, in the same context as K with his bloody jeans and bag of works stuffed deep down into the front pocket of his messenger bag, which smells encrusted with dirt and wear. Does he really have the gall to compare himself to us upstanding citizens? *It just happens to be socially acceptable that you need a few drinks to feel normal after a day spent interfacing with humanity,* he has said more than once. *What if I need a shot of heroin in the morning in order to even consider interfacing with humanity in the first place?* I roll my eyes, but some part of me understands what he's saying. My vice, somewhat arbitrarily, happens to be legal. But the gesture always repels me, makes me mentally cling to my husband, to pine for him a little bit. I miss the nights eyeing his empty IPA bottles, wondering whether he'd polish off a six-pack, knowing nothing about the evening was likely to substantively change if he

did. With a few notable exceptions, we were civilized. We cared
about our health. We had entire worlds to manage. And there was
the love we felt for our children, a force that bound us together in
spite of everything and forever.

·　·　·

K's substance use was incompatible with normal adult life. Alcohol
made him surly and unpleasant, then fun, then horrible, all in one
drunk. Either he was incapable of drinking it in a quantity that
would soften his edges, or he had a kind of allergy to it—AA frames
all alcoholism this way, as an "allergy of the body and an obsession
of the mind." There was no moderation. He slugged down hard
alcohol, preferably mixed with Red Bull or juice, in Big Gulp quan-
tities. If it was pills, he was droopy and smiley and unreachable, in
the kind of state in which people fall asleep holding a lit cigarette
and accidentally burn down their house. If it was dope he was nodding, his eyes rolling back in his head or closing intermittently. Or
speedballs—he got those beady eyes. I banished him when things
got like that and the frequent banishments stood in for the thing I
knew I should do: break up with him. But I was doing the thing that
codependents do: having a relationship with his potential. Having a
relationship with the fact that I knew if he could put down drugs,
he would be good. He could be great! I could perhaps love him into
a greater greatness. I convince myself that it's more damaging for
the kids for him to disappear altogether than to disappear and reappear as he had been. I do not break up with him. Instead, I further cleave the pieces of my life apart so that they can keep humming
along. For stretches of months, when the kids are with me, he is not.
I keep us busy with playdates and host dinners for friends. There are
grown-ups around, my sweet friends, who come with long baguettes
and pints of organic berries and vanilla ice cream and smiles for the
kids and keep us company. On switch day, I take them to their father's. We linger and make chilly small talk as they eat their chicken
nuggets, and I leave and am free to be with K. For years, I cry after
dropping off the kids. When I first get back into my own car, even
the sound of the door closing is poignant and sad, and the ensuing

silence is so total it chokes me up. I cry because I already miss them and I cry because I hate myself. I don't linger in this pain, which has a funhouse quality. To cope with it, I have already made plans.

.   .   .

Some days, I want the disease of loving him to be removed and I don't want to have to practice it. I don't want to have to walk up and down through the "searching and fearless moral inventory" of the Twelve Steps. I want something as swift and decisive as a bullet. As a drug.

But also, I am proud of the independence I've had to cultivate. I have learned to make a home by myself, have learned that I am resourceful, that I can spend a Sunday painting a Craigslist crib and keeping children entertained at the same time. I may not be able to free my mind from obsessing over him—whether he is clean, whether he's at work, whether he would cheat on me, whether this is worth it—but in spite of the changing weather patterns of his drug use and his affection, I have become a badass. Alone with both children, I cook, hike, take road trips, host parties and playdates and sleepovers. I fly home to the East Coast and look at myself in the mirror of the airplane bathroom during a turbulent spell, rocking my daughter and waiting for my son to finish on the toilet and I feel like superwoman.

.   .   .

K continues to test me and I discover there is apparently no limit to what I will tolerate. One night he asks if he can take the car— a phrase I bristle at when angry with him because *the* car is *my* car, a used Subaru sedan, and I pay for all of its gas and maintenance; I'm still paying off the car itself—to an art opening his friend is hosting in San Francisco. At the time, my car is in the shop being repaired so I am driving a loaner from the dealership, a brand-new white Subaru Forrester that I'm terrified I'm going to somehow fuck up in the few days that I have it.

Mmm, I say, like I sympathize. *I would say yes, but that car is brand new, I'm afraid of something happening to it.*

Nothing's going to happen to it, he says. *Well, maybe now it will, since you jinxed it.*

Funny, I say. *I don't think you should.*

Then a beat of quiet, an emptiness too uncomfortable for me to handle. He really doesn't have any other way to get there. Yes, but that's not my responsibility. True, but it's just one trip into the city.

Isn't there anyone you can get a ride with?

Not really, everyone's already in the city, he says, the implication hanging in the air that he would still live in the city, too, if he wasn't here with me.

If you have to, just please be careful, I say. The drag in my voice when I say the word "please"—in it lurks the knowledge that something will go wrong.

He doesn't come home that night. I watch seven or eight episodes of *The Golden Girls* in bed, my laptop baking my thighs. I text him a few times, a crescendoing string of unanswered blue message bubbles that culminates in my most loathed text, a standalone question mark. My thumb hovers over the send button but I do it. I hate myself. Each time I amble into the kitchen to refill my wineglass and my small bowl of pretzels, I walk into the kids' room and stand there for a few moments, listening to their shifting and peaceful respiration. Their breathing always makes me think of this word, *respire,* which I learned in college can mean building back hope or strength after a difficult time like a war. The house is so still. I walk up to each of them, reach my hand to their foreheads, feeling the dewy heat of their sleep, and I imagine that maybe we are all gathering and building strength. This little army. We will grow strong enough, the three of us, to make a better life than this.

In the morning, I am stirring syrup into oatmeal when K walks in the door, still drunk. I can tell by the delay in his movements. The ragged edge on his voice that he gets at the end of his high. His entrance lets in a patch of neon-white sky, cold sky, that imprints on my eyeballs when I look toward the doorway and I squint unhappily at it and at him. *Am I late?* he asks, which I assume is an attempt at humor, but I realize he might actually be proud of himself for bringing the car back in time for me to take the kids to school and day-care. *K!* the kids shout with joy, one right after the other. Every time he appears is like Christmas morning. That doesn't help my mood. *Hey,* I say bluntly.

I have good news and bad news, which do you want first? he says. He looks bloated with alcohol, his eyes slanted by substances and exhaustion. I wonder what in the fuck the good news could possibly be.

Bad, I answer. Always the bad first.

The car got broken into last night, I'm really sorry. His voice goes suddenly earnest on the words "really sorry" like a politician trying to connect with an audience, convince them of his humanity. *I'm sorry,* he says again. *Tim left his bag in the back seat. I told him he should bring it but he was like it'll be fine—*

I put a hand up to signal that I do not need the details, and begin to breathe like a dragon, a warm, seething, through-the-nose breathing that takes the place of speaking. The sensation of disappointment is as physical as a flu. I don't wait for the good news. While the kids eat their oatmeal, I get dressed. I wash my face, put on sunscreen, moisturizer, concealer, foundation, bronzer. All quick, automatic. I make the two, perfect liquid-liner wings on my eyes, dot on a dusty-rose matte lipstick, my everyday lipstick. I stand in the bathroom and look at myself for a long time. I picture screaming until the mirror and then all of the glass in the house shatters, the force of my rage popping the rest of the windows in the new white car, and the rain-like balls of tempered glass hitting the pavement in a violent downpour. Many times, complaining to my girlfriends about K, I've said I don't want to waste my "pretty years" in this relationship and be left with nothing. In the bathroom, I purse my lips and think: *fuck him.* I'm still pretty, there's still time. But time for what—another man?

There *isn't* time to tape a trash bag over the busted window and there isn't any tape anyway. I drive the kids to school under the sharp LED light of the morning sky, with the wind blowing loudly through the gaping open space where the window was. When I look in the rearview mirror, I see my son's face wincing against the almost comedically bitter wind, looking like he's about to cry. *Please roll it up!* he shouts from the back seat and I can barely hear him because we're on the freeway and the wind is blowing so strongly. I think about the cortisol pumping in my veins and wonder if he and his sister can feel from the back seat the stress and anger radiating from me like stink lines in a cartoon. *Oh honey, I would if I could,* I say. *I'm so so sorry, it'll just be another few minutes until we get to school, and Mommy will get it fixed today. The whole window broke, can you believe that?*

I tell my boss I need to work from home—car trouble—and I call around to auto glass places to see which one is cheapest. There's one company that comes to your house and replaces the window right there; I had them do it last time my car got broken into and the kids watched the whole thing from the window, it was better than TV, but it's more than I can afford now. Instead, I drive the brand-new Forrester to Alameda and sit in the courtesy area of an auto glass warehouse, staring at a microwave. A colorfully wrapped assortment of herbal tea bags has been shoved tightly into a Styrofoam cup. There's a cup of dark brown plastic stirrers, too, beside a two-cup coffeemaker and an electric kettle. A wall-mounted television is playing *The Ellen DeGeneres Show* and I think Ellen would probably make me feel better but the volume is all the way down and there is no remote and no human. I brought a novel, but I am too helplessly angry to crack it. Instead I text Claire.

ME: *new glass to replace the busted-out window in the new loaner car: $300. knowing you're responsible for a 40-year-old's shit-show of a life: priceless*

CLAIRE: *WHAT*

ME: *he didn't even get home til 7:30 this morning. i guess it's good he's not dead?*

CLAIRE: *i don't know how you manage to keep not killing him. where did he sleep?*

ME: *what's sleep*
i don't think he did

CLAIRE: *god girl*
how much can you take?

Not much more, I texted back, but who was I kidding. The window repair costs three hundred dollars—more than usual for a kind of glass they'd only just started using, of course—which I put on a credit card, as I did so often with all the little incidentals there was no real money for. With K, these had multiplied exponentially. When I get back into the car and reach down to bring the driver's seat forward a little, a tube of lipstick rolls out from underneath it. A white tube bisected by a thin gold band like a wedding ring. The color is a menstrual brownish red with a metallic sheen, those tiny bits of sparkle in it. A color I would never wear, and when I twist up the lipstick it is shaped crudely, worn down completely differently from any of mine, and the foreignness of its shape makes it somehow more disgusting. My heart races as I twist the lipstick back down into its case and I resume, with noisy insistence, my dragon breathing.

·   ·   ·

There are many ways to be with an addict, many different kinds of addicts to be with, and the disease has so many phases and degrees. For some people, it's a secret—no one knows or even suspects. For others, an open secret, like perverts in the church. And then there's the obvious version, the train wreck, the spectacle, when it cannot be hidden that your person is an utter disaster, which is how it often was with me and K.

I was a one-woman PR firm for him. My job, it came to seem, was to protect him from truths about himself and from others' judgments, bar the door, batten down the hatches, take care of it myself. And then when I hated and resented him too much to bear it, I became the opposite: his opponent, a shrew. I broke our contract, told everyone everything. I told my friends the things he said when he was drunk, told them exactly how much money he'd spent. I told them about the barfing and the crying and the apologizing. I weaved a story wherein I was the victim. His addiction wasn't a force preying on him; *he* was a force preying on *me*.

·   ·   ·

Once we were fully moved into the new apartment, I decided to host a housewarming party. I was growing sick of feeling like K and I led entirely separate lives, that we had separate friends. Because our relationship began as a secret, I had rarely brought him out into the light. I thought a housewarming party would be an opportunity to meld our worlds, establish a sense of normalcy. I set about making a long playlist and cleaning by throwing piles of clothes and stacks of paper into closets and drawers. Claire came over and we strung lights around the living room windows and mixed a large floral enamel bowl full of fruity punch, two different flavors of the cheap tropical juices in plastic jugs from Trader Joe's spiked with cheap vodka. I was uneasy about my social circle at that point: my graduate school friends knew I was on some kind of unspecified leave of absence. I was sheepish about having departed the halls of academia to take a corporate job in San Francisco to which I wore blazers and heels. Many of these grad school friends were quiet and well-mannered with small personalities— good, hardworking, honest people I selfishly imagined had lives that were distinctly non-disastrous. Furthermore, they had met my husband during our first and second years in the doctoral program and I feared they would be perplexed by his sudden replacement. Would they ask me what happened? Maybe we could all just avoid the particulars by drinking, cracking harmless jokes, and warming ourselves into a dreamy inebriation by the punch bowl. *Do you want to invite any of your friends?* I asked K when he came home from work late one night. I was watching a show on my laptop when I heard him pull up outside. I still thought about what I was wearing and the positioning of my body when his key began to turn in the door. I thought about the famous formulation by feminist film critic Laura Mulvey that women in film represented *to-be-looked-at-ness*. That was me. I wondered how I would look when he first walked in. At that point, I was aiming for something between seductive and domestic. I might be in lacy underwear and a T-shirt with a pastel face mask drying on my skin. A bare leg thrown over the quilted blanket. He came in and kissed me juicily, leaning over me on the couch, smelling faintly like other people's cigarettes. He stood in the kitchen and drank a tall glass of water, wiped sweat from his forehead. *I was thinking it would be fun to introduce some of our friends,* I continued. *Sure,* he said. *I guess I could invite Sam and Bill. I'll invite a few people.*

You sound unsure, I said. He rolled his eyes dramatically.

Really? Because I just said I would do it, he said.

Okay, I said. *I'm not trying to pressure you. Don't you think we should? Are you worried your friends wouldn't have fun or something?*

He walked over to the couch. *I'm not worried about anything,* he said definitively.

I just think it would be nice for us to join our worlds a little bit, I said.

His eyes sparkled as he looked into mine and said, deadpan, *I want to join worlds with you, Nina.*

I'm serious! I said as he laid his sweaty body on top of mine.

Oh, I'm serious, too, girl, he said in an extra-sleazy phony voice, grinding on top of me and kissing my neck as I giggled and screamed. *Let's fuckin' join worlds. I've been trying to get you alone all day so we could join worlds.* So many promises dissolved into laughter, into sex. I don't know if he was even listening to anything I said.

The following Friday, I made absentminded conversation as I tried on party outfits in our bedroom, stepping into and then out of half a dozen pairs of shoes. I had so many dresses that had seemed semi-appropriate for a young woman transitioning to motherhood, but were too slutty for a mother of two. No one here dressed up anyway. But as the hostess, I could get away with looking polished without having to endure the passive-aggressive singsong questioning I'd sometimes gotten on campus—*Ooh, what are you so dressed up for?* (A polite reformulation of the distinctly rhetorical question *Who do you think you are?*)

Who do you think will show up tonight? I asked K, stepping into some old wedge sandals I found at the back of the closet; they looked smudged, maybe even slightly moldy? *I should throw them out,* I thought. *I should throw all of this stuff out.* K stood behind me—he so often spoke to my back because I was doing something and he was standing around watching me.

I don't know, he said coldly, *who did you invite?* He seemed ex-asperated at having to be swept up in my anxious preparatory energy. He stood in place and I glided by him three or four times on the way to the bathroom, which had a wider mirror and brighter lighting, raising my voice so he could hear me.

No, I mean your friends, I specified loudly, smoothing the wrinkles of a skirt.

Yeah, I don't know, he said, and walked out of the bedroom and down the hall.

Well, who did you invite? I called after him. He made his way toward the couch and sat down. I asked again. *Did you invite people?*

My friends aren't really into shit like this, he said, gesturing dismissively outward with a hand motion that was almost like the jerk-off motion—toward the entire house, the décor and hasty cleanliness, which now looked somewhat desperate, overreaching.

Aren't into shit like what? I asked. Inside my body, the familiar tingling heat that prickled in the wake of these humiliations. A shame that bloomed like a case of hives. I pressed my tongue to the roof of my mouth, as I always did when I didn't want to cry. I heard my first question—*Who do you think will show up tonight?*—again in my mind and cringed at the booming, casual way I'd asked it, as though he cared how the night would play out. The presumption that we were in this, in anything, together. I sat down on the couch and looked at him.

Christ, now we're gonna get into a whole fucking thing? he said. *Please don't do this. Your friends are gonna be here soon, enjoy your party!*

I blinked back the hurt and looked into the kitchen. I'd bought handles of vodka and whiskey, even one of rum, at least half a dozen bottles of wine. A stick of Nag Champa incense sent a thin, dank spiral of heavy smoke into the space above the coffee table. Un-opened family-sized bags of tortilla chips lay fatly like blimps on the granite counter, to be adorned with jarred salsa and the guacamole Claire and I had made, which was Saran-wrapped and perspiring in the fridge. During the week, I had imagined what an encounter between my friends and his friends might look like, and in my mind, it had gone both ways. Enough punch to lube the silences, the room dark enough and music loud enough to make people feel loosened up and friendly. Or maybe it would be like a bad school dance, our people segregated into clusters. I hated the first uncomfortable moments of a party when the house feels too clean, too unmussed and falsely freshened. All of the effort that went into its presentation so painfully conspicuous, the first guests arriving and mingling mutedly in the kitchen. But now it would be neither. It all felt suddenly stupid. That we were doing this at all seemed stupid. There was no we. I had been the one who suggested we host a party. He'd never mentioned anything of the sort. He hadn't helped straighten or decorate the house. He didn't chip in for any of the supplies. And the one thing I had asked—that he invite some of his friends—he said he would do and then neglected to do, and he felt nothing at all. He *yes-ed* me and then did exactly as he pleased.

These moments illuminated the breathtaking scope of his disregard for me. There was no chance that he would ever apologize in the moment for something like this—would ever say, *I'm sorry, I knew you wanted me to invite people, too, but I'm just not comfortable* or *that doesn't actually sound fun to me.* (I was so good at thinking of the exact thing he could have said that he never said. I wanted to feed him lines from a teleprompter, I just wanted so badly for him to be how I wanted him to be.) He was emotionally gone. Closed for business. The evening stretched out before me, a span of hours during which I would not be able to access him, draw any kind of clarity or affection from him. I would host a party alone. He would be awkward, make people uncomfortable, possibly recede into the bedroom after a while to watch a movie on the computer.

I thought about my husband, who was so confident and comfortable in social settings, so portable, so translatable. We could drop ourselves neatly into any scenario. I thought about his office Christmas party, the one we went to the first year we lived in California, an ostentatious early-tech-money affair, how we'd dressed up and smiled broadly at his new colleagues, made conversation about real estate prices, a topic that meant nothing at all to us. We drank the company's liquor, ate oysters, and cracked each other up talking shit about the scene. But we looked good. We looked like a wedding cake topper.

The party was in full swing within about an hour, grad students getting loose, becoming slightly less painfully awkward, and texting their friends, who brought more friends, mildly standoffish, smart-looking people in itchy sweaters who locked up fixed-gear bikes and mussed asymmetrical haircuts as they entered, smiling, flat-lipped and guardedly. The house filled up, the speakers strained, the punch bowl was emptied ladleful by ladleful and then when I looked over was a third full again, a new concoction made from the Santa Cruz lemonade someone had found in the fridge and vodka, I presumed. With slight panic, I looked around for K. I wanted to have one of those moments at a party when you check in with your person and make that brief spark of connection, the eye contact and rhetorical *how are you doing* that serves no purpose except to confirm that of all the people occupying this space, you two belong most to each other. I had seen him in the kitchen at the beginning of the evening, but now I couldn't find him. I walked through each room leisurely, but with my eyes peeled. *I met your new guy,* said my friend Olivia in a high, teasing voice as I edged past her toward the bathroom. *He's hot,* she added, raising her eyebrows saucily. *Thaaanks,* I said, raising mine in return and smiling, although I was distractedly in pursuit of my hot new guy. I felt a chill. My extremities were cold. I batted away my most reliably recurring Bay Area thought—*Why must it always be cold?!* Even in the caramel light of a jam-packed living room at my own indoor party? Freezing. Just then, through the shadowy throng of guests, I caught sight of him at the other end of the apartment, opening the front door. *K!* I called his name, but he didn't turn around. The music was loud. I maneuvered through the haze of smoke, heard snatches of the conversation taking place around the coffee table as I followed him, turning the knob a moment after he'd closed the door behind him. When I opened it, he was walking away from the din of the party into the quiet of the night, toward a cream-colored sedan. His friend Sam got out of the car and walked around it to greet K, who hugged him, patting him roughly on the back. *Hey man,* Sam said, grinning. They pulled back from their embrace. *Duuude,* said K, laughing. *Get me the fuck out of here.*

I was about to call K's name again and ask where he was going, but when I heard that I froze, framed in the doorway. The porch light beamed down on me. The air outside was actually warmer than inside, even with all those people inside. Damp spring warmth. I wondered if I could pretend I was out there for a different reason, maybe to smoke, although other people were smoking out back and some were smoking weed inside, but then Sam noticed me. *Hey!* he said, surprised. *Hey,* I said. I must have worn the same humiliated expression I'd had earlier in the evening. I wouldn't show it, I wouldn't show any emotion at all. K smiled and played it off. *Oh hey,* he said, acting like I hadn't heard him. He was practiced at playing it cool even when getting caught. I tried to smile. My mouth made a thin straight line. *I'll be back later,* he called through the window as they drove away and a knot of shame settled in my throat. I tipped my chin up, a cool nod, no feeling.

The rest of the night is mostly a blank in my memory, like so many nights. K's disregard like a can of paint kicked over, whiting out the rest of the party. Claire stayed until everyone was gone, helping me wash the guacamole dishes and all the glasses the guests had used, even though we'd left a hundred plastic cups by the booze. People always end up opening the cupboards and taking what they need. I loved doing the postgame wrap-up with Claire—she was the keenest observer I knew, attuned to the minutiae of social interactions, and she could be savage in her appraisal of others, especially fellow graduate students. She was also better at cleaning than I was. I kept catching myself leaning on the counter talking while she was gliding around with a wet sponge, absentmindedly adjusting objects, sprucing. She did better than help return things to normal after a gathering at my house—somehow, her busy tidying made them glisten. We had that bloodshot, dehydrated end-of-the-night look, my grape lipstick settled faintly into the creases of my mouth, and our voices had grown hushed and a little bit hoarse, but we didn't want to separate yet. The house was still dirty and we kept making each other laugh. She stood pouring out the remaining beer bottles and putting them in the recycling as I swept the kitchen floor, which was sticky with spilled drinks and shoe prints and would have to be mopped in the morning.

So, not to—I don't know, she started, then took in a sip of air sharply. *Did he really just leave in the middle of the party?*

Yes, he did! I said in a false chipper voice. *I mean, what the fuck. He acted like he was into hosting a party together and then he told me tonight that it's "not his thing." Apparently, his friends aren't into parties.*

Ha—what could his friends possibly be into besides *parties?* Claire asked. *Are they busy curing cancer or something? I know maybe it doesn't bother you that much, but I think that's really fucked up.*

It does bother me, I said.

The man is fucking baffling, Nina. I just don't understand. You know the weirdest thing? He was so nice at the beginning of the night, he stood around talking with me and Danielle and Marissa and her boyfriend and he was being so charming and funny and asking about their research. I was like, Damn, someone's on his best behavior tonight.

Yeah, I said. *He makes no sense.* I stopped sweeping and stood with the broom in front of me like Cinderella, like I was about to slow dance with it, and opened my mouth to tell Claire what I'd heard him say to Sam, to tell her that it was even worse than just disappearing, he had called a friend to pick him up and get him out of here. The way he'd said that phrase—*get me the* fuck *out of here*—was still echoing. But I didn't tell her, either because I was too embarrassed or because I convinced myself in the moment it was unimportant. She knew he'd left and she knew it was fucked up that it was the two of us, and not my boyfriend, washing and drying the dishes, taking the overfull bags of recycling out back to the grey bin.

·   ·   ·

Hell hath no fury like a woman who's been taking care of a drunk. The *Big Book* calls alcoholism an illness that "engulfs all whose lives touch the sufferer's. It brings misunderstanding, fierce resentment, financial insecurity, disgusted friends and employers, warped lives of blameless children, sad wives and parents." In an undated memo, Lois Wilson succinctly described our plight: "Either we tried running things with too high a hand, weighted ourselves down with . . . guilt for another's drinking, tried too hard to stop it, or we soothed deeply hurt feelings with luxurious baths of self-pity—none of it good. In our own way, though not as obviously, we were just as excessive as our compulsive drinkers were. . . . Indulgence in hot anger, violent reproach, neurotic frustration, our attempt to retreat as completely as possible to avoid embarrassment or shame, was exactly as uncontrolled as our partner's drinking. Whether we acknowledged it or not, ours was a disease too—a mental disorder we'd let ourselves fall into."

In its early incarnation, AA and the auxiliary groups that came to be known as Al-Anon Family Groups promoted a view of the alcoholic marriage as dually flawed. In its honest reckoning with the financial, social, and emotional wreckage caused by alcoholism, the *Big Book* was downright radical, but many of its prescriptions were prim. A wife should refrain from nagging, lest she encourage her husband to drink. She should try to restrain herself from expressing disappointment or rage. Some wives had tried to be silent and serene in the face of their husbands' drinking, only to realize that it made them brittle and hostile. Or they suffered headaches, backaches, or other physical ailments related to stress. Anger did have a place within the Al-Anon paradigm, but it was widely encouraged that catharsis be sought by rendering it productive.

Many of the recommendations in "Dilemma of the Alcoholic Marriage" have to do with taking this sometimes murderous rage and putting it to use around the house or garden. "To get rid of my nasty feelings (anger gave me a lot of energy!) I would go out in the backyard and dig. I'd pretend I was digging a grave for my husband; I can't tell you how often I buried him in the backyard! Eventually I had a nice big patch of ground dug up to plant things in." This Al-Anon member grew flowers and vegetables. She continues, "All summer long I used to bring my resentments to Al-Anon meetings—in the form of bright bouquets!"

Another Al-Anon says, "You might feel like chopping somebody's head off; chopping a bunch of vegetables for making relish gives you just as much satisfaction and a good bonus besides." A third chimes in, "When you feel like 'rubbing someone out,' you can use that energy to scrub the floor or polish the furniture." Another suggestion was to bake bread: you "pound and pummel" the dough, pick it up and slap it back down, "stretch it as though you were pulling somebody apart and the result is a batch of delicious, sweet-smelling homemade bread."

chapter twenty-four

I n dissolving my marriage, I had made things harder for myself, had indeed made them unreasonably difficult—that fact was never lost on me. But I had also negotiated for the most precious commodity on the marketplace of motherhood: time. I remember reading a comment from a Swedish feminist while I was in college. She said the only hope for achieving parity in the home was through divorce. That had begun to feel true. I pay in pain, but I am free.

On free nights, K and I go out. We turn my car stereo up and careen around the city with cans of spray paint rattling in the back seat, screaming along to old punk songs. We hit every green light on Grand Avenue and I belt loudly, "*Oh yes, wait a minute, Mr. Postman.*" One finger pointed skyward. When we were just becoming friends again, I used to wonder if I would ever be comfortable enough around K to sing in the car, really sing, the way I did when I was alone, and now I sip from a paper-bagged bottle of New Amsterdam vodka, which tastes like rubbing alcohol, and really go for it, a sassily off-key crooning that I can't remember being too shy to share with him. We wear parkas and fingerless gloves to fight the bone-chilling cold of San Francisco nights. Through my weaker eye, rain on the car windows makes smears of the streetlights and I watch the wending drops carry the picture of the night down the panes. Walking down the street we take slugs off of a new pint of lukewarm vodka and order vodka sodas at the bar. The glasses milky with crosshatched scratches, the wear of a thousand hot dishwasher cycles. The soda is flat and the limes are rotten. We are full and happy and lifting off the ground, hot air balloons of hope and alcoholic grandiosity. We take a strip of pictures in the photo booth at Bender's. In one, his hand is wrapped completely around my neck and the vein in my forehead is beginning to show. A pantomime of choking that is actual choking. In another one, we are making out, my jawbone cutting a stark line through the center of the frame. I can tell that my tongue is in his mouth. A patch of a memory of someplace else, where we sit under light that is dim and warm, reddish, and concentrated above the wooden tables at each of its booths. Orbs of light down the wall of the bar. I run my fingers over the scarlike splits in the ketchup-colored leatherette cushions, reading the carvings in the tabletop. Decades of bored inanity, somehow made vaguely entertaining by having been preserved. Each tiny graffito is someone's charged night out, full of possibilities, jokes. There, I order vodka without ice and watch the bottle being upended, the liquid bubbling thinly as it is poured into the glass. I pay and start to drink. Its bite undiluted, every sip is a decision, and I pause just before swallowing to steady my focus. Like having a mouthful of semen: for a split second, a sort of primal panic—*What do I do with this?*—and then a deep breath and *ulp*. Swallow. Like medicine. While I smoke outside, I watch K order more drinks, take in his shoes and his coat, the hairline. My handsome guy, my old man. Does he look like an asshole? He is my asshole. I feel protective of him anytime I get even that much distance, a few feet and a window to watch him through.

These nights are like old New York nights, the bitter cold of early winter when the air smells so crisp, so freshly smoked it hurts to breathe, and the filthy piles of ice and snow at the edges of the streets look like clouds in a landscape painting, a dozen hues of white lined with a flat brush in twinkly mouse grey, then slate, then charcoal. At night in San Francisco, it's cold enough that my body feels flushed, itchy from the inside, cold enough to suck in and breathe out a happy mouthful of mist. We stay out until 3:00 A.M., 4:00 A.M. People are mostly safe in their beds and I like not being among them. I like feeling grit like white sugar on my teeth, behind my eyes, feeling exhausted, loosened up in my haunches like a race-horse, like I've been running all night.

At home, we undress and lay in bed exhausted. He admires the curve of my ass, feels over and over again the rise of it as though it contains the answers to the mysteries of the universe. I lay on my stomach, smiling in a way that feels sexy even in the inside of my mouth—this is the way he makes me feel—as he runs his hand up the backs of my legs, from my ankles up over my knees and thighs and pauses at the very place where my legs stop and my ass begins. He does it again and again. What does he want to know? He touches me differently, without the usual tyrannical certainty. I feel the kind of substance-addled happiness that spreads from the inside like an oil spill. And then we fall asleep.

Loving K is physical, a combat sport. Every day a different flavor. He is the butcher and I am the meat. Some days, I take to it ear-nestly like a kind of training, the way a freshly heartbroken person takes to kickboxing, reveling in beads of determined, purposeful sweat. Other days I'm aflutter, nervous and new, like I don't even know what sex is. I am living a fantasy of my own deflowering. On still others I'm afraid—in a curious ecstatic agony, witnessing mutely the shooting and darting and surging of real, bodily pain. Ethereal, glittering pain like the ice-hard bloom of crystal inside of a geode. The kind of pain I haven't felt since giving birth except it's good for a metaphor, not beyond metaphor, beyond language the way birth is. It moves through my body like lasers. Drags like scal-pels. Knocks me out like a two by four. "[A]re there not certain cir-cumstances where humiliation is not just horror, but is a route, a passageway, toward something else, something tranquilizing?" Wayne Koestenbaum asks in his volume on humiliation. We strug-gle, wrestle, hate fuck, we laugh and laugh and we fuck and then I cry and we fuck more. He slaps me, spits in my mouth, closes his meaty hand around my throat until my vision dims at its edges. "Split me like timber . . . beat me like egg yolks," Cate Le Bon sings on the song "I Can't Help You." I am a kitten he can carry by the scruff—numbed by helplessness. For blow jobs, he likes me backed up against a wall, not comfortably or even in any of the positions in which I think the act is customarily performed, but sort of crouched, squatting asymmetrically—one knee out wide to the side, the other tilting downward, wanting to kneel—and the full weight of my body bearing down on my chicken-bone ankles.

He squeezes my face so hard that for a week afterward I can see in the mirror the bruise of his thumbprint on my cheek, an imperfect little oval the color of grape drink. On a lunch break, I buy a bag of red licorice laces and a lighter shade of foundation, the cheap cakey kind, to cover it up. An excuse for a long trip to the women's room, where I suck up the sweet shoestrings like spaghetti while dabbing at the bruise with my own concealer, then some of the foundation, and then powder on top. It is fairly well camouflaged—the makeup is thick and too peachy, so it looks like a concealed imperfection, but at least it doesn't look like what it is. Each morning until it is gone I take great care with this new ritual—scrubbing my face, applying my usual arsenal of creams, and then the three-layer cover up. A couple times I put my hand right where his had been, squeezing my face as he had. My skin has the give of an overripe plum.

Fucking him is like a "session," like a whole thing, and afterward I leave the apartment and ride the train in the pleasant waking coma of the freshly traumatized—an exquisite removal, outside of time, like in the cartoons when a halo of stars and tiny birds circle one's head. I hum with a peculiar combination of satiety and wonder, an almost-angry perplexity. Like the visitors to the inside of John Malkovich in *Being John Malkovich,* who are spit out after their fifteen minutes inside his mind. Rudely ejected back into the world, exhausted and disoriented. Dropped into a ditch by the side of the New Jersey Turnpike.

.　　.　　.

So bound was K to some idea that he was connected to every other lowlife in the world that he walked the city streets with the swagger of a 1970s hustler, looking for trouble. Not even necessarily to get into it himself, just to prove that he would, just to nod knowingly in its direction, as if to say, *I recognize you*. Scarcity, beggary, filth: I recognize you. Vandalism, gangsterism, hooliganism, smut and grime and crime and darkness? I know you. I see you, and I am not afraid. It was part of his shtick. This was one of the ways that he compensated for his crippling vulnerability to drink and drugs; he spoke some international language of the underworld, and that made the city feel more his than mine. Walking past the dirty homeless, the greasy, wiry junkies mid-nod on others' stairs, the hookers on crank fixing their hair, fingering the grimy lace of their shorts, K would hold his chin high, and sometimes raise it an inch in their direction. A greeting. They didn't fuck with him either.

It wasn't all shtick, though. His experience with addiction had given him a window into deep, nonsensical suffering, and he approached the issue with surprising empathy. When a friend who had been trying his best to stay clean went to jail, K wrote a letter to the judge, attesting to the friend's character. Though he rarely had extra money, he always laced the bums on the corner with a dollar or two. *Don't waste it on food,* he'd say, which made them cackle.

To say that there was anything glamorous in his addiction would be simply wrong. I know addiction better than that. There was nothing glamorous, but to me, there was something compelling. A politics of disavowal I could see as punk rock. A cynicism so genuine it could be inspiring. Junkiedom has become so pharmaceuticalized in the past generation that it's hard to remember it was ever connected to any politics or aesthetics, to a more stylized nihilism. To any creative production, or anything remotely cool, like literature or jazz. There's something about getting your fix at CVS that really takes the rock 'n' roll out of it all.

A star debater, as he descended further into addiction he also became expert at defending it as an ethical position. Once, when he was strung out, we watched a documentary about the Syrian civil war and when he saw the image of the dead body of three-year-old refugee Alan Kurdi washed up on a Turkish beach, K began to weep. I'd never seen him like that. He said something unintelligible about the tiny bodies of my kids, probably that that kid, too, was some-body's baby just like our babies, and then he said, *Why would I want to be awake in a world where a three-year-old washes up on shore because no one wants to give him a place to live? I'm sup-posed to just go to work and act like that's not happening?* I had no answer for that question.

Being a junkie, if you really went all in, also eradicated insecu-rity. All of the worry that people wouldn't like him, that he wouldn't be able to sustain the artfully curated character he had become, his impostor complex, his fear that he wasn't good enough for me and that people around us could see it—all of that was gone instanta-neously. Once, he compared his late-stage high to the dull emotional window after jerking off. *People do that,* he said, *before going on a date or a job interview, so they can have a few minutes of calm, of getting to be blanked out like that. Why do all this other shit when I can go buy that sensation and put it in my arm?*

I always prided myself on my adaptability, a chameleonic capac-ity to move between social scenes and navigate their variable expec-tations with grace and charm. It was a thrill for me to have a foot in two worlds, to experience the polarity of this dual life. Like many codependents, I felt a charge of self-esteem when I surveyed the in-comprehensibly contradictory demands I put upon myself, just how vast and complicated and difficult a life I could "handle," just how many details I could keep in my mind at once, how many plates I could keep spinning. It was the same excitement I felt when I was young, carrying around the secret of having had sex all night, ex-cept now I sat in conference rooms in glasses, prim dresses, and tights, pulling my cardigan tightly around me as I listened to a pre-sentation, thinking about watching my boyfriend shoot crack, the moment when the needle went in and I averted my eyes, thinking about what I would make the kids for dinner. *Not many people could pull this off,* I dementedly thought. This was "keeping it to-gether."

K had a paradoxical relationship with the truth. On the one hand, he seemed to never *tell* the truth—he didn't give a shit about it, he lied to anyone. On the other hand, in his fatalism and nihilism there was something so brutally, undeniably true that it cut through the bourgeois bullshit of my existence. To aspire to lead an ethical life in an ethically bankrupt world was a joke to him. The cognitive dissonance of living alongside war, of living under capitalism—the endless phoniness of adulthood was something he simply could not, would not countenance. I related so strongly to this that sometimes it almost felt good to me that one of us should be able to bow out as he was, in resolute avoidance of the grotesquerie of the world. Why even try? Why not live instead, anesthetized, at the gritty intersection of art and sex and crime. I could see that as punk, as existentialist. A part of me might have liked being connected to that disavowal, funding its shadowy operations like it was some kind of sleeper cell.

Even as I write this, I acknowledge that it may also be ridiculous. Maybe I just wanted to read meaning into his inability to show up and be a good man. And isn't that just an extension of women's work, too? The excavation and analysis of men's trauma—unpaid work they won't do themselves—the ascription to them of some deeper reasoning, so that we may explain away the ways they mistreat us. How generous we are with context. I hear women do this all the time. But ever so slightly, it did sometimes soften the blow.

Opiates really are the great flattener. Heroin addicts don't often lead dazzling lives. Their interests and relationships steadily disintegrate and disappear. But representations of addiction are *so* flattened that addicts scarcely seem like people. I think we tell that story simply in order to continue to stigmatize and criminalize drug use, and in order to keep the addict in the realm of the nonhuman. It is easier to remain complicit in consigning opiate addicts to social death if we imagine they are zombie losers shooting one another up all day inside abandoned houses. It's far more challenging to consider the junkie with a job, the one who parents, the one still embedded in a social world, the one who wants to get clean. The sadness of the addict's family is also flattened, and typically shown in a simple way: they feel sad because drugs have robbed them of the person they once knew. The letters read by tearful loved ones on the TV show *Intervention* are the familiar template: Dear addiction, you have stolen the special person I used to know. Much more painful and uneven is the actual experience of loving an addict, because in certain ways, on certain days, they are still precisely, maddeningly themselves. It isn't all catastrophic. Life goes on. It is punctuated differently, by particular kinds of silences and deceits, arguments and promises, highs—obviously—and all-time lows. But life is also just life, boring and funny and complicated. Ever-changing and always the same. K and I had hours-long debates about the people we knew or about politics or television or books. We ate meals, watched movies, spooned. We drove up the coast, played each other song after song, one of us instructing the other in how to hear it: *This part right here. Listen.* We fought—a lot. Sometimes it felt like the disease he most acutely suffered from was being a dick. When I was angry with him, all of his problems seemed to spring from a fundamental narcissism, entitlement. *You are the most selfish person I've ever met,* I thought. *Of course you're a drug addict, what else would you be.* Other times, I saw it clinically: I loved a man with a fatal disease. It was eminently medical, physical. Arbitrary. Tragic. He could see it that way, too, particularly as it began to close in on him. The times we sat in the emergency room waiting for some poor early-morning nurse to lance and disinfect his pus-filled abscesses. The times he said he was ready to get better but we called every rehab and couldn't find a bed. People he knew kept dying. *This thing is gonna kill me,* K said once, lying in my arms, and it all seemed as straightforward, as terminal as a malignant tumor. Sometimes I wished it was cancer, something plainly unfortunate and irreproachable, a proper illness, which might introduce a clarifying mood, might make us want to appreciate the abundance around us, the richness of our own love. Something that would make us want to plant a garden, that would allow me to say to my friends something as simple as "the cancer's back" and suddenly open the doorway to their solicitous understanding, their casseroles. Addiction, beyond being stigmatized and criminalized, is a disease that mingles so maddeningly with free will that those of us living in its midst can swing wildly between sympathy and cruelty.

. . .

It whips you up, this love.

You can imagine, then, how the night he turns up with two of his front teeth in his right hand and one eye swollen shut, I don't even pause to consider turning him away. It is a night I've spent waiting for him to come home from work, texting him with no response, a night when my children are with their father and there is no one to fuss over. Alone with my thoughts and nerves, and a small flicker of something else—anger—just forming at the edges of my consciousness, I walk around the apartment, tidying, looking for a task to busy me. I have finally fallen asleep when the doorbell rings.

His mouth is blackly crusted. He's taken off his bloodied T-shirt, which is wrapped around his fist. Maybe the fist is also bleeding? His jacket is zipped halfway over his bare chest. He looks like G.I. Joe, except he is high as fuck and crying.

Alas, for the codependent, empathy springs eternal. His face is mangled, and looks like it hurts. When he opens his fist to reveal the teeth, I think immediately of the bombed-out cityscape of bone-grey teeth at the back of my own mouth, the two little carved-out caves. They are shells of my shamefully unfinished root canals, a most private despair. I trace these with my tongue instinctually and put my hand out flat in front of me. He drops his gaze, then drops the teeth into my open hand, and I lead him with my other hand to the bedroom. ("Try not to condemn your alcoholic husband no matter what he says or does," says the *Big Book*. "He is just another very sick, unreasonable person.")

But before this happens, I'll need to pay the taxi driver, who wants $58 for the drive from San Francisco. ("When he angers you, remember that he is very ill.")

He lies down in bed, saying, *Sorry, baby, I'm sorry, I'm so sorry.* I ask who beat him up but he doesn't want to talk about it. I look at the gaps in his new smile, though he isn't smiling, and tell him it doesn't look that bad. I'm lying. He looks homeless. Of course, the only thing keeping him from actually being homeless at this point is me.

I thought they were gonna kill me. I didn't even care, I just thought—

Thought what? I ask. He begins to sob. *You thought what?*

I thought I would never see you again.

Even from inside of it, I can see just how classic this moment is—it lives everywhere, from *M.A.S.H.* to *Raging Bull* to *The English Patient*. The man comes in freshly bloodied and the woman hops to, with a washcloth dipped in—what do you dip it in? Soapy water? Isopropyl? No matter, men think we're expert at this type of crisis caretaking, he won't even ask. He winces as I clean his wounds. Then he pukes. And then he sleeps.

In the wake of these minor tragedies, the house is suffused with fresh purpose. I vibrate with motivation. I have a reason, I am a reason. I am concerned, loving, and singularly useful. I am his war medic, smoothing my skirt as I close the door gently to let him rest.

Sometimes, in response to these reminders of my powerlessness, I find myself trying to make everything natural and calm. I make smoothies with kale, and cook hippie comfort food, gliding through the kitchen in a caftan, humming. I burn incense, bake bread, steep orange peels in vinegar to make my own countertop cleaner. A kitchen project, cooking or cleaning, is a particularly effective way to calm my nerves and imbue the space with an energy that is both healing and productive. I try to "green" my life in desperation. *Out, out, damn spot.*

But this time, the kids won't return for a few days. I think of the handful of teeth and I go the other way. (The *Big Book* again: "In desperation, we have even got tight ourselves—the drunk to end all drunks. The unexpected result was that our husbands seem to like it.") When he breaks out a baggie of Norcos the next morning—for the pain—I take two with my coffee.

I shouldn't do things like that, but the pills are for my own pain, and also for my panic—about my boyfriend, who is suddenly missing important teeth, about the knowledge that I might lose him any day, about my own rage, which is growing harder to ignore and about which I have never, ever known what to do.

("[O]nly by occupation in the day, by morphine at night, could she stifle the fearful thought of what would be if he ceased to love her." Tolstoy on Anna Karenina and her Vronsky.)

(Alternatively: "If you hang around the barbershop long enough, you're gonna get a haircut." My mother.)

I shouldn't do things like this, but more and more, I like to. What naughtiness and novelty, trashiness and tragedy in the sunny swaths of afternoon we've blotted out together on pills. There's the feeling of being high, but almost as good is the feeling of deciding to get high, drawing the shades and feeling the house darken, the pointless day unfurl.

When the alarm of life goes off, however, only one of us resumes being a responsible adult.

. . . .

Lois and Bill Wilson were married in 1918 just before Bill, who was in the army, went overseas. When he returned in 1919, he had no idea what he ought to do with his life. He tried taking small jobs but was ill-suited to them all, so the couple decided they would take a walking trip through New England. "When we were tired or unable to solve some problem, we would go off by ourselves in the woods or occasionally by the sea," she wrote. Lois wore "knickerbockers"— rare for a woman of the era, as was a cross-country walking trek—so the two drew the curious stares of all those they passed. In her 1979 memoir, Lois writes that she had feared that it might be awkward to be with Bill after a long stretch of independence, but as soon as he was back, they fell again into playful, happy love. She kept a diary during their walk, in which Bill himself asked to make an entry on one of the days of the trip. "Dictated to me by W.C.W," Lois wrote beneath his entry, "while under the influence of sunshine and two quarts of Maine blueberries. I disclaim all responsibility for the above and will not vouch for its authenticity. Signed L.B.W."

Early in our affair, K and I also dispatched ourselves, tired or unable to solve some problem, to other towns. We drove through the thick, English fog of San Francisco's beaches, down Highway 1 to Santa Cruz. Along the coastline, harsh winds battered the grasses and made the water slap against the bleached rocks. The sky grew bluer as we wound south. Under the influence of sunshine and a mint-chip milkshake, we drew with a pen fished from my purse on the back of a diner napkin. "Two mice, one milkshake," I wrote inside a banner, beside a line drawing of two nerdy rodents. "Be my ghoulfriend," he wrote, and then drew a little Ramones-style girl band, a cartoon of gangly rockers with long curtains of black hair.

Lois, who was the well-educated daughter of a Brooklyn Heights surgeon, writes in a staid manner and with restraint in her memoir, *Lois Remembers*. The reader doesn't glean much from her description of the couple's romance. But we do learn that she suffered three ectopic pregnancies, and by the third, Bill was often too drunk, "for days at a time," to visit her in the hospital. She writes that Bill always took the disappointment of being unable to have children with "grace and kindness"—what a guy—but his drinking increased throughout this period, often leaving her to shoulder the emotional burden. The pair pursued adoption but it didn't work out. As Lois wouldn't learn until later, it was Bill's drinking that deterred the agency from pushing the adoption through.

Even as Al-Anon posed a challenge to traditional femininity by urging its members to speak freely and honestly about their harrowing experiences with alcoholism, the program also reproduced and reinforced existing gender norms in many ways. Those with a cursory familiarity with the Wilsons' story know that Lois and Bill loved each other in that crazy alcoholic-codependent way. But their relationship was complicated by Bill's womanizing. A *New York Times* book review of Susan Cheever's biography of Bill Wilson calls Lois a "remarkable woman who married beneath her social station, devoted her life to Bill's personal salvation and crusade as a redeemer of lost souls, and nursed him as he died of emphysema in 1971." She is remarkable not only for her decades-long devotion to Bill, but because she reportedly also had to deal with Bill's affairs, including one extramarital relationship with an actress named Helen Wynn that lasted fifteen years. He even bequeathed to her a ten percent share of the royalties from the *Big Book*. The other ninety percent went to Lois.

If Lois was ever full of rage, she didn't show it. In her memoir, she tells a favorite story of being so fed up with Bill going to so many meetings (of the Oxford Group, which preceded AA) early in his sobriety that she threw a shoe at him, shouting, "Damn your old meetings!" That was apparently the peak of her anger, and a wake-up call to look at her own behaviors. Bill wasn't even drinking anymore—the solution that family members always say they most want—and still Lois was "self-righteous and smug" and was carrying around a lot of old resentments. She writes that she wasn't dismayed when she first realized Bill was an alcoholic. "I had faith in my own power to change him," she writes. "Living with me would be such an inspiration, I thought, that he would not need the balm of alcohol." It was a "great blow" to realize that that plan hadn't worked and that once sober, Bill didn't need her in the same way anymore. In his quitting drinking, her primary purpose in life had been "canceled out." Over time, she saw the ways "my ego had been nourished during his drinking years by the important roles I had to fill: mother, nurse, breadwinner, decision maker."

Lois found serenity through fellowship in Al-Anon, namely talking with other wives about the experience of living with men's alcoholism. Before Al-Anon had a name, wives would simply gather while their husbands were in AA meetings. "At first, we either played bridge or gossiped," Lois writes, "but soon we began to discuss our own problems and what we could do about them." In a CBS 2010 Hallmark Hall of Fame movie *When Love is Not Enough: The Lois Wilson Story,* in which Winona Ryder plays Lois, a long line of cars stands outside the Wilsons' home during an early AA meeting. The camera pans and the viewer sees that the idling drivers are the wives, who have driven their husbands here and are standing by, lest the men end up at the bar drinking their whole paycheck. In the film, the very first gesture of Al-Anon fellowship is Lois walking out to ask the nervous women if they'd like to come in for a cup of coffee.

I like that Al-Anon's origin story is in cake, gossip, and bridge, though I have sometimes marveled at the way these women funneled what must have been an epic store of cold resentments into warm womanly buzzing, thousands of rides and bundt cakes and pots of coffee for recovering drunks. Part of the reason why is that during this period, many recovering codependents had their eye on the prize of remaining married to their alcoholics.

The alcoholic dyad was at the center of medical and psychological thinking about alcoholism for a long time. And addressing alcoholism and the attendant problem of codependency was often seen in terms of managing (or at least managing one's responses to) an excess of feeling.

The project of men's sobriety in the context of AA was in part a project of rehabilitating the damaged masculinity of alcoholics. Though the program encourages a letting go of grandiose thinking about wealth or power in favor of a focus on humility and making steady, modest gains, many postwar men's recovery narratives reveal a "deep dedication to the role of self-reliant breadwinner." In many families, the work of restoring well-being lay in a return to normatively gendered balance.

chapter twenty-five

While he is sleeping, there is so much to be done. Doctors' appointments, dentist appointments, birthday invitations, school registration, lessons, sports, groceries, rent, gas, electricity, car payments, credit cards, student loans, debt collectors, holidays, library books, thank-you cards, classroom parties, presentations, playdates, science fairs, parent-teacher conferences, recitals, concerts, sing-alongs, photo albums, scrapbooks, Valentines. I forget sometimes that I am Mommy until I am jolted up at the first sound of their breathing. Who wants cereal, oatmeal, pancakes, banana, avocado, milk, juice? Time to get dressed, brush teeth, get backpacks, extra clothes, permission slips. These are the necessities. But wait, there's more. Because I sign up for things. I say *yes* to things. Bring dishes to potlucks. Assemble kale salads dusted with pecorino. I signed up to head the decorating committee for my son's preschool fundraiser just as my husband and I were moving out of our shared home and into separate apartments. Of course I did. Those first few days in that grimy sublet, while K lay in withdrawal in the bedroom, I made paper chains and crinkled hundreds of sheets of colored tissue paper into flowers to hang from the auditorium ceiling. I sat surrounded by them after the kids fell asleep, white wine warming at my side. I liked to throw a raspberry in the glass; it felt festive. I

stuffed the decorations into a black plastic trash bag and barely
made it to the school in time to hang them up.

Are you a parent? asked one of the haughty, wealthy preschool
moms with incredulity when she entered the auditorium and found
me standing on a ladder, clad in black, some black-metal band
sweatshirt of K's dragging almost down to my knees, with hair that
hadn't been washed in weeks, looking perhaps more like a drowned
rat than a mom.

A-parent-ly, I shot back, flashing her a big fake smile. A few minutes later, my husband arrived to help me hang things across the
high ceiling of the auditorium. The kids were with his mom.

Did you just drop them off? I asked.

No, they spent the night there last night, he said.

Oh. I let the strange, painful feeling of not having any idea where
he was coming from wash over me. We kept working. The room was
beginning to fill up with other parent volunteers, who arrived mostly
in couples and dressed to the nines in anticipation of this themed
fundraising event, which also included an auction. On long card
tables sat oversized plastic-wrapped baskets full of sundry "good-
ies" from local businesses.

God, I can't believe you signed up for this, my husband said a
few minutes later from the top of the ladder, holding fishing twine
between his teeth. I looked down. *Actually, I can,* he corrected.

*The main mom who organizes all this shit cornered me in the
parking lot and asked me if I would do it,* I said defensively.

So what! he hissed back. *You could have said no.*

I could have said *no* to a lot of things. When my husband and I
first met, I was working the desk at a yoga studio, in exchange for
free classes. There were guinea pigs below the desk so the stuffy
foyer smelled of human feet, wood shavings, and wriggling rodent
heat. I always showed up for that work shift, signed all the custom-
ers in, even when too many late nights and hangovers kept me from
actually taking a class myself. Hadn't he chosen me for exactly that
reason? That he knew I could be counted on to always put others,
put him, first? *Every alcoholic needs a codependent,* his mother
once told me matter-of-factly, as though she'd been holding the key

to our relationship all along and it wasn't love. I read her directness as viciousness, and only years later saw what she meant.

This is a theme. Unmanageability. I can't do all the things I set out to do so I do things shoddily, huffily, poorly, quickly. I am brittle. I slam the pan back onto the burner. I close my tiny fingertips in doors and drawers and yowl in pain and the sound of the yowling carries so much more than the warranted anger and I am instantly ashamed. In the little losses of control, I catch a glimpse of the fact that it—my life—is big-picture out of control, it's a little flash of chaos like touching the void for just a split second, and it is terrifying. The shame, most of all, is terrifying.

·　·　·

The night before my son's fourth birthday, K lets me do some of the methadone he has (*Why does he have methadone? Is he trying to get off dope?*). I've never done it before and I get higher than I've ever been. A couch-bound trip into a dimension of droning numbness I have only dreamed about. An electric blanket. The children are with their father and even though their sweaty bodies are twisting in sleep in his warmly lit apartment nearby, an image that typically has the power to make my heart feel like it's being wrested open, for a period of hours I forget even about them. I think about smoke, billowing and sweet, pumped in by a machine, filling the room. I think about a velvet-ceilinged planetarium. I think I'm in one. I think about methadone being called "government heroin" because it is heroin, it feels like heroin, how they describe the feeling of it and what I've seen it do to people's faces, their mouths so open, death-like, that bugs could crawl in. *Nonono don't think about that,* but then the thought is gone. The next day I can't stop vomiting. I vomited when I first took the drugs, too, but now even the slightest movement brings up a wave of spinning heat. The dampness in the air is cloying. I frost the chocolate cake I baked the day before and arrange the four little strawberries and the ring of blueberries outside its perimeter, and twice while I'm doing it I have to step away and open the back door to throw up. The frosting isn't that shiny shit-brown, it's homemade and more like a dusted-cocoa brown. *A pretty color for a sweater,* I think. I like all those rich-lady colors—mushroom, champagne. I have a vision of a different me, a new me, in dusted-cocoa cashmere, the me I could be today if I didn't feel this way, if I hadn't done what I've done. The birthday party doesn't begin for a few hours, and it isn't my responsibility to get the kids there, they'll be arriving with their dad—freshly cleaned and combed, surely, to make me feel even worse—but this sickness, this dizzy regret, I can tell, will last all day. In the moments when I'm not braced, nauseated, against the countertop, I am steeling myself instead against wave after wave of self-hatred. It's inescapable, this queasiness, the inside of my mouth stale, my saliva tepid and bitter as flat beer. *Shit, babe, I'm sorry, it's going to be okay,* K tells me, as though I've stubbed my toe. His voice too chipper, too accustomed to this hardship in the body. Does he wake up this way every day? I'm overwhelmed by the human capacity for feeling like shit. *It's just a rough morning,* he says, laying a hand on my shoulder, *but look at this amazing cake you made!* Being addressed directly is more than I can bear. I put my face in my hands. *You're a good mom,* he says weakly into the intolerable quiet, offering an answer to the question I don't have to ask.

Want me to come with you today? he asks, although we both know that today is not the right day to debut him.

No, no, it's all right, I say.

The party is a screeching, toddler-ful affair I've organized by Evite in a local park. The kids are still too young to be dropped off so all of the parents stay, circling a picnic table awkwardly, pecking at carrots and hummus as the sun rises in the sky, begins to beam down punishingly. Above the tinny music coming through portable speakers, I hear the din of dads talking about start-ups. Almost always, the air in the Bay Area is cold and warm at the same time, and though I've mostly grown accustomed to it, today it is infuriating. *Why would anyone want to live where it is never summer or winter?* I think. Never hot enough for a flowing dress nor cold enough for a real coat, where everyone insists on being outside in outdoorsy sandals with no socks even though when the wind blows, there is a bite in the air? A bite: the feeling of being snatched by cold, as if it had teeth, that ferocious little nip, nip, nip of the wind. The sun is hot on my forehead—I worry my makeup is going to melt, probably already is sliding around and looking orangey—but the armpits of my cardigan are icy cold with sweat.

Would it be better to be the mother who doesn't show up to the party? That's what a real addict would do. But that isn't me, or isn't me yet. The pressure to maintain is too strong. I still refuse to truly shirk, to give in to my weak side, to surrender to just being an absent mother, a shitty mother. And besides, I am so good at faking. My shirt is crisp and floral, purchased just for this purpose, and the ache in my cheeks from smiling reminds me to keep smiling. *You okay?* asks my husband while passing by me to retrieve a toddler-sized soccer ball from the bag he's brought, lifting his enormous blue eyes toward me and seeming to bring my gaze up with them, a pull I can't avoid, until we're making eye contact. We know each other's hangovers intimately. Sometimes we talk on the phone in the morning while we're both on our way to work and I can tell by the slightly nasal quality in his voice that he's had a rough night. In those moments, my pulse leaps. I feel protective, a hot bloom of familiar codependent concern, and I miss the pre-parenthood days of bringing him a cup of coffee in bed, and getting back under the covers with him to do the patchy arithmetic of recalling the night before and smoothing his existential unease. What would happen if I could say that to him right now? What if I could ask him for the same, for him to mollify me, ease this throbbing guilt? Just for a day, I want to be the alcoholic. I want a wife.

Yeah, I don't feel great today, I say, looking down, but then our eyes catch for a second. *Maybe I'm getting sick. I really hope not.*

That would suck, he says, because he has to say something. He knows I'm off-kilter, can surely see the yellowing depression in my eyeballs. But we don't look at each other too long these days—any sustained connection at all, even separated by a car window or screen door, opens a chasm of emotion and makes me cry. His awareness of my condition changes the air a bit, making me both a little defensive—*I really am fine, I baked a beautiful fucking cake!*—and a little sicker from the exposure, from feeling caught in this disgusting act. The act of living this new life, which is getting out from under me a bit more every day. My husband walks toward a gaggle of children and I feel pierced by his sudden absence. I want to lean on him, literally to stand against his massive frame and lean in, feel the broad, stiff warmth of his chest like the seat of a truck. But now he is standing over there, watching the little kids kick around a soccer ball the size of his palm, possibly thinking about the night I must have had with K last night. Maybe he's picturing us drinking and fucking. *But it wasn't like that at all,* I want to reassure him. I don't want to block any of the comfort he might show me, any of the solicitous feeling he might still have. I want his sympathy, even though I believe that he is well within his rights to hate me forever. It's something I still tell myself every day.

I am angry at K and at the darkness of the night we shared alone together on drugs. Heavy drugs, not weed or cute make-out drugs, party drugs. It is no longer romantic, the way this life is tawdrily closing in on us—for the first time, it's *us* I worry about and not just him. We've done drugs together many times by this point, but none like this. I feel angry that he's still at home, lying on the couch, maybe padding around in thick white athletic socks, or asleep with the remote hanging halfway out of his hand. He has the utterly maddening capacity to watch the same movie over and over and over again in the same day, a behavior I have never observed in any other human and that seems like an encapsulation of everything I think is wrong with him. I have the maddening capacity to ask him, *How many times do you think you've seen this movie?* when he's watching one of his classics. *Haven't you seen this like four thousand times?* It's like I can't not ask.

I don't want him here at the birthday party, but I don't want to be here alone. I don't want to be proving day by day that I left an only slightly dysfunctional marriage for a profoundly dysfunctional, indeed unworkable, relationship with a man who doesn't even have to do birthday party duty, doesn't feel like he has to show up for special occasions, who sends me out the door supportively, saying, *Good luck, babe, nice work on the cake,* and then gets to go back to bed. *But why would he show up?* I think. He doesn't know what any of this is like. He doesn't get it. Doesn't know the Trader Joe's trip for the little watery bags of baby carrots and the multigrain chips with flax seeds that nobody likes but that we all need to believe might nudge our little families slightly closer to health, doesn't know what an Evite *is,* for fuck's sake. Doesn't know that skinless sensation, the vulnerability of feeling judged and exposed around the other moms, how exhausting it is to corral the two kids into and out of the car. Knows only intermittently, momentarily, and as a witness, the car seats, the crumbs, the diaper bag. Of course, he can't know motherhood. But couldn't he at least get sober and become a real boyfriend, someone I could rely on, ask to carry things, ask to be with me in the joy and the heartache of raising these two small creatures? I get lost wondering whether he doesn't show up for me because he has a disease or because he's no good or simply because I don't demand it. I don't demand anything. I can't seem to create a world in which anyone feels they have to do anything for me.

For three hours, I stand with my methadone hangover among the other parents and make small talk and smile, occasionally clutching at my roiling stomach, and once, seized by an urgent need to throw up, crouching out of sight and barfing hot bile into the grass. My throat burns. My son seems none the wiser, bouncing around seated on a large ball, playing dinosaurs with his friends, and finally (after the birthday song, which, like me, he hates because it draws excessive attention toward him) eating the chocolate cake, over which the gathered mothers coo. It seems he is having a lovely day, an oblivious day. But I know the truth: that I am awful. That this—today—is beyond redemption. That as tightly as I have my hands wrapped around the reins, I have lost control. The party winds toward its end with painful slowness, as though someone is hanging from the hands of time, dragging them backward. The wind grows more bitter. We untie the balloons from the poles of the fence. I put the plastic jugs of juice, the bottles of sparkling water, and the half-eaten trays of faded supermarket crudité back into short paper bags.

Every individual has to decide for herself how fucked up she needs to get in order to manage the demands of a life. How fucked up she is willing to get, and what of that chaos she will allow the world to see. At first, it's a decision you can make. Eventually, you may become one of the ones who can't control themselves, who are lost to the disease and walking around drunk or high out of their tree. I have been there, but only occasionally. Those memories are indelible, like the time in high school when we went to the Chinese restaurant on Third Avenue that served unlimited white wine and I vomited on the PATH train between Manhattan and Jersey City, wondering about the faces of the other passengers on the train, imagining them recoiling, contorting in disgust, but too drunk, my vision too blurred, to actually witness it. I had been drunk in all of the theatrical ways young people can be. But with age my drinking had gone indoors. I did my heaviest drinking at bars close to home, at home with friends, or by myself. The day of my methadone hangover, a tempest of acid and bloat in my gut, I felt the thinness of the membrane between keeping it together and watching it all fall apart. This was too far. But I still hadn't had enough.

The rank sweat in my armpits and the crotch of my jeans grew warmer once I got in the car and turned the heater on. My temperature in the Bay Area: cold and then artificially hot. Cold and hot, cold and hot. My face flushed as the dry air from the front-seat vent began to thaw me out. *That was a fun party!* I said to my son, eyeing him in the back seat.

·   ·   ·

One message of Twelve Step recovery is that we must set aside ego. After believing ourselves to be the star of the show for so long, believing that we could and should exert our will to manipulate the outcomes of relationships, it's time to sit down and shut up. Each of us must become willing to be "a worker among workers." But K just wanted the good shit out of life. He was raised to seek la dolce vita by Italian parents who made their own sausage. Out of every stew he plucked only the pieces of meat. He left the toilet paper roll on the holder after the toilet paper was gone, he drank juice until only a drop was left and returned the carton to the fridge.

The angry energy this brought out in me was tantrum energy, the same thing I recognized in my toddlers when they were hungry or tired or didn't want to share. Squirming, full-diaper anger. I'd always been angry—a low-grade ire always bubbling, simmering away like a pot of rice on the back burner of my consciousness—but sometimes something else, a ferocious, hot anger would burst forth inside my body. It was especially likely to happen if I was moving my body, pushing it or taking care of it, as though that action jarred something loose. Just noticing that I was in a body, exerting some control over my own movements, brought up either the memory or the hope of a kind of freedom I seemed to have abandoned. I cried while running with pop music piped into my head through pink earbuds, cried at the bubblegum voices and the bass, timed to my sneakered steps, cried at the facile narratives of female empowerment wrought by heartbreak, all that phoenix-rising-from-the-ashes shit, all that "since you've been gone I can do whatever I want." The couple times a year I got to a yoga class I cried in half pigeon, folded over myself feeling a knot of rage begin to untwine, a tight, tangled ball of emotion like the contents of a bird's nest. Wire, wool, and hair.

He couldn't help it. Could he? Couldn't he have tried harder? Couldn't he just stop? I felt as confused about him as the kids often did about characters in movies when, trying to get the moral lay of the land inside a particular film, they turned to me and asked, *Is he a good guy or a bad guy?*

It's almost like there are names for the number of times the sun comes up, K once joked after revealing he didn't know what day of the week it was. How lost I must have been to have laughed. It was resigned, eye-rolling laughter, but there was also genuine surprise. Stark awe. It was incredible to be able to live so free of the burdens of adult responsibility, to be connected to the vast network of obligations I navigated daily by only a few thin strands.

He was a baby or an old man or both. His clothes smelled like urine sometimes. I washed them, let him sleep. I began to rail at him in anger and he let me and even apologized. *This has to stop,* I'd say. *Promise me, promise me you'll try to stop*—and he'd promise.

He was sickly, but also angry. He yelled, raged, caused havoc. I retreated, reading Norwegian or Japanese novels where nothing happens. Novels of blankness and bowls of soup and quietly bubbling tension in relationships between shy people. The characters looked out windows onto lush expanses, they thought their small everyday thoughts, fed cats whose personalities were also sweetly described, and met at a Tokyo bar for sake and pickled snacks. They struggled to really know and understand one another because they were decent and quiet people who wouldn't see the point in shouting and swearing at one another. *There are so many possible lives,* I thought. *This one is mine.* If a satellite zoomed down to snap a photograph, these windows, saffron-yellow-lit at night, in this building on this street in this city, were the ones behind which my pinprick of an existence was tormentedly ticking away.

Every relationship is a kind of world-making, and the one we'd said we wanted to make in the beginning wasn't the one we made. Why couldn't I be in a Tokyo bar, or at a film screening at the Kulturhuset in a second-tier Scandinavian city. I was working at a branding agency. Claire, still in the doctoral program, had moved to Moscow to do research and Skyped me weekly from the glamorously crumbling Soviet apartment building where she lived. That reality was supposed to be mine, too—Russia, research—but I'd frittered it away. I felt small as a speck, trapped in West Oakland, folding and refolding children's clothes, my once-dazzling "potential" now diffuse and remote as a passing cloud. *I can't live like this forever,* I thought. But as the days wore on, a more frightening realization dawned: that I could. I absolutely could.

There was nothing to stop me, no bottom low enough. And nothing would kill him. Nothing would grant me the true status of widow, a lifelong entitlement to suffering. A stamp of approval on just how bad it was. Instead, the experiment of our love would sputter forward, threatening collapse but never properly collapsing.

He still had ideas about what he would do. He lay on the couch, scratching his face and telling me about his plans. By that point, I'd largely been scoffingly cast out of K's social life, such as it was—peopled with castaways and urchins, feral characters with laughably big dreams, delusions of grandeur, when their reality was so small it could fit, literally, in the palms of their hands. A plastic bag not half the size of his palm, the network of lines, heart lines, life lines, that mapped his fate. And the trip to get it. That was all there was. Still, he couldn't always see that, so I heard about the butchering apprenticeship, a book he was writing, getting really into martial arts—he thought he'd really like that, just had to save up for a few months to be able to afford the studio. He just needed to make some fucking money. Even the way he said the word "money" had changed, *fucking money,* with putrid spittle flying from his teeth. Those were the upswings—coke, speed, crack, meth?—that punctuated days and days of nothing.

chapter twenty-six

Alone with the kids, I traveled east to visit my family a few times a year. One of those trips happened during the summer, when my father would spring for the rental of a Jersey Shore beach house for the week and my sisters and I, our children, and our divorced parents gathered.

The airport was bustling, and the line to pass through the security machinery wound around and around the black poles with seatbelt material stretched between them for crowd control. I was always turned on by the parade of men removing their belts. When the ride was smooth, the plane was loud and calm, like a room in which an enormous fan is whirring. The pleasant forcedness of white noise. As soon as the slightest turbulence hit, it seemed to be hurtling with great uncertainty, as though being pursued. It wasn't just me, the machine itself seemed frightened. Outside the window was not the reassuring majesty of the horizon line of whipped clouds topped by the thick pastel blue icing of sky; that vision always suggested to me the magnitude of human mastery over nature. But that confidence could be rattled in an instant, as soon as I felt the smallest rocking, the slightest bump in the air. The first time I ever heard a flight attendant instruct passengers to take their seats and fasten their seatbelts because we were coming up on some "bumpiness" I was twelve and on my first-ever flight. I looked at my mother and said, *Air doesn't have bumps.* This air had bumps. We were not securely flying above the cotton-ball clouds; we were instead surrounded as though submerged in a vaporous milky solution, something poisonous-looking. I watched the kids watching their screens and wondered, as I so often did, whether they could feel my anxiety, whether they were absorbing it. I was all smiles whenever they needed me.

The eagle has landed, I texted Kat, who lived in Brooklyn with her husband and kids. As much as I hated flying, I loved arriving in New York City in the summer—the cloying, muggy air, iced coffee and ice cream, air-conditioning blasting through every sagging corner store, seeing my kids and Anya's kids together. We added Kat's kids to the mix and then there were seven children all together screaming across the asphalt of the playground. Before we left for the Shore, I heard from a friend of a friend, a cute musician I had met in California. He'd asked for my number and invited me out for a drink. We had five drinks apiece, expensive cocktails at a gorgeous hipster bar, and flirted until last call. I hadn't meant to seem quite so available. I was careful to make mention of my complicated relationship at some point in the night, but I also let him give me a peck on the mouth when we said goodbye, and we kept texting, drunk, until I fell asleep. The next day I piled with my mother, my kids, and our suitcases, plus towels and linens from her apartment, into her car and drove us in stop-and-go traffic down the parkway to the beach.

Anya stood on the shoreline, looking out. I sat on the deck, watching her. Amid the beach crowds, the tilting umbrellas and erect coolers, the greased barrel-chests and taut tanning teenagers, she was a most discernible dot, unmistakable in her like-me-ness: the same height, broad back, ropey braid of misbehaving summer hair. A hot breeze blew, and she put her hand to her head to steady the wide brim of her straw hat. I turned to settle the small stack of paper napkins on the picnic table, setting my drink down on top of them to keep them in place, and then returned my gaze to my sister's lean form by the sea.

Near her, her small, bronzed children played. Three little sun-warmed caramels, their hair whipped by the salted air. The older two were digging feverishly, making something. The baby sat shirtless, with his own shovel, senselessly smacking the sand. I could see his sugar-sack shape, the blocky, meaty, diapered heft of him. It occurred to me that he was wearing an actual bonnet.

My sister's posture was slack, and though she was momentarily alone she held herself almost as if there was a baby in her arms. Or, rather, something in her posture said that she'd held babies—many, for many hours, on airport security lines and while stirring the big Danish white enamel pot in her kitchen, her phone squeezed in the crook between her ear and her shoulder. She stood rooted on the shore with legs locked, her hands on her slightly overextended hips, elbows splayed out to her sides. Her body inhabited, haunted, by exhaustion. It was diffuse, but indelible, permeating everything. I wondered if we had ever been lighter on our feet, or if that's just how we enjoy remembering youth. Even from the deck, fifty yards behind her, I could imagine the damp furrow of her brow. I thought of crying out to her to let her know I'd made lunch, but I knew she wouldn't hear me so I texted instead: *Turn around*. She didn't move.

The sliding door suctioned open.

Why don't you just walk down there? my mother asked. *She's busy with the kids; she'll never check her phone.*

She's not busy with the kids, I can see her. She's just standing at the water's edge.

Who's with the kids? My mother tried for casual, but could rarely conceal her alarm.

They're just playing, I said. *They're fine, Mom, I see them. I counted them. The baby's wearing a bonnet? I didn't know they still made bonnets.*

Well, Lucia went to the surf shop, I'm sure she'll be heading down when she gets back. Put your suit on and you can go with her.

Yeah, I said halfheartedly, heading back into the kitchen to top off my screwdriver. *I might.*

The beach week was when we did all of our old family things. My dad bought shellfish and cooked it. Anya and Lucia and I baked and cooked together, and made runs to Dunkin' Donuts for tall plastic cups of iced coffee and to CVS for sunscreen—high SPF for face, low SPF grease for legs, self-tanner in case the sun wasn't working fast enough, and nail polish to do mani-pedis for one another and the kids. My dad knew to bring an old stack of issues of the *New York Times Magazine* so that Anya and I could do a month of crosswords together under the blazing sun, getting the pages greasy with fist prints as we took turns writing. At night, after we put the five kids to bed, the original five gathered again to eat cookies and talk about politics. It was comforting to watch our mother make our father laugh in the same way she always has.

By day, we entertained the children, or watched them as they entertained themselves with imaginative cousin games. A bunk bed was a ship. Dolls were bathed in mixing bowls. In the downstairs bedroom that my mom shared with Lucia for the week, we sucked on e-cigarettes and tried on one another's bathing suits so we could rally the troops to head down to the water. The kids were kids by this point, my son five and my daughter nearly three, and though my body had gone back to its previous weight, it was forever marred by stretch marks. For the drum-taut tummy and wobbly, baby-deer legs of my two babies, I had traded some of my own suppleness. Anya had made the sacrifice, too. Lucia still had flat abs and wore mismatched combinations of seemingly endless bikini pieces she pulled from her bag. First I put on one of Anya's high-waisted two-piece bikinis, one with a paisley top and solid red bottoms, but it made me look bloated and round, so I donned instead the black one-piece suit I'd brought.

This suit is to a bikini as a nun's habit is to normal clothes, I said as I climbed into it.

Oh please, my mom said. *You look great.*

God, are we already there? Anya said. *Mom, no one wants to look great. That's what Rob tells me when I ask how I look before we go out and he doesn't even look up, he just goes, "You look great, babe."*

Well, you do. You don't want to look great?

She wants to look hot, Lucia chimed in. *"You look great"* implies there's more to it. Like great for your age, great for a mom.

Great considering you were recently maimed in a hunting accident, I added.

Ah, forgive me, said my mom. *You look hot. Not for a "mom"*—she added air quotes for comedic effect—*just for an . . . anything.*

You do, said Anya. *If I didn't know you, I would hate you on sight.*

Aw, really? I said. *Thank you. I would hate you, too.*

The easy intimacy of our family made me feel both deeply grateful and also closely observed. Throughout the week, in various combinations, we caught up, discussing and comparing our bodies and lives. K and I texted while I was away, but he was often slow to respond. Though he had never accompanied us on a trip to visit my family, he had told me that it made him insecure when I was out of town, especially back home, which he imagined as a hotbed of ex-boyfriends. *It's really just me and my sisters, and maybe some old friends I try to see when I'm home,* I'd said. Still, he was suspicious, and suspicion always made him cold. It had been the same when I was away on business trips. I tried to stay calm, not to check my phone every few minutes, but the stress of not hearing back from him spun me out. *You're on that phone a lot,* said my mother as we passed each other on the stairs. *I guess,* I replied.

The week passed lazily, without incident, and by Saturday, after a long hot car ride, we were back in Brooklyn. The kids and I were flying back to California the following day, and my sisters asked if they could take me out for a drink that night.

What about the kids? I asked.

Rob already offered to watch all the kids, we'll just go down the block, Anya said, as though the plan had already been made.

At a bar on Grand Avenue, my sisters sat me down, with suddenly grave and nervous expressions on their faces, and told me they were worried about me, about the life I was leading, and especially about the extent to which my relationship with K had taken over my universe.

You're obsessed with him, Lucia said, *and I think it's really damaging you. And I'm afraid it could damage the kids.*

Let's just say it, Anya interjected.

Say what? I asked.

What we're really afraid of is that your kids will be taken away from you, Lucia said.

Taken away from me? I said incredulously. *Are you kidding?*

We knew this would make you defensive, Anya began.

I'm a good mother. I'm an amazing mother! Under what circumstances would my children possibly be taken away from me?

Now Lucia tried, *I knew you weren't going to like hearing this*, she said, *no one would—*

So why are you saying it? I asked. *My relationship has been a struggle, and if it's too difficult to hear about it, I can stop sharing, but it's a little alarmist to suggest someone is going to take my kids away. Who—cops?*

It is possible, said Anya. *You have to grant that. All it would take is their dad calling child services, or K getting arrested, or—*

That's not going to happen. I've told him hundreds of times he's not allowed to come to the house when he's using.

He lives with you! You're living with a heroin addict, Lucia said.

You were *a heroin addict!* I countered. *Now I'm the fucked up one? So fucked up that I require an intervention? I'm sure Mommy was in on this. Was she?*

She's also worried, replied Anya. They were taking turns with that practiced calm. It was rich, I thought, the tables turning this way.

What exactly are you asking me to do? I said. *I don't think you understand how hard I've been trying to keep everything together. All I do pretty much is work and take care of the kids and there's barely even time for my relationship with K. I'm kind of shocked, to be honest. I don't know what you want me to say.*

I'm surprised to hear you say you're shocked, said Lucia, with the calm of a thousand years of therapy. *You're so stressed, you've been on your phone all week. It's hard to even get your attention.*

So the problem is that I'm texting too much?

I know you know what we're talking about, said Anya. *You don't have to agree, it was just important to us that we say this to you so we know we did.*

Well, now you have, I said, and walked to the bar for another drink.

I flew home the next morning, hungover, in an emotional fog, withdrawing from my bag at half-hour intervals the peanut-butter-and-jelly sandwiches, the goldfish, the markers and coloring books, and the little Ziploc bag of gummy bears for everyone who was *being so good!*

．　．　．

Soon after I got back to California, my sisters' admonitions still ringing in my ears, I told K I had gone out for drinks with another man while I was in New York, and he strangled me on the bed. He wrapped his hand around my neck and stared into my face, with an evil, death-dealing gleam in his eye— some pleasure and some terror mixed in with the rage. My eyes bulged like in the movies and I felt myself going blue. I was nearly unconscious when he finally let go.

How long were we like that? Twenty seconds? Thirty? It would have taken longer to actually kill me, but not much longer.

So all of the pockets of calm were a lie. We were living right there, at the edge of something irreversible, poised to experience something truly, blackly final. To fight the feeling of helplessness, he was about to make something happen. To make the end of me happen. And I had put myself there. I'd seen him punch a wall, break a window, seen him throw things, and I had put myself there in bed with him.

Afterward, he cried. He appeared physically sick. He seemed to have shown himself something about himself that he hadn't known. I coughed as soon as he let go of me, my hands instinctively jumping to hold my own throat. K staggered backward, a caricature of a man newly aware of his own brute strength. In the visceral rushing return of my breath and my consciousness, it all looked like a performance to me, like he was kidding. It was the way a murderer, stricken, drops the murder weapon in a bad police procedural, and looks at the blood on his hands, thinking, *What have I done?*

.   .   .

My mother once told me that I should be mindful of how far I went with boys. I was a teenager, and she knew that every weekend brought the promise of crossing some fleshy threshold. *There's no going back,* she said, sounding more foreboding than I think she intended. I understood what she meant, but only once I'd gone far enough to understand. She meant once you've gone to third base, you never just go to first base again. Or you rarely do. Why would you stop at kissing? You have no reason to. Third base has become the new baseline. *Once you have sex, sex is just the thing you do,* my mother told me.

This would be like that, wouldn't it? I had to either find a way to leave or become someone who is regularly strangled, who fears for her life.

Never again, he told me. It never did happen again. But still, it was a new bar, an event that had moved the poles of our relationship. I pictured an explorer in the arctic, picking up a flag and trudging farther into the snow to set a new marker, some brutal new extreme.

There is no poetry to be found in the moment when a man has his hand wrapped around your neck and it might be the end for you. In the afterword for her memoir, *Heart Berries,* writer Terese Marie Mailhot is interviewed by poet Joan Naviyuk Kane about the stakes of being a Native American woman writing about her life. They talk in particular about Mailhot's stories of abuse. "People seem so resistant to let women write about these experiences," she says, "and they sometimes resent when the narrative sounds familiar. It's almost funny, because, yeah—there is nothing new about what they do to us. We can write about it in new ways, but what value are we placing on newness? Familiarity is boring, but these fucking people—they keep hurting us in the same ways."

What value are we placing on newness? Why should it be new?

The entire point of writing it down is acknowledging how profoundly, heartbreakingly not new it is. How obvious.

I openly flirted with the idea of leaving him. *It's what I should do,* I said. What any sane woman would do. *I wouldn't blame you,* he replied. But I stayed.

I felt I'd provoked him. Helpless as I felt watching his irrational anger flare, I sometimes enjoyed playing my part, pushing him to his edge and watching him dangle there. He instinctually clenched his fists when he got that angry. He tried to leave the room but I followed him, continuing the conversation, continuing to escalate.

Walk away from me, he said slowly through gritted teeth.

No, I said, fitting as much hurt and haughtiness into that tiny syllable as possible. *Talk to me,* I pleaded. *Why are you walking away?* He was walking away because he was afraid he would hurt me, and a part of me wanted him to. If I could push him far enough, he would do something or say something that would confirm again immediately that he was the bad one, that he was a savage. Maybe he would do something that would break this spell once and for all.

Soon after this incident—"the incident," it is called, still, in my head—K started talking about sobriety with renewed conviction. He let the justifications go—his philosophies of heroin addiction as some kind of ethos, some punk removal from society. He stopped explaining away his behavior or even talking about it and began to turn himself toward help, texting old friends in the program, going out in the evenings with a paperback *Big Book* and coming home with a Starbucks cup.

Are you gonna try again? I said.

I have to, he said.

There was so much hurt, so much damage between us that the entire pursuit was shaded with told-you-so energy, as early bids for sobriety often are. *I'll show you,* I could practically see him thinking. I didn't care. Whatever it took.

chapter twenty-seven

When I talk about the vomit, blood, and piss of addiction, the lying and the shouting and the strangling, I am speaking in the idiom of drug addicts, of addiction memoirs and AA meetings with their "I-was-*so*-fucked-up" bravado. If you know these people or read these books, you will have heard these tales. They are some combination of ghost story (meant to haunt you), fight story (meant to entertain you), and humble-brag (meant to impress you). A shock that gives way to healing. If you get around a certain type, they will go *on*. Blacked-out road trips, pills plucked from puke (lest they go to waste), reluctant trick-turning, overdoses in Burger King bathrooms, burglary with babies left home alone. One constant is failed love affairs, the list of names that could be dashed off like tick after tick scratched into a prison wall or a bedpost. Each one of those names representing an elaborate web of hope and misery, a Greek tragedy. The trail of people like me left in their wake.

I write in this idiom, I think, to be taken seriously as a member of this tribe. And yet I am not one.

The paradox of living with a drug addict is that you can never really "get" what it's like; then again, neither can they. K was the person with the most acute expression of this disease that I'd ever seen, the person whose life chances seemed to plummet by the week. He was the one doing all the vomiting, who knew what it was like to wake up dopesick on a slate-grey rainy morning and have to go out into the cruel world to find his next shot. He was the one who, on the way to the bathroom at seven-fifteen in the morning, took long, frigid slugs from the handle of vodka in the freezer and then shut his eyes tightly, snapping his fingers through the brain freeze. He was the one who logged months—one time more than a year— sober, doing push-ups in the living room, incessantly meeting his sponsor for coffee, toting the spiral notebook in which he wrote down his feelings. The clean-smelling, gum-smacking wholesome- ness of that hope against hope! Only to go back out—more drugs, more lies, back in the same grinding routine. Hundreds of days of effort seemingly gone within seventy-two hours. Only he knew what it felt like to fuck up that grandly. He was also the one who got to be high.

But he couldn't see what I could, couldn't see his own fallen face when he was really strung out, the maudlin sad-clown downturn of his cheeks and mouth, which made him look like the man who used to sleep outside my office building. He couldn't see the predictable arc of his drunk, from flushed and manic and loving to slurry and angry—usually around 11:15 A.M., when I could expect mystifying, hateful text messages alleging that I'd cheated or deconstructing one of my character defects—to apologetic later, though often a bit too exhausted to be truly contrite. He couldn't see just how pain- fully obvious were the wounds of his childhood, nor how lovable he was, nor how much he shone when he rose to the challenge of doing right by the world. It was easy for me to believe that in fact I knew the contours and the impact of this disease every bit as well as he did—maybe even better.

I started to mentally prepare for K's death—to brace for it, and maybe even to hope for it a little. It's humiliating—a form of neglect—to be the widow of a living man, a man who would just as soon be dead. His absence at my side began to feel flagrant, con- spicuous. It was infuriating. So there were days, I admit, when the idea of his death, viewed from a certain angle and in a certain light, looked like it might offer relief. I was always waiting for the phone call at that point anyway.

I let the movie play in my head. I knew I couldn't prepare for what it would feel like the moment I heard that piece of news and knew it was really true. You can't prepare for that. So I imagined everything after that—the Internet friends who would surface to tell their stories in tiny type beneath photos of him in his youth. I imagined that it would be lonely, that the future—a kind of forever quiet—would open like a trapdoor in the floor.

We didn't share any friends. He'd burrowed deeply into some underworld where I wasn't welcome, and he adamantly kept me from that world. One day he texted me while walking from a record store down to the Mission. *The cops are talking about me. They're after me*, he wrote. *Meet me.* I told him I was in the city with Claire and that we weren't heading home for a little while, but if he wanted to meet up with us, he could get a ride back to the East Bay. I told him where we were parked, across from the Whiz Burgers on Eighteenth and South Van Ness, and said we'd meet him there. He got in the back of the car when he got there and started telling us a story we couldn't quite understand, speaking in junkie tongues, a paranoid tale about being pursued by the cops, by a rival, some graffiti writers who were looking for him. Everyone was looking for him, and he just had to get out of the city, he was so grateful that we could take him. *Thank you so much,* he said. Next to each other in the driver's and passenger's seats, Claire and I exchanged furtive glances. With the windows down, we muttered to each other and he was too distracted or too high to hear. *What is going on?* Claire asked nervously. I looked over at her. *He is beginning to lose the thread,* I said. *He's losing his mind.*

· · ·

When K gets sober, we enjoy a couple months of unadulterated relief. Joy. Glee, as I watch him transform back into the gorgeous boy I fell in love with. He is rewarded—with steaks, with sex, dates, and drawings from the children. He moves back in. It's as though he has returned from a mission to space.

For dish towels and picture frames and a rug for the kids' room, we go to IKEA and inhabit briefly every small space decorated with sample furniture, every other imaginary life. It feels, finally, like we are a normal family. *It's good to be back,* he says, as we sit awkwardly on a too-firm sofa, and I can feel my wide, happy smile drawing back either side of my face.

Then, more time passes. He goes out all the time ("Damn your old meetings!") and is on his phone all the time. I find that I am angry at him every day for not doing the dishes, for not even thinking to clear the table, to put away the clean plates and bowls and mugs in the dishwasher, to dismantle the jagged, many-tined and -tonged horizon line of the silverware holder, the part of unloading I most hate. We have the usual, timeworn conversation:

ME: [banging around the kitchen passive-aggressively, dropping a ladle into the utensil drawer from a considerable height]

HIM: *Do you need help?*

ME: *Uh, yeah, I do.* [Sigh.] *I need you to occasionally do the dishes.*

HIM: *Right. Well, all you have to do is ask.*

ME: *But I don't want to have to ask. It defeats the purpose if I have to ask—that means I'm still entirely in charge of the household and am simply delegating a task. It's not the same as you taking the initiative to do something.*

HIM: *You want me to want to do the dishes?*

ME: *Yes.*

HIM: [Laughing] *That's never gonna happen, honey.*

But then one day I hear him doing the dishes, and here's what I do *not* think: *Yes!* No, there is no *yes* at all. I think: *He is running the water too long. He'll damage my nice pan. He doesn't know where anything goes.* I am so accustomed to thinking of him as unwilling and unable—useless—that I find it is very hard to stop. And, of course, he has not exactly become useful overnight. *Wanting* to do the dishes, to lighten my load? That was never gonna happen. He is, as ever, comfortable with my exhaustion, depletion, frustration. He is doing the thing I wanted but surely he can't be doing it right. I have to fight the impulse to go into the kitchen and take over, or oversee. The impulse is not an abstraction. It feels like an itch inside my fingers.

Sometimes, even this degree of unremarkable domestic discord pleases me. Months later, I hear about the impending separation of a couple I know. They are seemingly perfect—wealthy and attractive, with a large, clean, beautiful house and one small child. ("Big house, no sex," my mother used to say.) Their separation will surprise everyone, but I soon learn the even more surprising details—that their marriage is dissolving quite like mine did. The husband has been unable to extricate himself from a long affair with an ex. *How immature!* I think.

The revelation of the couple's separation happens the same week as the anniversary of my wedding to my now ex-husband. I wake up that August morning with a feeling of confusion that lingers through coffee and only resolves once I realize what the date is. I stand in the bathroom looking into the mirror and I think about how different my face looks from the one I saw in the mirror on my wedding day. It isn't possible to trace exactly how it's changed. Well, a few new lines are, in fact, quite traceable, but otherwise it's just a knowing, a sense of temporal weight gathered in the cells of my skin. "Tragedy plus time equals comedy," I always read in profiles of comedians. It's a pithy formulation, but not always true. Tragedy plus time is just a strange, stoic silence, the hovering grey of a Bay Area morning—the sadness of the toast crumbs, but many years on, at the relieving but ultimately still wearisome point when the crumbs don't make me cry. I find I can accommodate all the small, sedimented griefs of my life, and I know that more are coming. Isn't tragedy plus time just adulthood?

I feel bad thinking about their kid, who will have to endure divorce. At least mine didn't have years of memories of the family together to sift when we split. Then again, they didn't get to enjoy those years of having an intact family. I think back on the depression I felt in the first year or two of marriage, which manifested largely as shattered perspective. A hypersensitivity that made me tear up at the crinkling sound of a stranger's bag of chips. I couldn't see people's faces properly. I would home in on the under-eye bags of other passengers on the subway.

Sarah and Justin are splitting up, I tell K later that night as I'm preparing dinner. I mention it casually, though I have known for a while that it was really happening. In truth, the other couple's split has been reverberating like a cymbal crash throughout my week. But I haven't wanted to share it with him and subject it to his laser-focused scrutiny. Moreover, Al-Anon reminds me that it has nothing to do with me. It's not my life, not my business.

I haven't mentioned my wedding anniversary to K either. He is sober and at this point the mention of my ex-husband isn't likely to start a fight, but still I stay silent. I keep opening my mouth to say something and then think better of it. Why do I want him to know?

The life we are leading by this point is one that for so long lay beyond my wildest dreams, an outgrowth of that seedling of a fantasy I planted so many years earlier and set about watering in my psycho hothouse way. The picture of my life I stared at so long, like a madwoman, willing it to change, to grow. Here it is, at last: K and I, sober, cooking dinner and dissecting other fucked-up people's relationships like a real husband and wife.

He takes a long pull from one of the bottles of cherry kombucha we bought at Whole Foods just the day before—two for five dollars on sale. *One for me, one for you,* he'd said as he put them in the cart. But he's already drunk one—I know because the empty is in the recycling bin—and the one he's now opening is the second one. My bottle. I have to try to pry the tentacles of my mind off of each of these things as they happen. Convince myself that they are insignificant. I cannot stop myself from noticing them. Or (often) mentioning them.

That one mine? I ask casually as he wipes his top lip. I move browning cubes of eggplant around in a frying pan with the turquoise spatula from my old wedding registry. It has also browned around the edges from years of use. A hundred pancakes. A million eggs.

I don't know, it was just in the fridge, he says.

Does he really not know? Surely, he remembers *one for me, one for you.* He leans against the counter and continues to take long, annoying man-sips. *Who wants the divorce?* he asks.

What?

Who wants it, Sarah or Justin?

Oh, I say. *Justin, I guess? Well, actually, probably Sarah. He's been having an affair with an ex-girlfriend. He just can't quit her. So much for the perfect family.*

K laughs gruffly, unsympathetically. *What an idiot,* he says. *Haven't you told them we're the absolute best-case scenario and we're still miserable?*

That's cute, I say, but inside I relish the comment. That we could have made it this far, to this other form of misery, the one borne of stability, familiarity. I think of the poor divorcing souls, how she'll probably call me soon, as the moms do. I think about an affair: the torment, the hidden texts, the clandestine calls, the sense of stealing something forbidden. I have empathy; I can understand how such things happen. But I am dizzy with gratitude that the urgency powering such an idea seems remote, that I can no longer really relate.

·   ·   ·

Just after dinner, my ex-husband calls. He is still at work. I picture him at his office desk, though the memory of what it looks like is years old. I haven't been there in ages. I wonder if he has a photo of the kids somewhere visible and if so, which one it is.

Where are my diamonds? he asks when I answer the phone.

What diamonds?

It's our diamond anniversary, he informs me. *Ten years.*

It's ten years? I ask, stricken. *God,* I groan, *I thought today was nine.*

Ten, he confirms playfully. I can hear him smiling. He is newly engaged to his girlfriend, whose ring I've seen in person recently and looked at again on Instagram.

My parents used to do this, too, talk on their anniversary even after they'd split. It became complicated by the fact that their wedding day, also in August, fell on the same day as Jim's birthday. I imagine my mother had to sneak away, or wait until Jim was out of the house, to call my father and sigh the heavy, reciprocal sigh of the divorced. It can be such a comfort, that sighing, but the shared history and information it wordlessly communicates is a threat to all but the most confident partners. Around them, we are careful not to relax too much into that old proficiency. Tragedy plus time plus comfort equals something our current partners don't find particularly cute.

For our paper anniversary—one year—I commissioned a friend to tattoo on me the image of a love letter, a small envelope sealed with a heart above a banner with my husband's name. It was done shallowly, shakily, a bit drunkenly, in our kitchen one night while our then-five-month-old son was asleep. I straddled a wobbly chair and eyed the sticky patches on the cream-colored linoleum floor while our friend worked with the buzzing gun, outlining the tattoo on the back of my right shoulder. Once it healed, he'd come back, he said, to fill in the violets in purple, the heart in red. We never did finish it, though. It's still without color, and now badly faded.

Sometimes when I see that tattoo I feel sad, my son tells me when he is eight years old. Not gingerly, but matter-of-factly, the way children who've been raised with permission tend to speak about their feelings, announcing them baldly like a weather report. *When you're driving and we're in the back sometimes we can see it and we hold hands because it makes us sad*. I brace for more but he stops. That's all he wants to say.

It makes me sad sometimes, too, I offer. *You know, I thought maybe I should cover it up with a different tattoo, but I think that would actually be even more sad.*

He agrees. For a moment, we hold each other's gaze, our big, matching eyes telegraphing twin pain. He is too much like me.

I want to keep it because your daddy and I will always be family, I remind him. *I love him very much. And we both love you like crazy.*

He gives me the pursed-lip-line of an agreeable half-smile, a gesture I've come to think includes a modicum of pity for me.

The idea of my children holding hands to weather that sadness makes me feel, actually, like I'd like to sit down on the floor and wail for a couple hours. But navigating the untimely demise of my marriage has meant growing the capacity to take in my children's occasional expressions of anguish peacefully, responding to them calmly and lovingly, validating their pain without showing too much of my own. They think the tattoo is sad? I think about the hardbound album of wedding photos that they've never seen and make a mental note to make sure the book is hidden in a place they won't find it until—when? Until I deem them ready? This is a sad truth for them, that the love that forged them preceded them, that they can't capture more of it. It's like a fairy tale they can hear that becomes familiar, but never real.

There are moments of your childhood that stay with you forever, moments that for some reason imprint themselves on your consciousness. I wonder what those moments will be for my kids, and how many of them have already transpired. I imagine them, those memories, stacked in manila file folders like the ones that used to sit on my father's desk. I wonder how many are piled in the attics of their minds.

.　　.　　.

K stays sober and his entire being is altered: He stands taller, his voice has lost its murkiness and sounds as sonorous and warm as when we'd first met, those nights in the nineties when I twirled the telephone cord around my finger and tried to draw out his buttery laughter. He is funnier, more handsome. His jokes make me double over. His kindness feels like a miracle.

One day, because he has been sober long enough, because I am beginning to trust him almost reflexively, to take trusting him for granted, I ask him to pick up the kids from school so I can stay at my office a bit later. He's never done this errand alone before, and he accepts the request with enthusiasm. *Moi? Really? I'd be honored,* he says. I overexplain the details of the mission, where he can park and how to sign them out of the after-school program, and he cuts me off to say, *I got it, I got it, I know exactly what to do, I've been with you to pick them up a hundred times.*

From my desk, I watch the clock and when I think they're likely to be back at the house, I send K a text asking how it went.

Fine, they're great, we're all at home, he replies.

Thank you! It's a new day, I write back, with the sunshine emoji and the praying hands. A few minutes later, I bring my notebook and pen into the office conference room and sit distractedly among my colleagues as we discuss the monthly traffic to our website. I should be listening, but briefly, I allow myself to bask in the pleasure of this moment. I have a boyfriend, a *partner,* as Bay Area denizens are careful to say, who can help me. Maybe none of this has to be complicated anymore. Maybe he could start picking up the kids regularly a day or two a week.

But when I get home, I discover that he is gone, or rather, that he is that other person, the one I hadn't had to see for months. *Mommy!* say the kids as they wrap their tentacles around me and I kiss them hello. *Baby!* he greets me, but he looks cockeyed, his face somehow askew. He smells rancid, like sweat and alcohol, like carpet in an old saloon. *How was your day?* he asks, and his voice bears that undeniable inflection as if it is out in front of itself, getting away from him a bit.

My day was fine, I say. The warmth has drained from me already but for the kids' sake I keep my voice chipper as I utter one more line: *Can I speak to you in the kitchen?* As I walk through the living room to get there, I catch the beginning of K rolling his eyes in the periphery of my gaze. I swivel around to confront him as soon as he's over the threshold of the kitchen and accuse him of being drunk, my voice quiet but drenched with hostility.

Oh, I'm not doing this again, says K, putting his hands up as though to physically block my words from reaching him. *I'm not doing this with you.* He is already exasperated, growing irate; it's as though I've been accusing him of being drunk every day for the past year. He laughs a little to emphasize how ridiculous he finds this suggestion.

You're saying you're not drunk, I offer rhetorically, my voice breaking from the effort to remain calm.

That's what I'm saying, yes, he spits back. *And I'm saying that you are obsessed with tearing me down. Nothing I ever fucking do is good enough for you—*

Please keep your voice down, I interject, but I should know he finds my near-whisper particularly maddening, and he raises his own voice to say that I *would* do this, I would call the *one* good thing he has accomplished into question.

If you are about to say your sobriety, you can stop there, I say and I can feel the blood rise in my cheeks, the heat spreading through my body. The idea that we've been laboring under these past months—that we are at peace, reconciled, that the iceberg of resentment is melting—is exposed in this split second as an utter delusion as my old rage comes flooding back. *How stupid do you think I am?* begins my tirade. I strain not to yell but my voice warbles as I tell him that I actually trusted him, believed he wanted to do me a favor, and he endangered my children. It is one thing to fuck with me, lie to me, let me down, but now that he has driven with the kids, slurring drunk, there is no apology in the world that will make a difference. *Drunk with my children in the fucking car! Were you drunk when you got them or did you get drunk afterward?* I yell, but I don't wait for an answer. I put my head in my hands and say, *I can't, I can't, I can't! I can't.* An incantation meant to carry him away, out of my sight. *Do you hear me? I cannot do this,* I thunder. *I cannot fucking do this for one more second. I have been waiting and waiting for the thing that will finally make me say this and mean it.* I lift my head up and look right into his eyes and shout, *Get. The fuck. Out. Of my life,* at a volume the kids and the neighbors can certainly hear.

I can't fucking wait, he snaps back, shaking the frame of the house when he pulls the door shut behind him.

chapter twenty-eight

On a bright sunny morning, I go for a run instead of lingering in my apartment, now creepily quiet when the kids are with their dad. If I stay inside too long in the mornings, I'll end up watching television or crying. On Pleasant Valley, I turn to start the steep jag, a hill that marks the triumphant threshold of three miles and means I'm halfway home. The windows of a shitty Honda are rolled down and inside two junkies are either sleeping or dead. There's a high-hat and another drum bag in the back seat. They're collapsed unnaturally, like corpses. The woman folded sideways and back, the man with his head bent forward, his chin almost touching his chest. I take in the scene as I jog past them, up to the top of the hill, feeling a wave of sadness and disgust, and then guilt, my familiar friend.

At the top of the hill I turn around and run back down to see if they're okay. I crouch by the window and watch the woman to see if she's breathing, to see if her breath is moving the strawberry blond wisps hanging in front of her face. It is. Inside the car is an entire world. The man is sitting in the driver's seat, slumped over. A bit of foamy white saliva is gathered in one corner of his mouth.

Hey, I say. *You okay?* Then again, louder. *Hey, you guys okay? Just making sure you're alive.* I knock a couple times on the car door.

In my purse at home, I have NARCAN, the overdose-reversing drug. The man is roused and mumbles, *Yeah yeah, we are, we are.* And I run as if spring-loaded, bounding back up the hill nearly tearful with gratitude, away from the man's dirty, bloated sausage fingers lying gently on the steering wheel, feeling his way into wakefulness as if blind, as the very, very opiate-high do, the little Chihuahua curled in the crook of the passed-out woman's waist like a hairy growth, wriggling almost imperceptibly to nestle more deeply into her creases, the smell of metal and cigarette smoke baked into the hot upholstery.

Later that day, I drive to the San Francisco airport to pick up Lucia and my mother, who still come in a pair. They visit California together a couple times a year, usually once for Halloween, which is today. Their Brooklyn apartments are a few long avenue blocks apart and they talk every day. Their relationship is no longer as one-sided as it was years ago. Lucia is now my mother's emergency contact, too. They go for manicures together. Lucia helps move heavy things and meets my mom for coffee at the nice pastry place on her block. My mom loans Lucia her car when she wants to get out of the city, and the two brave Whole Foods together to shop for Thanksgiving dinner, which Lucia has started hosting at her place in Gowanus. They have a kind of symbiotic relationship—my mother still sometimes answers the question "How are you?" with "Lucia had a date last night"—but I no longer find it grating. Their bond has only grown more beautiful. They always looked the most alike in our family—Anya and I bear more of a resemblance to our father's side—and now they have grown into a vibrant kind of sisterhood built on the thrill of Lucia's survival. They make each other howl with laughter. They laugh in the retelling of stories and sometimes one has to finish the tale while the other catches her breath.

Lucia's path has not been easy, but she has prevailed in a most inspiring way. She has built a career working for artists and is a performance artist in her own right. She's gained a following for an oeuvre that focuses on many of her harrowing experiences. We bond over the fact that we both continue to iterate on the same themes, on the same traumatic material: drugs, death, and what she calls "the calamity of being female."

On this visit, my mother regales me with a story of driving out to a Lowe's to buy bags of soil with Lucia because she was burying herself alive for a performance. It's one of those stories that's so ridiculous it makes my mother laugh and shake her head in the telling. It's the happy version of the incredulity of many years ago. She even shows me a photo on her phone of Lucia looking pretty in a white tank top, floral skirt, aviator sunglasses, and Pumas, holding a shovel. Behind her, my mother's trunk is piled high with forty-pound bags of dirt.

Did you watch the performance? I ask.

No! says my mother. *I draw the line there—you know I support your work,* she says, turning to Lucia, *but I draw a line at watching my own daughter bury herself.*

Well, it's kind of your fault, Mom, I say. *You're the one who showed us all the crazy art in the first place. And you know what you always told us—*

She finishes my thought, reciting the well-known Carrie Fisher quote: *Take your broken heart, make it into art.*

. . .

It's been a while now since the night my sisters expressed their fears for me, and my own life has settled into a quasi-suburban normalcy. Lucia is nonjudgmental and loving about my breakup with K, perhaps more than anyone else in my life, but she also doesn't hide her relief. *I know how painful this is,* she says. *But you had to do it,* she adds gingerly. *He gave you no choice. And now look at you.*

Look at what? I ask flatly, unimpressed with myself.

You've taken back the narrative of your own life.

Years earlier, I had worried about introducing Lucia to K. I felt jealous thinking they'd share some dark understanding, a commonality that would crowd me out and make me feel like a little sister to them both. And they did get along well, though they never spent much time together. Sometimes, irrationally, superstitiously, I'd thought of Lucia and K as being on a kind of pull-cord—if one of them was doing well, it meant the other couldn't be. Now K was gone again, and Lucia was clean, successful, merry as ever.

At night after we put the kids to bed, a round-robin of stories and snuggles and kisses that finally settles them after the gleeful family day and a night of trick-or-treating, Lucia and I lie on my couch, feet to feet, and pick through the pillowcases full of Halloween candy. I tell her it struck me as ghastly, then sad, that when K left he took the old, funny, black-and-white photograph of his father out of the small silver frame on the mantelpiece. Then I noticed he took the photo of himself, too, off of the refrigerator. A handsome young one, also black-and-white, mostly of the back of his head as he screamed into a microphone, his hair sweaty and slick as a seal. And the photo of our hands clasped together, Instagram faux-faded, where you can see his tattoo that reads *Promises*. Though he said he would, he didn't move his things out. He didn't leave his key. But he took these few photographs, to help him draw a through line, to continue his life's project of crafting and sustaining a persona, to double down on the antihero shtick, to save for the next woman ("girls," he still calls them) the crumb trail of his life. *This is my father. This is me when I went on tour thirty years ago. This is a girl I loved and lost because I'm bad bad bad and unreformed, unrepentant, unfixable. I know you think you can fix me, new girl, but you can't. You shouldn't even bother to try. This girl here in this photo, with the baby-blue manicure and long fingers clasped happily, desperately, around the Promises tattoo: you should see what happened to her.*

It occurred to me that I had given almost a decade of my life to a man who would always prize his family photos over mine, who would scarcely linger over a black-and-white photograph of my beautiful mother, my beautiful grandmother, the cluster of immigrant relatives in fur coats and heels on a cement stoop in Brooklyn, my uncles swimming, my grandfather looking like Tony Soprano playing big band music. The things he found bewitching on TV and in movies—in real life he doesn't care that way. We hadn't joined our worlds the way lovers, families, are meant to. He took back the bits of himself, right out of the frame, when he left.

In the morning, Lucia gets up with the kids before I do, and by the time I rise and shuffle toward coffee, she's sitting, hugging her knees in the middle of a circle of stuffed animals. Home in New York, she regularly spends time with Anya's kids, inviting them over individually for takeout and sleepovers, but my kids don't often get to see her, so when she and my mother are in town they rise at dawn. Lucia has that same magic quality she did when we were kids. It's the same thing K had, the thing that made you feel you couldn't get enough of him. And like him, she is willing to really play with my kids, to submit to any game or charade or to sit and talk deeply about anything that's on their minds. Sometimes when my son is upset, he'll say, *I want to talk to Lucia*, and disappear into his room with my phone.

This morning, she hops up as I enter the living room, grumbling myself awake, and says, *Sit, I'll get you coffee*, pointing to the couch.

My mother makes a move from her seat on the couch, too. *I'll do it, Lucia*, she says.

No, no, sit! Lucia insists.

Jesus, what are you on this morning? I ask, amazed at her energy.

Just high on life, she replies, smiling back.

part 4

chapter twenty-nine

I t took me two months to make a Tinder profile. First, I made play-
lists, and careened down the freeway crying and belting out the
songs that reminded me of him, and the songs I'd collected while
angry at him or lonely or longing or hopeless or exhausted. I
coasted, singing, along the Bay Bridge, holding long wavering notes
like a wounded wolverine. When it felt like I couldn't cry anymore,
I uploaded five little thumbnail images of myself in which I thought
I looked young-ish, vaguely normal, and vaguely cool, and went in
search of oblivion in the form of a stranger, a new man on whom I
would hang no hopes at all.

I need a palate cleanser, I told friends, trying to sound cavalier,
and stayed up nights fielding messages from men who wanted to
meet me or text me or show me their dicks. Confirming my own
relevance—or the timelessness of men's urges—made me feel desir-
able in a way I hadn't realized I'd been longing for. I had a marriage,
two kids, and the catastrophe of K behind me, but I was not damaged goods! Or perhaps no goods are too damaged to repel male
desire. No matter. I was still likable. Hot, even. My phone vibrated
through the night.

But compared with the barreling ease of my texting with K,
most of the communication I had with this new crop of potential

mates lay along a sad spectrum from stale to horrifying. Some were scarcely literate and seemed to have learned to spell correctly only the words for body parts; others seemed to cope with the discomfort of phone-flirting by performing a strange formality: *How does the evening find you, madam?* Others acted like self-satisfied sleuths confidently pacing an interrogation room: *Well well well, tell me, Nina, what's a girl like you doing here?* What is anyone doing on a dating app? It all made me cringe with embarrassment. I hated my own tone, too. It felt like it had been a lifetime since I'd been engaged in that kind of casual self-presentation, and I didn't like squirming under my own microscope, rereading my messages to see how I'd played a particular question, assessing the extent to which I'd mastered affecting a cool-girl air. While I was waiting for them to text back, there was nothing to do but read over the conversations I was in the middle of having and judge them. I tried to come off as busy and independent. I had an arsenal of self-deprecating, semi-serious ways to say that I had just emerged from a disastrous relationship—*lol*—and was looking for fun but not commitment.

Once, I revealed I had children in the middle of a playful text exchange and immediately felt a chill. *Oh really?* the guy wrote after a minute-long pause. *Shit,* I thought. Then: *No, not shit!* That's the truth! I shouldn't have to hide it. *Don't worry, they're not looking for a new daddy,* I replied. *Just I am.* The guy blocked me ten seconds later, and I guffawed loudly and shouted, *Oh, come on!* into the empty room. *That was funny!*

The first spell-breaking fuck with not-K chased three double vodkas and two tequila shots and lasted about six minutes. It was with James, a lean, craggy, handsome man who was also stumbling out from the cave of a long-term relationship and still adjusting to the light. We texted incessantly for a few days, then met at the darkest bar in town. He knew the bartender, a girl with dyed-black hair and tattoos—another me; another everyone—who gave us shots for free and did one with us. She'd just gone through a breakup, too, that very day, meaning we all had an excuse to drink, an excuse to do whatever we needed to do to blot out our feelings. How good I was at that: feeling entitled. Letting my hair down, giving myself permission, and then melting tipsily into it. *Fuck love,* she said saltily as she upended hers. The bartender gave James a lingering, knowing look each time I ordered another drink. *They've definitely fucked,* I remember thinking. I don't remember what he and I talked about that night, just that it led to clumsily urgent making out against the driver's side door of my car. The homeless man sitting in a sleeping bag just outside the city's main library looked on silently. I'd put the booster seats in the trunk.

Someone else's breath. Someone else's mouth. It was a clammy November night, the air damp and chilled and the streets puzzlingly empty. We sealed ourselves into the silence of my sedan and continued kissing, pulling back every now and then to make the kind of flat, questioning eye contact you do with a near stranger. There was a blankness behind his eyes, these new eyes, a look that satisfyingly reflected exactly what I felt in that moment: *I don't care who you are.* I wasn't even sure I liked it, I just knew that he wasn't K, that I'd tried everything else and this was all that was left.

I so frequently thought about K and me in terms of narratives that already existed, pictures I'd collected since I was a little girl. There were so many scenes I'd imagined myself into—canvases and film stills, old photographs, even cartoons. There were scenes of captivity, desperation, and lust, and after our breakup, scenes of freedom, Disney sunshine, the whole village of my life alive in exultation, birds holding in their beaks the banner announcing my survival.

That night, freedom was pure escape. I imagined myself at the bottom of a luminescent sea, a movie ocean, chained to a shipwreck, eyes darting nervously around in what the viewer quickly realizes are the moments before drowning. My pretty hair flowing mermaid-like, turbid, grey-blue water sending Renaissance waves undulating through the length of it. In the back seat, James peeled my pants off and I unbuttoned his pants and we were drunk and stupid and we laughed a little bit and I straddled him under the weak streetlight and it was too fast to be good, too fast to be anything, but his face was rough and he smelled like a man and it was like taking a pair of bolt cutters to that chain around my ankle. I swam up, up, up toward light.

"Reader, I fucked him," I wrote, paraphrasing *Jane Eyre,* on my girlfriends' text thread the next morning, and they returned the requisite emojis of enthusiasm and love.

James and I quickly became each other's security blankets. Somehow, his was the house I ended up at after all the other bad dates, watching reruns of *30 Rock* in his sweatshirt and pajamas while his pitbull snored in the corner. In the dark early morning, before donning his construction vest, he brought me coffee in bed and I could tell he thought it the height of chivalry. Sadly, after the relationship I'd just escaped, it did actually impress me.

James gave way to others. There were bad dates: the milquetoast Midwesterner who told me he was recovering from alcoholism while I callously downed three drinks at the bar. He never called again. The boyish girl who I wanted so badly to take me under her capable, sporty wing but who didn't even try to kiss me at the end of the night. I feared I emitted some toxic straight-girl desperation: the kind that just wants relief from men, to be put out of my misery. There were flings. A tall and brilliant Russian man I'd had a brief, intense relationship with years earlier came to town on business, and we drank red wine in a bizarre Airbnb under the gaze of its owner's mask collection and had dinner and then tender this-is-what-could-have-been sex in a small, dark bedroom. There was the beautiful, frustrated academic with a penchant for Bushmills and Southern sludge metal. The drug dealer. The chef. It was like dating bingo. Not K, not K, not K, not K: that was the only real criterion.

You deserve to have some fun! I told myself. But it mostly wasn't. The work of getting to know someone, even briefly, felt both exhilarating and perfectly pointless. I emerged from these trysts the way one does from a long conversation on a transatlantic flight: refreshed, yet ten minutes later disorientingly incapable of remembering a single detail about the person whose life story you just heard, at whom you nodded so vigorously, *mmhmm*-ing in solidarity for hours. Where was it he said he was going? What does he do for a

living? And wasn't there something important about a brother, or
was it a son?

Fortunately, sex often felt just like when I was younger. A vigor-
ous diversion. And not just sex itself, but its lazy aftermath. The
sumptuous pleasure of stretching out into the freedom of my own
home like a corpulent cat. That hadn't been ruined, not by marriage
or divorce or children or depression. As it turned out, it was all still
just right there for the taking. You only had to be selfish and crazy
enough to reach out and grab it, to fondle its balls. I enjoyed getting
up to pee and returning to my room to find in it not the same body
I'd been fucking and fighting with for years, but a new slab of humanity. Someone happy to see me, who pulled me back into bed,
who lit a joint for me. Someone who wanted to impress me. Why
shouldn't I be impressed. *So, love was dead—so what?* I thought.
Lust, happily, was not. The sharp, hormone-rich aroma of someone
else's armpits filled the air of my apartment and it felt like sweet
revenge. It also broke my heart a little, but very little.

When people asked me about K, I replied with seriousness, *He's
dying.* Occasionally I found myself saying what I really meant: *I
hope he dies.*

.   .   .

During this period, K was gone but not gone. I heard from him occasionally and he was how he was: funny, regretful, angry, confused.
We treated the dissolution of our relationship as something both
tragic and ineluctable. Just like the beginning of the relationship, it
didn't feel like a choice we'd made or could unmake. I got used to it
after a month or so. It wasn't like the days right after he left, when
every clap of thunder or flicker of light startled me, made my eyes
dart nervously around like a dense babysitter in a horror movie,
as though he was about to reappear. Now I just casually heard his
voice in my own voice, as I made jokes that sounded like his, and felt
surges of him like ocean waves in my body, in the atmosphere.

He had competing narratives: that he was dying alone in a room
at his mother's house, and that he was painting the town, meeting
people, working, moving and shaking, dating. We still saw each

other occasionally. I would make the drive out to the suburbs after work, talk with his mother in the kitchen for a while, the same hushed conversations, the two of us, both expert at this role, making our folk prognoses. I'd watch TV with him in his room for a while like he was a patient in a hospital. He was growing fatter and bloated, trying to kill himself with alcohol and drugs. *I look like a monster, I know,* he said once as I sat on the edge of his bed, probably looking sad.

You've looked better, I said.

Wow, he laughed, *that's very honest for you, Pimentoloaf. I've never heard you say anything like that. Good for you.*

I laughed. *Please don't die,* I said.

Oh, honey, he said. *That's the sick joke of it all. I'll probably live to be a hundred. And really have decades to soak in this breakup.*

If you want to try to stop, I'm here, I said.

I know, he said. *Wanna watch a* Chopped?

.   .   .

Eventually, I met a good one. Josh, a kind, good-looking, successful man with a softness in his eyes and just enough mystery to be interesting, but not enough to make me wonder if he was bullshitting me. He owned his own house and a big, beautiful dog whose anxious, bounding joy and loyalty to him seemed to be harbingers of good.

He took me to a bar I'd never been to and let me drive his nice new car afterward. I was drunk, and weaved downhill to his house feeling unhinged, like he would have let me do anything at all, high on the power of being hot. We fucked against the butcher block in his kitchen and then I excused myself and threw up. Once, I sent him a text message with a red heart and a black heart at the end, and he began adding the two hearts in that order to the end of a lot of his messages, particularly if they were romantic or involved making plans. I understood instinctively that mine was the black heart. His was red: pulsing brightly and healthily, ready for love. He was a gentle soul. He once worried aloud that he wasn't enough of a "bad boy" for me. He wanted to meet my kids. Over the course of a few weeks, he did more for me in the way of practical assistance than K had in the entirety of our relationship. He was a love-is-an-action-verb problem-solver, who noticed my refrigerator door was broken and swiftly fixed it the next time he came over, with a replacement part and tools he'd brought from home. He bought me small gifts. He talked about the future. Once, as I was writing on a deadline from his bed, he came in and said he was going to run out and get us some dinner.

You don't have to do that, I said.

I know, he said. *I'm hungry. Aren't you hungry?*

Yeah, I said. *But you don't have to go all the way out. I'm sure there's something here I can make for us when I'm done.*

He looked at me like I was an alien. *It's just dinner,* he said. *You get so weird anytime I do anything for you. It kind of freaks me out.*

It kind of freaked me out, too, how uncomfortable his easy affection and care was, how even as I appreciated it, it made me squirm like a bug under a magnifying glass. When he left to get food that night, I opened the diary on my computer and wrote, "Lying on Josh's bed finishing some work. He went to get dinner. It's calm, quiet, clean, Conway Twitty playing and the sound of the dog licking peanut butter out of a toy. Remember this feeling. Your life could be this peaceful if you let it."

.   .   .

I didn't tell him when my period was late, and a week later, I ended the relationship. We were supposed to take a trip together. We had begun to make those kinds of plans, but every day the pressure of being with someone like Josh—someone good, who was actually paying attention, whose antennae were focused intently on detecting my signals—felt more overwhelming. I felt less suited to it, paralyzed by it. Even as we were breaking up, he was so present and honest, he revealed so many of his own feelings with such disarming clarity. But ever since breaking up with K, my body's response to a display of male feelings was akin to the unleashing of histamines after exposure to an allergen. I couldn't take it. I was curt. I said, *I'm not ready,* all the things people say.

The morning after we broke up, I peed on a stick and found out I was pregnant—with another globule, a not-yet-lentil-sized bundle of cells that I would have to send back to the seas, the stars, the sky. Where do souls go? If one even inhered in this miniscule mass. I pictured it: a bloody seed.

I wrote it down in my diary: *I am pregnant.* It looked as heavy as it felt. *I feel like a Gauguin,* I wrote. *My tiny breasts have acquired an awkwardly triangular, 2-D flop. They're sore, stuck haphazardly on my increasingly square body. I feel rooted, fat, pathetic.* I knew immediately that I wouldn't tell Josh. I wanted to, but it wouldn't be fair. He was too invested, too smitten. The pregnancy would be something to bind us, bond us, a reason or an opportunity for him to show up. I dreaded an abortion, but not more than I feared Josh appearing on my doorstep and insisting we go through something together. Worse still, he might try to get me to think about it differently. I could imagine him holding my hands, fixing me in his good-guy gaze, and saying, *We could do this, Nina.* And we could have.

No, I had no time for tenderness. I had to get to the hospital and blot out the possibility of a life, of more motherhood, another detour into dowdy obsolescence, sleep-deprivation-induced psychosis. I didn't need a gooey, soft-hearted *partner,* I just needed a ride to the clinic. Only one person I knew could carry it off with the requisite cynicism, nonjudgment, a little dark humor sprinkled like stolen Splenda into the tall cold glass of sorrow I was about to drink. Fuck tenderness—I wanted Doctor Death. Before I called K, I texted him.

ME: *I need you.*
K: *I need you too*
ME: *Hi*
K: *Hiii*
ME: *No like i need ur help*
K: *Oh ok. i got u*
ME: *thank u*
K: *anything for u pimentoloaf. what is it?*
ME: *it's better to talk about in person*

K: *come over then. but i'm not in great shape, i warn you*
ME: *that's okay. we can talk about that. or not. i'll be over later, after work*

Anything for me, I guffawed, from the privacy of my own bed. K loved such proclamations, loved them so much more than the daily work of love, than making the coffee or taking the dog out to pee. After work, I gathered my belongings, which always seemed voluminous and unwieldy at day's end like I'd been living at the office, and drove out to his mother's house, where he was camped out in the small bedroom that I knew every inch of. I could picture his exact positioning on the bed, the only place in the room to sit. I had missed this slow, long drive from my office in the city in rush-hour traffic all the way to the suburbs, with a seltzer in the console and loud music I could sing along to. I loved driving and I loved the suburbs and other people's moms, the brief respite from responsibility I'd enjoyed so many times as K's mother unloaded a recent Costco haul and fed me. That day, I stopped at the liquor store on the way like I used to and bought a cheap bottle of white table wine and a bag of Cheetos. I prepared to see K and to enlist his help.

. . .

It's strange to be here for me and not for him, I think, as we take our seats in the hospital waiting room. Three times we've sat in the ER, waiting to be seen for his abscesses. The nurses with clipboards would shuffle around in medical scrubs and Crocs. They would say things about insurance that he wasn't listening to. I listened. When they asked certain questions, he let a silence hang in the air until I stepped in and answered.

While we waited, K would ask me to take a photo of him, for posterity or sympathy or social media. There was something amusing to him about his own suffering. Ever since he'd had cancer in his twenties, he'd treated his own life cavalierly. I joked that it didn't matter, he'd been granted nine lives. *Isn't that sad?* he said. *You know so many good people and I'm the one who's going to live the longest.*

Now, in the sterility and brightness of the hospital, amid corporate signage promoting the hegemonic wellness imagery of active, bright-toothed families throwing Frisbees in blurred green parks, K looks extra Other. Extra punk, extra grim, extra tragic. He looks like he both belongs and doesn't belong here. He looks like a street person, like someone who ends up in a hospital, but also like someone who doesn't fit in, here or anywhere. I thought this about him the sicker he got, the farther from the straight world of doctors and nurses and other normal people. He dwelled in a permanent exile.

Usually, after a trip to the hospital for an abscess, we argued. Before my anger could sediment, it had to bubble over, be spit forth like lava. I hated feeling responsible for him but not being able to rely on him. There was no reciprocity. *What would happen if I got sick?* I hissed. *What if I needed you?*

Do you honestly think you couldn't rely on me if you were sick? he said, sounding affronted.

You have nothing, I said. *You have no resources. You have no money. No, I don't think I could rely on you. I can't rely on you. Look around—I don't rely on you for fucking anything. If something happened to me, I would be completely fucked.*

But here we are, a damp spring day. I'm filling out paperwork at the check-in station while he sits in a chair in the waiting room. I keep thinking I should have worn drawstring pants, something more akin to pajamas—athleisure wear, all the rage—instead of tight jeans. I imagine the thick, rough menstrual pad I will have to situate bulkily into my underwear before we can leave this place, and the thinner pads I will buy at the drugstore afterward, the kind with wings that I have only worn after births and other gynecological traumas like this one. I will have to button my pants gingerly, ease the button through the hole with my fingernail, trying to suck in but not being able to in the bloated aftermath.

And you have a ride home after the procedure? the woman at the desk asks.

Yes, I reply.

And where is that person? she asks.

I point to K. He is sitting fifteen feet away, looking at his phone.

He looks especially bedraggled, a bit grimy in the face, his greasy hair—still majestic, now streaked gorgeously with grey—is hidden beneath a beanie. Couldn't he at least take his hat off? The hair has the power to sway public opinion. He has tucked his chin into his windbreaker and is chewing on the zipper. He seems to notice us looking in his direction and looks up. His eyes have that darting, beady quality. I can picture the slick wet of his pupils like spilled inkpots. I look back at the woman checking me in. Her expression hasn't changed, her fingernails are clack-clacking over the keyboard and I know she doesn't give a shit but I have a strong urge to say, *It's not his*. A desire not to seem like the kind of person who would get knocked up by a guy like him.

In the waiting room, I return to my seat to wait for my name, like the woman told me to. K takes my hand and lays it in his, face up, like a dead bird. The awkwardness of the waiting area closes in—its maroon-and-grey-patterned carpeting, its modular ersatz walls and colorless lighting, a scattering of elderly Asian couples who cannot be here for the same thing I'm here for.

Senior discount day at the abortion clinic? K mutters quietly just as I notice the demographics of the place, and I smile with half of my mouth.

It's a good thing, I say, my voice sounding jagged with anxiety. *It means they're treating this like any other medical procedure, which is exactly how it should be treated. I mean, that's what it is. I assume these people are here for other*— I meet his eyes and catch him sizing me up, hearing the escalating panic in my voice, his mouth softening in a minute gesture of sympathy that immediately knocks me off-kilter. He takes my other hand so he is holding them both and he clasps them between his two giant hands like Beauty and the Beast.

I know I said this last night, he begins in a low, gentle voice.

Don't, I say, feeling a lump rising in my throat.

If you want to have this baby, he goes on, *even if you go back there and you decide you want to have this baby*—

No, don't, I say again, shaking my head, beginning to cry.

I'm there, that's all I'm saying. If you can't . . . do this. We've done the baby thing—we could do it no problem.

Yeah, it wasn't a big deal at all, that whole baby thing. I laugh, wiping snot on the sleeve of my sweatshirt.

Well, we fucking pulled it off, he says.

I eye him.

You, he corrects. *You pulled it off. Because you can do anything. You're amazing.*

I know that it's a real possibility that I could decide not to do it even right before I do it, that I could sit up in the hospital bed and declare that I've changed my mind. That may seem like a comfort to him. It doesn't feel comforting to me—it only exacerbates my anxiety to think of this decision as active or incomplete. To think that I've taken the insurance-mandated, in-office pregnancy test, slept like shit for a week, made it all the way here, filled out the paperwork, and that still a crisis of conscience might loom in my immediate future. I just wanted the certainty of it being done, over. There would simply be a moment beyond which it would be final. The chance for that particular life could never be recovered. I just had to get to that moment.

But I let myself imagine it again, as I had for days. One last time, I picture keeping it. The tiny hand wrapped around my finger. The heat of the BabyBjörn as I sway back and forth. I remember K holding my baby girl above his head, bringing her nose down to touch his nose in an Eskimo kiss, setting off her inimitable trill of a giggle, the same one she still has.

No, I would not invite another life into this scene. Another baby, this one belonging to someone I scarcely knew, to be raised by me with my ever-deepening under-eye circles, the gusts of air that blow my nightgown out around my legs as I resentfully tear into the kitchen to rinse the bottles. It takes a lot of resentment to whoosh through my house: it's a small space. K would be where, couchbound in his dirty jeans? Watching television and drinking from an extra-large glass of iced tea? *Maybe this would get him sober,* I find myself thinking, and I actually have to shake the thought—the delusional, insane thought—out of my brain.

I am going through with it, I say decisively, looking past him, over his shoulder to a panel of windows that lead to a courtyard of some sort that isn't even outside. It's still part of the medical facility, one of those echo-y terra-cotta-tiled inside/outside spaces where built-in potted plants and an information desk sit awkwardly side by side.

Well then, we'll tuck you into bed with a rom-com and I'll go get wonton soup, he says. *I have to run another errand quickly, too. I know I said—*

Hey—I interrupt him, holding my hands up to my chin as if in prayer. *I don't care if you get high,* I say. *I meant that. I don't care anymore. Just come back and be with me.*

At the end of this is a bad movie and wonton soup, I think. I try to relax into that, but feel myself tighten remembering the contours of K's care, thinking that he'll need my car and my credit card in order to procure the Advil, the curative soup—no act of altruism is independent for him. No act of generosity pure frill, he is here—sitting beside me assuring me that any decision I make will be okay, that he would raise a stranger's baby with me. I appreciate him so much. I also know this is not enough. Not right. I think about Josh and wonder if he will go by himself on the trip we'd planned. I picture him crestfallen, contemplative, alone. I think about the fact that he probably thinks he has it pretty rough at the moment. He has no idea where I am and what I am about to have to do. The life of a healthy bachelor is so staggeringly easy it is stupefying.

I feel a wash of deep gratitude as I'm led by a nurse out of the waiting room, away from the check-in lady, away from K, back into the linoleum ring of rooms where I'll be granted the fog of a mild sedative and this impossible pregnancy will be ended. After the procedure, K comes back into the room where I'm lying lightly drugged and smiles when he sees me. He stands next to me and the nurse who has brought him draws the curtain to give us some privacy. *You always look like a little girl when you're in here,* he says, and when I faintly smile I feel the largeness of my face, a puffy deliberateness to the movements of my cheeks. The look on his face is the one he gets when, during an argument, I start crying from some deep, unsettling place and he goes entirely soft. He looks at me sweetly. His scruffy face makes him look tired. Even his facial hair is beginning to go grey, and he looks like a man who has lived a hard life, who "has put a lot of mileage on the car," as he would say.

When have you ever seen me in here? I ask.

I don't know, you sent me a photo before your eye surgery, he says. *Remember that one crazy dilated eye? I had that on my phone forever.*

I smile weakly, turning my head toward him more and he takes my hand. *Yeah, but you weren't actually there,* I think. *You were never there.*

I do feel like a little girl with my skinny limbs tucked into the soft printed cotton of the hospital gown. But as soon as I'm back in my clothes, I am a woman again, a grown woman who will glaze over while watching a week's worth of television in one night, who will well with emotion for months longer, weighing the choice she's just made, wondering what one more baby might have been like, might have looked like, might have felt like with its gummy mouth against her skin. I am, at least, a woman with a man to drive her home. I lean my weight into K a little and he guides me toward the door, the car, our bed. *If you're going to let yourself need him, just need him,* I tell myself. *He can show up this once.*

For the rest of that day and the following day he takes care of me. He gets the soup and tea and all the other snacks I like and three rolls of SweeTarts and makes a nest for me on the couch, cozier than anything he would make for himself. He used to sleep on that couch beneath a single sheet and I would want to manage and control even that. *Aren't you cold?* I'd say. *How can you sleep like that?* He knows I'm cold, always, so he brings the duvet from my bed and another light blanket to go on top of it, like I like.

Can't even imagine how many dicks have touched this thing since we broke up, he says as he brings the comforter up and then down on my head like he used to for the kids, tucking in the corners around my body.

Oh, shut up, I say. *This isn't really the time.*

Oops, right. Sorry, m'lady, he says, tucking me into the second blanket. *I'll be back with your seltzer.*

He gets up to go to the liquor store, to go shoot up, he borrows the car to go buy more, and for the first time in years, I feel nothing. No sense of panic or fear of abandonment. No rage. My body feels like an empty cavity. I imagine that I have been scooped clean, disinfected somehow. These years of rot, of toxicity.

I will never change him, I think. His greying beard, the slackening in his not-sober, never-sober, and still-beautiful face. He is only a person, like me, trying to survive. When he returns and settles back into the fort of fabric and snacks, I set my mug down on the coffee table, then reach for him and say, *I love you.*

He moves closer and lays his head on my shoulder and I feel the minor exertions of his breathing against my collarbone.

It's you, Pimentoloaf, he says. *It's always been you.*

chapter thirty

"**S**erenity is giving up the hope of a different past," says someone in my Tuesday night Al-Anon meeting. I take out my pink notebook, a gift from Claire (how many notebooks and nice pens have we given each other over the years, how many do all girls give to other girls, so that we might facilitate one another's truth-telling, might imagine we will one day write it all down and find catharsis there?), and I write it down, along with all the other corny slogans that have by now, in the corniest of all possible conclusions, accumulated to actually alter my thinking, to begin to change my life. "Happiness is an inside job," I have written. My mother-in-law's line, which I could only hear as smug until I really needed it. "In recovery, we let go of burdens that were not ours to carry." And "You didn't cause it; you can't control it; you can't cure it." And I jot down my favorite, one I had never heard before until a fellow Al-Anon pointed it out in our group binder: "If you're eating a shit sandwich, it's probably because you ordered it."

When I was ready to go back, worn down and exhausted, it was all still there. The coffee, the placards, the unsettling warm welcomes, the cardigan-clad knitters, although now they are young, pierced, and tattooed. It can be harder for codependents to hit "rock bottom" than it is for addicts. Often, there are few material consequences for our actions. Our lives fall into a devastating psychic, emotional, and spiritual disrepair—the "epidemic of wasted life" the doctors wrote about—but it may not be obvious. As with a chronic pain disorder, the suffering is typically invisible. Our expertise, after all, is in enduring and managing hardship, not showing what we're going through. Rock bottom for me did not feel like the end of the line, as I'd imagined it would, a moment when I'd run out of hope or options. I'd tried Al-Anon in those moments before, and it hadn't quite worked enough or meant enough to me to stay. This time it was, rather, a droplet of curiosity, only possible to register once K and I had split, about who I might be without the albatross of others' addictions. Into the hollowness where he had been, one small bead of wonder collected about what a day might feel like, how I might spend my time.

I had by then come to understand that people-pleasing extended far beyond my most intimate relationships. It was evident in the way I took on too much at work, the way I came to someone's rescue even in conversation, trying to fix and smooth, laughing a little too loudly or too long. The way I would always say, *Yes, I would love to come to your poetry reading, baby shower, birthday party*, even though I wasn't sure it was true. I overpromised and underdelivered. I dodged responsibilities and issued breathless apologies that left no room for response or repair. Like alcoholism, codependency is, at its core, a form of insincerity, of bullshit. And it feels terrible to be insincere.

I went back to meetings and began to read the Al-Anon literature again. It wasn't perfect, and some of the program's literature—specifically admonitions to behave mildly and with restraint—feel woefully outdated. For example, the informational brochure given to newcomers in Al-Anon has a handy bookmark inside it, a list of things the Al-Anon member vows to do "Just for Today," like take things one day at a time, spend a half hour alone, focus on happiness. "Just for Today," it still reads, "I will be agreeable. I will look as well as I can, dress becomingly, keep my voice low, be courteous, criticize not one bit. I won't find fault with anything, nor try to improve or regulate anybody but myself." I hated finding lines like these in the literature. But I believed in its heart, in a strength to be found underneath my skepticism.

None of this crystallized, however, until I did the even harder thing, which was to get sober myself. That happened unexpectedly. I flew east for Claire's wedding and made a toast in a long camel-colored dress and bright red lipstick. I spent five days among people I adore, drinking without ever managing to get properly drunk. Instead, I felt bleary, blurry, bloated, disconnected. I wondered at my own apartness. I wondered, too, whether the kind of happiness that my friend had found with an especially warm, wonderful, dependable person could ever be possible for me. Could love feel like that? Something solid that you know will be there? It was as though alcohol had stopped working, or my self-hatred was finally strong enough to counteract its effects. On that trip, I woke in the mornings vowing to myself that I wouldn't drink, but each afternoon I was drinking again. I even drank on the plane ride home and, close to the heavens, said a prayer I thought someone might hear. *Please help me feel better than this.* When the plane landed in California, I decided to try sobriety again.

Drying out felt just like what it is: becoming more crisp, attenuated, economical. The taut electrified string of my own attention felt at times like a high of its own. To be able to think, focus, notice emotion: I didn't know how strong those sensations could be. I also got sad. I got bored. I began to clean out some of my closets and drawers. But I was newly alive in all the ways the addiction memoirs I've read over the years said I'd be. A little surly, newly tender, frequently brought up short by an uneasy sense of wonder.

The shift that took place in my thinking was subtle at first, and it hurt. It felt uncomfortable, physically rough like sitting on a pile of rocks. In Al-Anon, people are often struggling not to act—not to immediately seize upon a situation and try to manipulate it or fix it or exert control over it. Not to hide, lie, or manipulate. Another slogan: "Don't just do something, sit there."

We repeat these simple slogans incessantly, but it's because they don't always get through. They can't when our brains are buzzing or when we're still caught up in feeling sorry for ourselves. If you hear them enough times, they are bound to stick one day, to catch you off guard with their usefulness, their depth. They remind you, at least, how many others have been through it. In the silence and stillness we learn to be alone, we learn to listen to ourselves, and we learn humility. The surge of confidence we felt while thinking we knew what was right for everyone else was actually arrogance, the cheap high of self-righteousness. Also like a drug, it's surprisingly hard to put down.

Nothing about my struggle has been unique. I can see that so clearly now. The singularity I ascribed to my feelings for K was both real (in that I felt it) and a delusion. The thought is painful. Could any two souls, any alcoholic and codependent, have collided and produced this exact tragedy? Probably. Like the monkeys locked in a room who eventually write Shakespeare. The grief over the end of the relationship is nothing compared with the mourning I must do for the thing I long believed to be love. Breaking up with that love fantasy is what brings me to my knees. I still grieve for the dyad— that desperation, obsession, distraction. I grieve for the belief, nurtured against all odds, that I could save my sister or K. I really did believe I could save K. But a man is not a house. You may be able to carry out small renovations, but you can't re-pour the foundation.

As one of the women in *Women Who Love Too Much* says, "I kept hoping I could find someone who would make my life turn out the way I wanted it to." I still pine for the perfect logic of that victimhood. I remember the torment of some of those years with K as a time so abjectly lonely and raw that I am nostalgic for it. I felt hummingly, almost dangerously alive. To believe that it was only a matter of finding the right person—I miss being that naïve. I miss the simplicity of that worldview, of being that poor put-upon girl. She had it so rough, and with no one to rescue her properly. So many tried, but none got it right. I miss that victim but I had to let her go. I had to let even the idea of her go.

I believe the way we tell stories about addiction matters deeply— it informs the way we act, from the level of public health discourse to the kitchen table. It informs the degree of empathy we can bring to those suffering with this disease, the extent to which we can protect ourselves from its destruction and embrace living in spite of it. And it shapes the way we understand love and care—what can be justly expected of us, and when it has gone too far.

At first, though I hear myself in what other Al-Anon members say, and though I am vaguely comforted when I leave the church and head toward my car—a certain feeling of pleasant solitude that takes hold as I mull all the personal information they've just lobbed into the room—I still question how it can be applied to real life. My real life. Still, I go. Once during every meeting, some stranger is briefly graced with a kind of genius tuned perfectly to that day's need in me. I still don't, can't believe in God, so I just believe in that—that when I show up, some lightning bolt of essential, tailored wisdom is delivered directly to me, piped right into my ears. It may as well have my name on it.

I find I don't know how to share in the open-ended way that certain others are able to, to take up space with a mumbling, meandering comment about what's transpired in my week. The few times I do speak up in a meeting, I curate my thoughts carefully beforehand, making sure there's a narrative arc to what I'm going to say, a few small self-deprecating comments for laughs, a point to make. Even the emotion I submit to a support group must demand little of others.

Embedded within so much self-help literature is the notion that a more real version of yourself is buried beneath some emotional rubble. Your "true self" is there to be found and treasured, under all the hurt and pain and damage. The genesis of the concept of codependency is so bound up with our American thinking about the power of the individual, and the "true self" makes sense in this context. Substance abuse recovery as we are most likely to experience it is just a set of concepts, developed in a particular time and place. The heterosexual couple is at its center: a broken man whose wounds must be healed so that he can return to the helm of the nuclear family, to the role of the self-reliant breadwinner, and an angry woman who should make even her rage productive, knead it into the bread dough, so that she might forgive him and restore peace to her marriage and her home.

I haven't wanted to uncover or to recover anything and I haven't experienced my path to greater peace this way. After so many years clinging in fear to various identities, I prefer to think of the space of me as empty space, the way I did on the couch with K, freshly vacuumed out, with the hope of him changing, getting better, finally stilled. Once and for all. A moment of no hope and no future. Of perfect acceptance. Recovering implies a doubling back, a recuperation, but my path away from destruction has not entailed a recovering of anything. Everything is new.

For a long time, I believed that if I took care of myself, I would necessarily, organically move farther away from others. In the binary logic of individualism, you fortify the self at the expense of the other. But in filling the empty space of me, I have found that actually the complete opposite is true. The more I love myself, the more my heart opens, the more present and sensitive I become, so much so it hurts.

Frequently while driving, I reach my hand into the back seat and make a "gimme" motion with my fingers, just like my mother used to. My daughter lays her hand in mine and I smooth her small knuckles with my thumb. I hold her hand and then my son's. Both are clammy, soft, utterly trusting. My son lifts my hand to his face to nuzzle against it or give me a gentle kiss. I do short then long squeezes, twice, then three times, and they squeeze back the same pattern. We've always done this, but I don't know that my clutching always made them feel as safe as it does now. Perhaps it felt more frantic those hungover mornings in the back seat; perhaps they thought I needed something from them. My love for my children has always been fierce and it has always fed me, which is why I thought I was a pretty good mom even when I was drinking, even when I was with K. I was doing my best with the tools I had. But now that I have better tools, I know that I am a good mom, maybe a great one, and the comfort in that is profound. I think about the fact that they can now trust me entirely, the way I trusted my mother—to be even and reliable, to be awake and alert, to live with integrity—and a sense of fullness spreads through my chest, warm as whiskey.

I feared I would become less fun in recovery. What a relief it has been to discover that the fun wasn't alcohol or drugs, it wasn't me being crazy: it was just me. We still dance in the kitchen to The Go-Go's and The Marvelettes. We do a pretend cooking show, try to beat the timer as it runs down, one of us stirring, one pouring, one plating. My daughter tells me she's learned to sing "Lean on Me" in her school choral group, so I put on Bill Withers and we sing it together and tears fill my eyes. My daughter tilts her head compassionately in these moments and says, *Mommy, you don't have to CRY,* which makes me cry more. I am awed daily by these rewards of recovery. Nothing flashy—all small, contained everyday moments like lights on a string. The rewards of a well-tended life: the clean new house bursting with plants, the dog their father and I rescued all those years ago now grey-haired and snoring in her bed, and this book, almost finished. So many meals together where we share our rose, thorn, and seed: the best part of our day, the worst, and something we're looking forward to. *What is romance anyway if not this?* I find myself thinking. Nothing feels more romantic to me now than believing I deserve this joy, this love. The one it turned out I was looking for all along. By the grace of some god or goddess or the ocean or the moon or dumb luck, we have survived this monstrous disease for now.

I can't let go of everything, all my old ways. For me, recovery, the filling of the empty space of me, is not a renunciation of dependency. Love is still my drug, the potent intoxicant I believe gives our lives their meaning. And the relationships of dependency I enjoy on this planet—with this planet, with books, with the incredible people in my life, and especially with my children—are still what give me purpose. The thing I have renounced, have tried to set down once and for all, is suffering. Unnecessary pain. A belief system that conflates misery with authenticity. I discovered that I could stop obsessing, stop controlling, stop victimizing myself. I only had to want to, to sit down and learn how. I remind my sponsees of the poster that John Lennon and Yoko Ono made in the 1960s to protest the escalation of the Vietnam War that read "WAR IS OVER! (IF YOU WANT IT)." It ought to hang wherever the Twelve Steps go.

The rain comes and goes but the Bay Area cold still lives in my bones. All ten fingers never warm. On Tuesdays, I stand outside the church basement entrance and wave to the people coming in, the ones who want the kind of life I want now, whose stories I have been following for nearly two years. I hold the door open for one of them, a young woman in her twenties whose girlfriend is a violent drunk. When she looks up to acknowledge me, I see that she has tears in her eyes already. Inside, I pour the shitty coffee into my cup and sit down in the least creaky pew.

acknowledgments

Thank you first and foremost to my family, who let themselves be written about and showed nothing but love. You continue to prove we are unsinkable.

Thank you to my parents for imparting a lifetime love of words. To my mother—my North Star—who reminds me to also write my joy. To my father, for steadily keeping the beat and for always listening. To my sisters: you complete me. Thank you for being the funniest people who have ever lived and for your unflagging belief in me. To Leah, for living to fight another day with grit and grace and for turning it into art with me. To Alexa, the other half of my black-and-white cookie, for understanding me in ways people only dream about.

Thank you to Sylvia Yules. To the Brauns, Arons, and Lermans. To Deanna Steele, Beth Holland, Jersey Lynch, and especially Zac Judkins and Erica Nagel for all their support.

To Elise Herrala, my forever first editor and rom-com costar, who was there at all hours and who read every word at every stage, from the very first sentences, which dropped from the sky in the middle of the desert.

To my first loves: Beth Blofson, Ryan Hawke, Medb Marsceill.

My grrrls, my heart. Keepers of my memories. I would hardly have any idea who I am without you.

To Tai Power Seeff for our love everlasting, for too-late nights, cemetery walks, and coupons.

To Tre Wallace for being a rock, my favorite bookworm, and an endless source of comfort.

To Carvell Wallace, the most reliable source of wisdom I know.

Thank you to Flip Brophy for always telling me I could do this and for calling to make me laugh throughout the whole painful process. To Jim Rutman, interlocutor extraordinaire, for your expertise and for engaging with my ideas—good, bad, and ugly—over all these many years.

To my editor, Alexis Washam, who got it from the very beginning and who has shown this book such care. To Jillian Buckley, your knowledge is deep and your enthusiasm contagious. To Gwyneth Stansfield, Melissa Esner, Julie Cepler, Dyana Messina, Nicole Ramirez, Anna Kochman, Annsley Rosner, and everyone at Crown who helped bring this to life. Thank you to Louisa Dunnigan at Profile Books and Jason Richman at United Talent Agency.

To the friends who read this book in drafts for their brilliant, funny, and, above all, useful commentary: Brian Gallagher, Anna Godbersen, Melissa Richer, Laura Smith, Yael Stiles, and Diana Thow. You kept me going and made this book better.

To Nora Reilly, Jessica Egan, and Christopher Roebuck for answering research questions.

To loved ones near and far who light up my mind, and who have too many gifts to begin to count: Ryan Calder, Ethan Hawke, Ben Dickey, Patrick Marsceill, Cal Light, Lindsay Leopold, Kara Urion, Rebekah Witzke, Mary Beth Keane, Rian Dundon, Charlotte Buchen Khadra, Zachary Levenson, Rahfee Barber, Lawrence Barth, JR Geisler, Yael Gottlieb, Lia and Felicia Halloran, Michael Weber, Summer Brenner, Gloria Frym, Patricia Kubala, Leila Nichols, Rachel Goldman, Robin Meyerhoff and Michael Ryan, Ariana Wolf, Hall McCann, Judy Zinis, James Spooner, Lisa Nola, and my sisters in rock: Rachel Sager Sales, Kristy Morrison, and Christie Call.

Thank you to Teresa Sabatini and Tracy Helton Mitchell. To Lilly Gage for freedom and time. To Felicia Keller-Boyle for wisdom beyond.

To K: there are no words.

And finally, to Emmett & Iona Mae, my brightest lights, true loves of my life. You are the key to the map of my existence. Thank you for showing me who I can be.

GOOD MORNING, MORNING, DESTROYER OF MEN'S SOULS

Nina Renata Aron

Random
House
Book Club

Because
Stories Are
Better Shared

™

A BOOK CLUB GUIDE

Questions and Topics for Discussion

1. Addiction—particularly male addiction—is often glamorized or venerated in literature and popular culture. Do you think that there is a kind of cultural fascination with addiction and addicts? Is this part of what draws Nina to K? If so, in what way?

2. Nina Renata Aron observes that "our cultural view of female addicts has long been dim, to say the least," while addicted men are often given a pass or even celebrated as "tormented" geniuses (both p. 188). What cultural factors might contribute to this difference in treatment? Do you see any of those factors at play in Aron's life?

3. How does Aron link the temperance movement and the rise of feminism in the United States? Why do you think the two are so closely intertwined, and why has the contribution of temperance women been "dwarfed" (p. 82) by that of suffragists in the historical account?

4. Aron notes that as a child, she "often played the role of another parent in our unfolding family saga" (p. 39). How might that dynamic have impacted her relationships as an adult?

5. Aron feels that she "made a better mistress than a wife," the true "have to have" lover as opposed to a wife who "is leftovers in the fridge" (p. 140). What factors might have contributed to her feeling this way? How might these elements have affected her marriage?

6. Aron associates true love with darkness and danger: "tumult" (p. 124), "obsession" and "mad flower" (both p. 177), something "a little bit evil" (p. 171). What factors might have contributed to this perception? Do you agree with these connotations?

7. Why do you think K fails to invite friends and then leaves the housewarming party in chapter 23? Is there more to his actions than his assertion that he and his friends weren't *really into sh*t like this* (p. 205)?

8. For Aron, a quote from temperance crusader Carrie Nation—"I represent the distracted, suffering, loving motherhood of the World, who, becoming aroused with a righteous fury rebelled at this torture"—contains "the whole of the codependent experience" (pp. 166–67). What do you think Aron means by drawing this comparison? What are some contemporary parallels between the early temperance movement and the current conversation around codependency?

9. Throughout the book, Aron is shot through with opposing tensions—a yearning for a more "normal" life (p. 90) and her tendency to create "the chaos I lived in" (p. 131); and her modern feminist ideal of autonomous, individual fulfillment and the bonds of romantic and familial love. How do you think factors like upbringing, culture, self-perception, and motherhood might have contributed to these tensions? What other external factors might have created this opposition in her life, and how might they have impacted the nature of her codependency?

Recommended Listening

What follows is a list of songs that Nina Renata Aron recommends that readers listen to while reading *Good Morning, Destroyer of Men's Souls*.

"Over" • Alice Boman
"You Are the Sunshine of My Life" • Chokebore
"Days of Nothing" • Chokebore
"Get Well" • Nothing
"A Night in the Nursery" • Jonathan Fire*Eater
"Half-Lit" • Single Mothers
"Let Me Come Back" • Girls Against Boys
"They Live by Night" • The Make-Up
"What She Said" • The Smiths
"Axemen" • Heavens to Betsy
"Twisting the Knife" • Sorcha Richardson
"Parallels" • Big Knife
"Tonight" • Sibylle Baier
"Anteroom" • EMA
"Needle in the Hay" • Elliott Smith
"Whiskey Sour" • Molly Nilsson
"Sisters" • Cate Le Bon
"Harsh Realm" • Widowspeak
"Spill Yer Lungs" • Julie Doiron
"Swoon" • Tanya Donelly
"Aspirin Kid" • The Nation of Ulysses
"Send Him Back" • The Pointer Sisters
"Lust to Love" • The Go-Go's
"Feels Blind" • Bikini Kill
"Try a Little Tenderness" • Otis Redding
"Nothing But a Heartache" • The Flirtations

"Reel Around the Fountain" • The Smiths

"Only Love Can Break Your Heart" • Saint Etienne

"(Sittin' On) The Dock of the Bay" • Otis Redding

"Close to Me" • The Cure

"Speed Trials" • Elliott Smith

"Cigarettes and Coffee" • Otis Redding

"Miss Misery" • Elliott Smith

"White Flag" • Jay Som

"Please Mr. Postman" • The Marvelettes

"Lean on Me" • Bill Withers

"The Hunter Gets Captured by the Game" • The Marvelettes

about the author

NINA RENATA ARON is a writer and editor living in Oakland, California. Her work has appeared in *The New York Times*, *The New Republic*, the *Los Angeles Review of Books*, and elsewhere.

This book was set in Sabon, a typeface designed by the well-known German typographer Jan Tschichold (1902–74). Sabon's design is based upon the original letter forms of sixteenth-century French type designer Claude Garamond and was created specifically to be used for three sources: foundry type for hand composition, Linotype, and Monotype. Tschichold named his typeface for the famous Frankfurt typefounder Jacques Sabon (c. 1520–80).

RANDOM HOUSE BOOK CLUB

Because Stories Are Better Shared

Discover

Exciting new books that spark conversation every week.

Connect

With authors on tour—or in your living room. (Request an Author Chat for your book club!)

Discuss

Stories that move you with fellow book lovers on Facebook, on Goodreads, or at in-person meet-ups.

Enhance

Your reading experience with discussion prompts, digital book club kits, and more, available on our website.

Join our online book club community!

randomhousebookclub.com

Random House Book Club™

Because Stories Are Better Shared

RANDOM HOUSE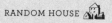